Sol Power

The Evolution of Solar Architecture

Sol Power

The Evolution of Solar Architecture

Sophia and Stefan Behling
in collaboration with Bruno Schindler

Foreword by Sir Norman Foster

A Publication for the READ Group
(Renewable Energies in Architecture and Design)

Prestel
Munich · New York

Based on research carried out for
Sir Norman Foster & Partners and the European Commission
Renewable Energies Division DG XII Directorate General for
Science Research & Development

Concept and design: Sophia and Stefan Behling

Drawings, illustrations, and graphics:
Nina Berkowitz and Dirk Lange

Contributions to the text were made by Bruno Schindler, Josephine
Smit, Klaus Bode (on comfort), and Simon Pinnegar (on urban planning)

Front cover: The Autonomous House designed for Richard Buckminster
Fuller and his Wife by Foster Associates in 1982. Photo: Richard Davies
Frontispiece photo: Bavaria Bildagentur

Photo credits see p. 239

Die Deutsche Bibliothek – CIP-Einheitsaufnahme:
Sol power : the evolution of solar architecture ; based on research
carried out for Sir Norman Foster & Partners and the European Com-
mission Renewable Energies Division DG XII Directorate General for
Science Research & Development ; a publication for the READ Group
(Renewable Energies in Architecture and Design) / Sophia und Stefan
Behling. In collab. with Bruno Schindler. Foreword by Norman Foster.
[Drawings, Ill. and graphics: Nina Berkowitz and Dirk Lange]. - Munich;
New York : Prestel, 1996
  ISBN 3-7913-1670-2
NE: Behling, Sophia; Behling, Stefan; Berkowitz, Nina

Prestel books are available world-wide. Please contact your nearest
bookseller or write to either of the following addresses for information
concerning your local distributor:

Prestel-Verlag
Mandlstrasse 26, 80802 Munich, Germany
Phone +49 89 381 709-0
Fax +49 89 381 709-35
or
16 West 22nd Street
New York, NY 10010, USA
Phone +1 212 627 8199
Fax +1 212 627 9866

Production: Konturwerk, Rainald Schwarz, Munich
Typesetting: Sheila de Vallée, Windsor Forest
Offset lithography: Repro Line, Munich
Printing: Pera Druck Matthias GmbH, Gräfelfing
Binding: Conzella, Munich

Printed in Germany
ISBN 3-7913-1670-2

Contents

Acknowledgements

This book is intended to provide comprehensive background information as well as illustrating the effect solar energy in architecture and urban planning might have in the future.

We have had the privilege to meet some of the most amazing, fascinating, and enlightening people during the course of our research.

Initiated by Wolfgang Palz and his work in the: Commission of the European Communities, Directorate General for Science, Research and Development the READ Group was founded in 1992. Core group members are: Sir Norman Foster, Sir Richard Rogers, Thomas Herzog, Renzo Piano, and Norbert Kaiser. The task set by this group of architects and designers was to join forces to pursue a policy based on sustainable solar architecture. At the 3rd European Conference for Solar Energy in Architecture and Urban Planning in Florence, 1993, Sir Norman Foster as the President of READ announced the following:

The time has come to redefine architecture and urban planning for the next millennium:
1. For our species and civilisation to maintain a sustainable relationship with the earth, our activities, including our architecture, must harmonize with natural cycles, rhythms, and resources.
2. The current knowledge and skill of architects can meet these conditions within the financial constraints of today, and should be supported by appropriate economic policies based on a broader and longer term rationale.
3. Since solar energy is the most fundamental resource and powers all natural cycles and living systems, it is obvious that solar architecture is not only the necessary response, but also the most promising vision.
4. As architects we must take responsibility for this in our art and in our politics, learning to draw from the experience and knowledge of our colleagues in all our disciplines.

Architects, designers, engineers, scientists, clients, and all other parties involved have to work in a productive relationship. They depend on each other. Like most projects illustrated in this book, the outcome is a result of a more extended team effort than might be apparent.
We want to express our deepest gratitude for all their help, advice, and support to our the closest collaborators on this project: Andrea Belloli; Nina Berkowitz; Dirk Lange; Simon Pinnegar; Bruno Schindler; Rainald Schwarz; and Josephine Smit.

The book would not have been possible to make without the support, time, and patience of the following individuals: Jochen Behling; Klaus Bode; Barry Cook; George Deschamps; Office Design Services; Patricia Drück; Norman Foster; Thomas Herzog; Verena Herzog-Loibl; Reinhard Holsten; Pilkington Flachglas AG; Norbert Kaiser; Bobby Michael; David Nelson; Wolfgang Palz; Stefan Robanus; Hermann Scheer; Jürgen Tesch; Sabine Thiel-Siling; Wolfgang Wagener; Athouros Zervos; Thomas Zuhr.

The following group of individuals and organisations have given generously of their time, information, advice, and picture material: Aerovironment; Arcosanti; Solarex; Christopher Alexander; Calthrope Associates; Christoph Behling; Ulrich Behr; Etienne Borgos; ID Büro; James Carpenter; Solarex Corporation; Kyocera Corporation; Obayashi Corporation; US Department of Energy Washington; Canon Design, Buffalo; Richard Diamond, Berkely Laboratory; Danielle Engle; Claude Engle; Asahi Glass, Japan; Cathy Harris; Volker Hartkopf; Joachim Helmle; Jörg Hieber; NEDO Japan; Canon Japan; Sanyo Japan; Kraemner Junction Corporation; Yoshio Kato; Prof. Kimura, Waseda University; Gregory Kiss; Yuichiro Kodama; Sabine Kraft; Heinz W. Krehwinkel; Nikolaus Kuhnert; Ian Lambot; Harry Lehmann; Vivian Loftness; Elke Moeller; Jürgen Markwart; Paul MacCready; Kjc Operating Company, California; Prof. Dieter Kimpel; Martin Pawley; Renzo Piano Building Workshop; Caroline Rochlitz; Richard Rogers Architects Ltd.; Julius Schulmann; Peter Seger; Nikken Sekkei; Nippon Sheet Glass Japan; Ken Shuttleworth; Paolo Soleri; Prof. Sobeck; Sinisa Stankovic; Koen Steemers; Future Systems; Prof. Tanabe, Tokyo University; Huw Thomas; James Wine S.I.T.E.

We especially would like to thank Pilkington and the Flachglas AG for their generous and unconditional support.

Most of all we want to thank our new born son, who had all the patience in the world.
Thank you Leon. This book is for you.
Good luck!

Preface

Sol Power. Why such an ambitious book, and for whom? The subject of architecture and solar power is presently a central part of all our agendas for a better future, a future in which life will be easier and more satisfying and in which our economies and society at large will achieve a better harmony with nature.

We all spend a major, if not the largest, part of our lives in buildings, and as Europeans we consume more than a third of our energy in these buildings on heating, cooling, and lighting. This is why we all welcome the prospect of dwellings, buildings, and urban developments offering greater comfort, while at the same time being more economically viable than those of today — relying far more on natural energy, particularly solar energy, and being designed to respect rational and aesthetic criteria, building traditions, and progress in modern architecture.

All this is the menu of solar architecture. This book has the merit of going systematically back into the history of architecture, which until two hundred years ago was solar architecture. It investigates the values of old principles and traditions still alive in vernacular architecture. These are the roots of solar architecture in its modern expression, which integrates both the new 'solar' technologies and modern architectural concepts.

It has taken an extraordinary effort in terms of imagination and study to create *Sol Power.*

This work was supported by the European Commission in Brussels by means of a research project with the READ Group (Renewable Energies in Architecture and Design), which comprises some of the most prestigious architects in Europe. As such, this book is a landmark for the READ Group's work and ambitions.

Dr Wolfgang Palz
Head of the Solar Energy Research Programme
Commission of the European Communities

Foreword

I am writing this in the Engadin Valley in Switzerland, a region that is world famous as a skiing playground. Although the scale of the mountains dwarf everything that is man-made, the urbanisation that relentlessly follows the pursuit of leisure is everywhere apparent and leaves permanent scars on the landscape. Although I am privileged to share the pleasures of this sport, I cannot help contemplating, as I ride an elegantly functional chair lift, that it consumes a huge amount of energy.

For nearly every kilometre that we wish down the slopes with the force of gravity, our quilted bodies, heavy boots, skies, and poles are hauled back up the mountain for a similar distance by a mixture of cable cars, gondolas and lifts. Hardly surprising that those ski passes cost so much money when we consider the outlay and running costs to power the system that for most of the year will lie idle.

Downhill skiing is well publicised, and almost everyone knows about this region and its associations with the sport. Less well known is another world of skiing – cross-country. The Engadin Valley has hundreds of kilometres of ski trails which traverse frozen lakes and climb up and down through forests and across fields. In all kinds of weather throughout the winter months, the valley is alive with two kinds of cross-country skiers, those who will glide along grooved tracks 'classic' style and those who will ski 'freestyle' on the smoother strip next to the tracks.

Once a year there is an annual event called the Engadin Valley Marathon, which is a Mecca for more than 12,000 skiers who come together to celebrate their sport. They start at nine in the morning from the southern end of the valley and travel for five kilometres, climbing and descending several metres over the course. The race, like the activity itself, embraces all generations – from Olympic-level athletes at the front to the retired grandparents and less serious addicts who will follow behind. The leaders will complete the course in about one hour and twenty minutes.

The warm outer clothing that the competitors strip off at the start will be moved to the finish line by trucks which average about the same speed. In the relatively brief history of this race, the speeds have increased dramatically – partly through technique and partly through the development of higher-technology equipment. Regardless of their finishing times, the event is a fun-loving celebration for the vast majority of those who participate.

On a typical winter day, it is interesting to compare the activities of those skiing own the slopes and those traversing the cross country trails at the bottom of the valley. Aside from the outlay for equipment, the downhill group pay a high price for those facilities which lift them continuously to the top, unlike the other group whose sport costs them virtually nothing. But how do you quantify the poetic difference between a stroll through the woods and queuing for a ski lift?

The comparison of equipment is interesting. My downhill skies, sticks, and boots, which are agony to walk in, weigh much more that cross-country gear. Because there is no waiting around in queues or sitting on open chair lifts, the clothing and boots for the cross-country skier is similarly light and also very comfortable. Despite being able to cope with extreme conditions of winter chill, air and body temperatures, perspiration, and freedom of movement, it is only a fraction of the weight of those bulky parkas and ski suits. The differences between these two kinds of skiing may be partly philosophical, but there is no escaping the fact that the performance of the independent cross-country skier is directly linked to the advanced technology of the equipment and clothing. The cross-country skier is liberated from the need for an all-consuming infrastructure. Even the ski trail itself is ephemeral. Almost invisible in winter, by spring it has disappeared into lakes and routes for walkers and mountain bikers.

It was Buckminster Fuller who drew attention to the revolution in the world of communication, which has some parallels with my skiing example. He compared the inefficiency of all those tons and tons of copper cable – the infrastructure which not so long ago rested on the sea-bed to connect continents – with the electronic freedom that lightweight satellites and invisible airwaves now offer. Fuller never lived to see the tiny mobile telephones that were a logical extension of his many optimistic predictions about society's ability to achieve more with less. In an article that he wrote in 1969 Fuller makes the point thus:

> To demonstrate this fantastic improvement in performance, we witness that one communications-relaying satellite of only one quarter of one ton of material is now outperforming the transoceanic communications message capacity and fidelity capability of 175,000 tons of copper cable. This constitutes a seven-hundred-thousand-fold step-up in communications performance per pound of invested resources.

Sol Power picks up on the importance of reference points from the contemporary worlds of recreation and communication. In chapter one it charts indigenous buildings from the past. I am reminded about Bernard Rudofsky's observation in 'Architecture without Architects' that 'the philosophy and know how of the anonymous builders presents the largest untapped source of architectural inspiration for industrial man.' The true vernacular of its time was often on the cutting edge of available technology –

far removed from the romantic associations that might follow in a later age. It is easy to forget that the concept of what is an acceptable level of thermal comfort has changed over time. Many examples can be found from the past of solutions which control summer overheating, but there are few which face up to the difficulties of heating in winter. The environment for a king in the Middle Ages would be unacceptable to those in many of today's societies who are classed as the poorest. It is an irony that the threat of global warming, corrosive pollution, and depleted resources of non-renewable fuels should coincide with a rising demand for thermal comfort.

So what is it that connects the non-building references of our time with those indigenous structures of the past? Surely they were all pushing the frontiers by showing ways in which the maximum benefits could be obtained from minimal resources. In the case of those earlier builders, they were, in the best examples, creating synergies between climate, resources and place. Stefan and Sophia Behling trace the rise and fall of that tradition up to the present day, showing the pendulum swings of awareness and excess. The non-building references could be interpreted as reminders that current building technology lags behind other sectors and could benefit from greater cross-fertilisation and long-overdue research.

The READ Charter of 1996 is a step in the right direction. The first three sentences set the scene by noting that 75% of energy consumed in Europe is accounted for by buildings and traffic — 50% and 25% respectively — most of it from non-renewable sources. The evolution of a solar architecture, the only kind of building that will cultivate renewable forms of energy — must therefore be inevitable. It is not about fashion but about survival, given the enormity of the challenge. The group of 27 European architects signing this charter and its promotion through this book is a provocation — a small but important addition to the voices of growing concern.

In his book *Critical Path*, Buckminster Fuller wrote about the first flight by a man-powered craft, demonstrating that improved technology would produce more effective results with fewer materials and less energy, and in less time. Some years ago, I met the designer of that aircraft, Paul MacCready, at a conference in Aspen. He talked about how he had achieved the seemingly impossible by going back to the basics of early flying machines and using advanced materials from other technologies. When congratulated, MacCready did not think that he was the most creative one — he believed that the truly creative act was that of a man called Kraemer, who set the challenge and offered a significant price for the first flight to be powered by human energy. I believe that this understatement came partly out of modesty, but his point is significant.

The designers, whether architects or engineers, can only act on the political initiatives of those who set the priorities. I carry much hope that this work by Stefan and Sophia Behling will help to bring those initiatives closer and stimulate all of us with an appetite for the challenges that lie ahead.

Norman Foster
Pontresina
February 1996

The Need for Change

Crisis, What Crisis?
Towards a sustainable future

The concern regarding environmental crises on both the local and global levels reflects a general acceptance that the present form and degree of resource exploitation and our associated consumption practices are unsustainable. The continued disappearance of forest cover, land degradation, the loss of biodiversity, air and water pollution, and the changing chemistry of the atmosphere all clearly reflect the inappropriateness of our present activities and the need for more effective environmental protection.

Concerns over the relationship between human activity and development and their influence on the environment are long-standing. The Earth is rapidly becoming a more crowded place: the less-developed countries experienced exponential growth rates that led to a doubling of global population in just 25 years. In advanced economies, growing evidence of environmental destruction has made people increasingly aware of the potentially irreversible damage being caused as a result of dominant development and consumption practices. The pictures of the Earth transmitted back from American space missions provided a profound symbol of the Earth as an interconnected, dynamic system, yet at the same time illustrated its fragility.

The significance of global interdependence was further highlighted by the energy crisis of 1973: the life-styles that had been fostered by an unhindered rise in energy consumption in advanced economies were directly challenged and called into question. Essentially, the economic rationales which had led to 25 years of continual growth had become problematic. There was an increasing loss of faith in the ability of science and technology to overcome any potential difficulties in the pursuit of progress. Instead of remaining committed to a belief that technological innovation would continue to enable our energy consumption and life-style requirements to be met, it was recognised that we had to come to terms with the realities of finite resource levels and the carrying capacities of ecosystems at both local and global levels.

In the last 20 years, our knowledge of environmental systems, and their interaction and relationship with human activities, has evolved through the development of national and international research programmes and more sophisticated methods of prediction enabled through increasingly accurate modelling techniques. At the same time, environmental devastation has been witnessed first-hand: forest die-back and euthropication of lakes in Scandinavian countries and southern Canada; the occurrence of widespread famine in Africa during the 1970s and 1980s; ongoing poverty and malnutrition for a significant proportion of the world's population; the depletion of rain-forest hardwoods, resulting in the loss of biodiversity and the destruction of traditional shrub woodland due to the pressures of fuel gathering; the increase in the occur-

rence of skin cancers associated with atmospheric ozone depletion; and the increasing number of asthma sufferers found in congested urban areas linked to low-level ozone and smog pollution.

Despite this, our life-styles and consumption patterns have failed to reflect our concerns. Indeed, although energy efficiency has continually improved, the growth in consumption levels has outstripped any potential gains made in this regard. Although new technologies have enabled fossil fuels to be utilised more efficiently and in cleaner forms, the costs involved in making such improvements have largely put them out of reach for the newly industrialising nations, where the growth in emissions is taking place at the most startling levels. There are difficult issues to be addressed by advanced economies in this regard, as the 1992 Global Summit in Rio highlighted. How do you avoid placing restrictions on, or hindering, economic development yet promote the struggle against environmental destruction?

The potential of nuclear energy, once regarded as the natural successor to fossil fuel, has been curtailed as a result of environmental concerns, and the true costs involved are becoming increasingly apparent. The meltdown at Chernobyl in 1986 and the continued inability to find a resolution to the problems posed by radiated waste disposal have focused public concern on the viability of this energy source. Thus it can be argued that we have reached a moment of transition in both our production and consumption of energy. New technologies must enable us to work with and for the environment rather than be utilised as tools that allow us to conquer and dominate. The notion of sustainable development is increasingly stressed in this connection. Central to this concept is the requirement that current practices and policies should enable (according to the 1987 Brundtland Commission) 'development which meets present needs without compromising the ability of future generations to achieve their needs and aspiration'. In moving towards more sustainable relations between development and the environment, three interrelated components of human impact need to be recognised. Based upon Paul Ehrlich's 1967 formula, this impact may be regarded as a product of population, consumption, and technology, components that exist together everywhere. Thus:

Environmental Impact = Population x Consumption x Technology.

This equation illustrates the actual environmental costs of particular life-styles, making tangible what is so often invisible. Exposing these costs is paramount if people are to be encouraged to move towards more sustainable forms of living.

The global environmental crisis is a question of survival. Never before in history have human beings had such an impact on Earth. The resulting problems are a product of the size and growth of population, quantity of consumption, and quality of technology.

1

2

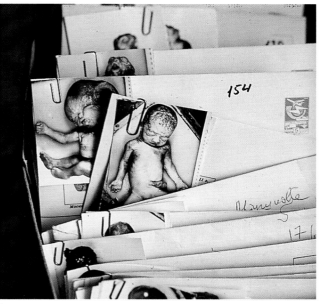

3

Deforestation
The gathering of wood for fuel is one major cause of the destruction of savanna trees and scrub forests. Wood is the principal source of energy for most people in poor countries, where women may spend large amounts of their time and energy finding and harvesting it. In many regions, wood harvesting exceeds rates of re-growth.

Pollution
Between 1970 and 1990, whilst sulphur-based emissions declined from 65 to 40 million tonnes per annum in the wealthy OECD countries, emissions from the rest of the world rose from 48 to 59 million tonnes. The future development of these industrialising countries, including the 1.2 billion inhabitants of China with their vast reserves of coal, places the environmental crisis in clear perspective.

Nuclear Waste
Nuclear waste is accumulating at an alarming rate. So far, the problem of waste disposal has not been solved anywhere in the world. Construction costs for nuclear power stations rose from £250 per kWh in 1971 to £2,000 in 1985, reflecting the risk factor involved. Cancer and birth defects are caused by exposure to radiation from nuclear waste.

Population
New centres of growth

The Population Explosion
Since 1900, the world's population has tripled in size, the world economy has grown 20 times bigger, and industrial production has increased by 5000%. The continuing rise in the world's population today is a major concern.

World Population
The exponential growth of world population is a very recent phenomenon. Before the organisation of agricultural production and the formation of city-states by the early urbanising civilisations, population levels were relatively static for more than 30,000 years. These new forms of social organisation enabled greater numbers to be supported given the resources available (1).

Industrialisation and the large-scale migration to towns and cities from the 17th century on represented a further period of sustained increase. It has only been in the last 40 to 50 years, however, that the pressures of population growth have taken on new dimensions. It is difficult to predict the future; however, the fastest-growing areas show little sign of significant decline in their growth, and those areas where population growth is being reduced already have vast base populations (2).

The rapidity of contemporary demographic change makes it unclear whether the patterns of growth and urbanisation being experienced in the developing world are replicating traditional patterns of industrialised economies or whether they are fundamentally different. Whilst actual and future predictions are hindered by difficulties in collecting accurate data, the environmental consequences and increasing strain placed upon both natural and social resources are becoming clearly apparent.

United Nations projections estimate that total global population by the year 2000 will be between 6 and 6.5 billion persons. To put this into perspective, the total population stood at just 250 million, 2,000 years ago. Until the advent of industrialisation in Europe during the 18th and 19th centuries, population growth was gradual and inconsistent, characterised by high birth and death rates and periods when population levels declined through poor agricultural organisation, famine, and disease. It was not until 1820 that global population reached one billion, and despite European industrialisation, migration, and the resource exploitation and diffusion of new technologies overseas through imperial expansion during the 19th century, it was another hundred years before it reached two billion.

Since 1945, exponential growth has led to a rapid expansion of numbers on an ever-increasing base population. Whilst the rate of population growth has declined and stabilised at very low levels in a number of advanced economies, the fall in death rates but persistence of high birth rates in developing countries has ensured a rapid expansion of global population. Death rates have been reduced through the introduction of modern preventative and curative medicine, including immunisation, water sanitation, and antibiotics, as well as improved agricultural techniques, which have enabled higher crop yields in certain areas of the developing world. Presently, with a growth rate of 1.7%, approximately 190 million births and 95 million deaths occur each year, adding a further 95 million persons to the Earth's population annually. Of these births 95% are in the less developed countries, 20% —19 million — in India alone.

The growth in population levels is paralleled by the rapid urbanisation taking place in many developing world cities. In 1990, 43% of the world's population was urbanised, comprising 73% of people living in developed countries and 33.6% in developing countries. It is estimated that by the year 2000, the total proportion of urban dwellers will have reached 50%, this increase being almost wholly represented by the growth of cities in the developing world. Forecasts indicate that within 10 to 15 years, few cities in the developed world would feature in a top 20 table of the most populous urban agglomerations. Mexico

City and São Paulo already vie with New York and Tokyo and, if they have not already done so, will soon overtake them, as will many others in terms of absolute numbers. The strain such a rapid increase has placed upon the cities' social and physical infrastructures is indicated by widespread un- and underemployment, burgeoning slum districts, and the proliferation of squatter settlements on available land, typically in peripheral locations. It is estimated that a third of the urban population in developing countries live in such conditions; when new dwellings are considered, shanty-type dwellings comprise two-thirds of all new households. Although urban pressures are clearly not as dramatic in advanced economies, many cities, particularly in the more dynamic regions, continue to face urban development pressures as a result of migration and, more significantly, the changing number and form of household structures. Rather than a simple growth in numbers, changing social relations and life-style choices have created a larger number of household units, for example through later marriage, cohabitation, and increasing proportions of divorced and remarrying couples.

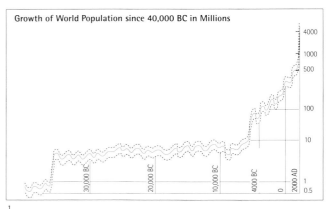

Growth of World Population since 40,000 BC in Millions

1

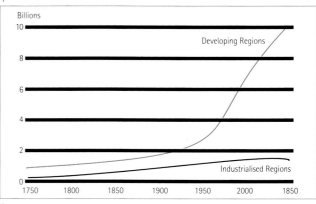

2

Two demographic trends are presently being experienced at a scale that has no historical precedent: an explosive growth in the total global population, and the increasing urbanisation of that population. The demand for housing for new urban dwellers is greater than ever.

3

Urban Centres

The dramatic growth of population in developing regions is giving rise to a new urban hierarchy and an increasing number of mega-cities with populations of 10 million or more. Indeed, the UN estimates that by 2025, there will be 12 cities with populations greater than 20 million. This growth has not been uniform, and the variation is leading to a profound shift in the urban balance. In 1950, the large majority of the world's largest urban agglomerations were found in developed countries – for example, New York, London, and Paris. By the year 2000, the list of the 25 largest cities will be dominated by rapidly growing cities in the developing regions (4, 5).

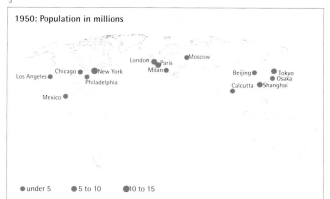

1950: Population in millions

- under 5
- 5 to 10
- 10 to 15

4

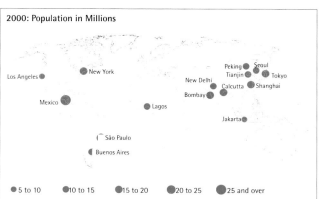

2000: Population in Millions

- 5 to 10
- 10 to 15
- 15 to 20
- 20 to 25
- 25 and over

5

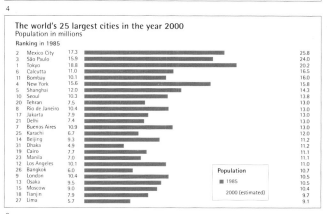

The world's 25 largest cities in the year 2000
Population in millions
Ranking in 1985

Ranking	City	1985	2000 (estimated)
2	Mexico City	17.3	25.8
3	São Paulo	15.9	24.0
1	Tokyo	18.8	20.2
6	Calcutta	11.0	16.5
11	Bombay	10.1	16.0
4	New York	15.6	15.8
5	Shanghai	12.0	14.3
10	Seoul	10.3	13.8
20	Tehran	7.5	13.0
8	Rio de Janeiro	10.4	13.0
17	Jakarta	7.9	13.0
21	Delhi	7.4	13.0
7	Buenos Aires	10.9	13.0
25	Karachi	6.7	12.0
14	Beijing	9.3	11.2
31	Dhaka	4.9	11.2
19	Cairo	7.7	11.1
23	Manila	7.0	11.1
12	Los Angeles	10.1	11.0
26	Bangkok	6.0	10.7
9	London	10.4	10.5
13	Osaka	9.5	10.5
15	Moscow	9.0	10.4
18	Tianjin	7.9	9.7
27	Lima	5.7	9.1

Population
- 1985
- 2000 (estimated)

6

Informal (Squatter) Settlements (1980s)
Number of people living in squatter settlements in selected major cities (figures in thousands)
Over 1 million squatters

City	Squatters
Mexico City	7,000 (44% of city population)
São Paulo	4,333 (32%)
Calcutta	3,530 (37%)
Bombay	2,985 (35%)
Delhi	2,800 (56%)
Bogota	2,393 (59%)
Manila	2,000 (40%)
Karachi	1,852 (37%)
Lima	1,545 (33%)
Addis Ababa	1,418 (85%)
Bangkok	1,200 (26%)
Ankara	1,104 (51%)
Caracas	1,052 (34%)

7

Housing Demand
Rapid urbanisation of cities in the developing world places great strain upon housing and infrastructure resources (7).

The urbanisation of world population has put enormous pressure on those working in the fields of urban planning and infrastructure. The building construction industries have not yet found solutions for major urban problems (6).

Consumption
A matter of balance

Urban forms help dictate, and are dictated by, changing transport modes. The development of trams and cleaner urban railroads promoted suburban development at the beginning of the 20th century in Europe, Australia, and North America, for example. High-density transit-oriented neighbourhoods were encouraged as new development concentrated upon these linkages. The car has succeeded the tram and train, offering personal mobility at the cost of poor energy efficiency and high levels of pollution. The rise in car ownership and the encouragement of low-density settlements has ensured that households have increasingly become dependent upon the car to negotiate sprawling urban landscapes.

Concern about the pressures applied by exponential population growth to the environment is not simply about numbers, but also recognises the widening disparity in consumption patterns and life-styles between rich and poor. Traditional economic models of development have made explicit the link between progress through industrialisation and increasing levels of energy consumption. Indeed, the direct correlation between per capita energy use and the wealth of nations provides evidence of this association. Industrialisation both necessitates and stimulates greater energy consumption levels, in converting raw materials into manufactured products and in stimulating the development of new products through technological innovation that add to energy demands. For example, whilst the production of electricity was originally intended to provide lighting in buildings and streets after dark, utility owners have searched for ways in which their in-plant investment could be utilised at other times of the day. As standards of living for a large proportion of the population increase, technological innovations gradually become regarded as essential. The telephone, the refrigerator, the car, the television continually increase the energy requirements of the average consumer.

The inequalities recognised between industrialised and developing countries are reflected in their respective energy consumption levels. Economically advanced societies — for example, most European countries — consume approximately a hundred gigajoules of energy per person per year, the equivalent of three and half metric tonnes of coal. In the US and Canada, this figure is closer to 10 tonnes per person per year. At the other end of the scale, countries remaining at low levels of industrialisation typically consume just 0.1 tonnes — 1% of the amount of the highest-consuming societies. If conditions enable developing societies to reach the consumption levels presently recorded in the industrialised nations, then with the vast population bases these countries represent, the implications for global energy requirements are immense.

The energy crises of 1973 and 1979–81 illustrated to industrialised countries the dependency on high levels of energy consumption required to support their life-styles. The message has become more urgent as growing environmental consciousness has recognised the implications of air pollution, ozone depletion, and acid rain for future generations. This greater understanding has translated into support for more sustainable forms of development, which work within environmental constraints rather than trying to overcome them. An important component of this debate has focused upon a re-evaluation of urban form and function and contemporary industrial practices and procedures. In this regard, there has been an increased willingness to recognise the importance of issues such as urban densities in determining energy efficiency and the

value of moving towards environmental concerns and the more efficient use of raw materials with less negative output and environmental damage (from cradle to grave).

Although public support for environmental issues is often highly vocal, actually translating these beliefs into changing life styles is a more complicated matter. Importantly, this necessitates an understanding of the possible motivations for change: how can an individual's decisions be valued? As dominant economies have placed overriding faith in the principles of the free market, the position of placing value — a private judgement — on the environment, traditionally regarded as a public good, is a complex one. A further paradox is introduced: whilst the global significance of environmental stress is recognised, these issues must be tackled at the local level. Many have argued that our ability to combat problems this complex requires a reassessment of social values and communitarian principles. The environment is a common concern and must be tackled as such.

Energy Consumption in Relation to Gross National Product

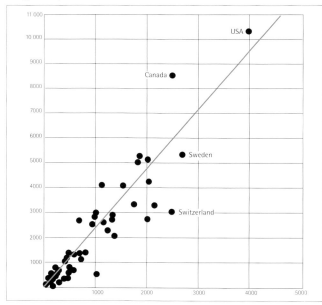

1

The Haves destroy the atmosphere through their waste of energy; the Have Nots increase in number and suffer because of the lack of energy. Only through a radical increase of efficiency and a refocusing on renewable energies will it be possible to provide the desired lifestyle for all people on this planet.

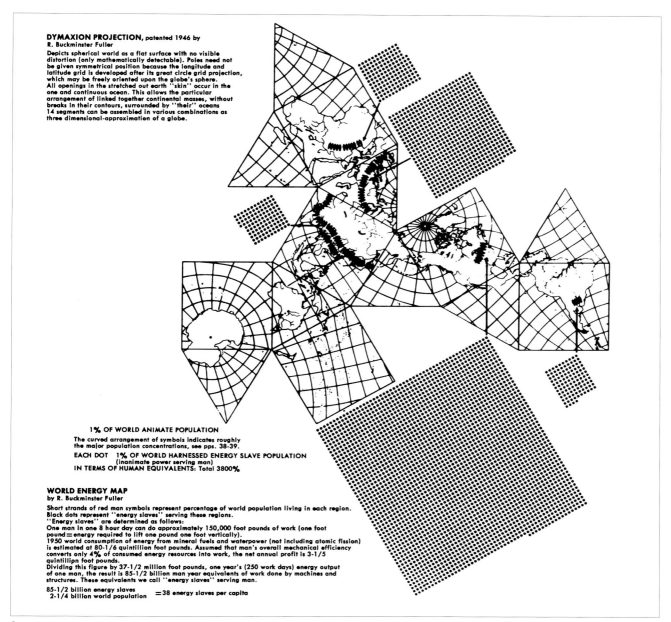

DYMAXION PROJECTION, patented 1946 by R. Buckminster Fuller

Depicts spherical world as a flat surface with no visible distortion (only mathematically detectable). Poles need not be given symmetrical position because the longitude and latitude grid is developed after its great circle grid projection, which may be freely oriented upon the globe's sphere. All openings in the stretched out earth "skin" occur in the one and continuous ocean. This allows the particular arrangement of linked together continental masses, without breaks in their contours, surrounded by "their" oceans 14 segments can be assembled in various combinations as three dimensional-approximation of a globe.

1% OF WORLD ANIMATE POPULATION

The curved arrangement of symbols indicates roughly the major population concentrations, see pps. 38-39.

EACH DOT 1% OF WORLD HARNESSED ENERGY SLAVE POPULATION (inanimate power serving man) **IN TERMS OF HUMAN EQUIVALENTS: Total 3800%**

WORLD ENERGY MAP by R. Buckminster Fuller

Short strands of red man symbols represent percentage of world population living in each region. Black dots represent "energy slaves" serving these regions. "Energy slaves" are determined as follows: One man in one 8 hour day can do approximately 150,000 foot pounds of work (one foot pound = energy required to lift one pound one foot vertically). 1950 world consumption of energy from mineral fuels and waterpower (not including atomic fission) is estimated at 80-1/6 quintillion foot pounds. Assumed that man's overall mechanical efficiency converts only 4% of consumed energy resources into work, the net annual profit is 3-1/5 quintillion foot pounds. Dividing this figure by 37-1/2 million foot pounds, one year's (250 work days) energy output of one man, the result is 85-1/2 billion man year equivalents of work done by machines and structures. These equivalents we call "energy slaves" serving man.

$$\frac{85\text{-}1/2 \text{ billion energy slaves}}{2\text{-}1/4 \text{ billion world population}} = 38 \text{ energy slaves per capita}$$

2

The Haves and Have Nots
Buckminster Fuller's representation of the world (2) illustrates the great inequality between the energy consumption levels of rich and poor nations. The wealthiest 25% account for 75% of total consumption and similar pollution production levels, whilst the other 75%, representing the poorer developing countries, account for just 25% of total world energy use.

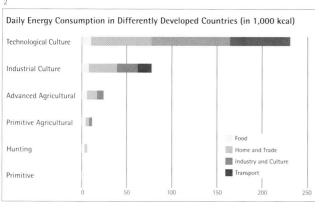

Daily Energy Consumption in Differently Developed Countries (in 1,000 kcal)

Technological Culture
Industrial Culture
Advanced Agricultural
Primitive Agricultural
Hunting
Primitive

Food
Home and Trade
Industry and Culture
Transport

0   50   100   150   200   250

3

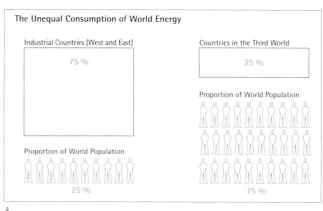

The Unequal Consumption of World Energy

Industrial Countries (West and East)   Countries in the Third World

75 %   25 %

Proportion of World Population

Proportion of World Population   25 %   75 %

4

Energy consumption and pollution clearly correlate. Countries with high gross national products are the largest producers of fuel-based pollutants, CFC propellants, and nuclear waste (1). Although new technologies have enabled fossil fuels to be utilised more efficiently — for example, through desulphurisation processes — the costs involved in such improvements are largely out of reach for newly industrialising countries (3).

Technology
A question of sustainability

By harnessing energy through agriculture, humans have transformed much of the natural world to suit their requirements. Since energy is neither produced nor consumed, only transferred, all potential energy sources available to us represent a form of solar energy, stored as biomass in trees; as fossil fuels in oil, gas, and coal. Technological innovations have enabled each of these sources to be discovered and utilised, typically leading to a great expansion of production capacities at each stage and promoting new uses and consumption patterns. Dominant forms of energy use reflect an evolution from muscle power through the discovery of fire and the combustion of wood and dung, to the extraction of non-renewable fossil fuels and their conversion to electricity. Muscle power and wood burning still provide a proportion of the energy requirements in the most industrialised societies.

Prior to the Industrial Revolution, our energy sources were primarily renewable. The form and design of towns and cities took into careful consideration characteristics of the local microclimate, typically oriented to take maximum advantage of solar activity. The onset of new forms of industrial organisation during the 18th century was largely enabled by the development of steam-powered engines driven by coal instead of charcoal. The continual refinement of this new technology opened up new vistas for development, increasing the demand for energy even further.

The Industrial Revolution was a fossil-fuel-based revolution: the two went hand in hand. Although it marked a dramatic step in terms of innovative progress, at an early stage the detrimental implications of these technologies were apparent: cities were blackened; the skies continually filled with dense smog; poor health ensued, with children developing bone deficiencies through lack of exposure to sunlight. The pursuit of progress and demand for ever-increasing energy consumption to feed new life-styles has typically offset such concerns.

In the period of reconstruction following World War Two, the role of energy in rebuilding and redefining national industries was paramount. The market for petroleum surged through the growth in car ownership, encouraged by governments and concretised in urban, and increasingly suburban, forms of living. The nuclear industry grew in parallel with militaristic objectives of the Cold War period: electricity suppliers in the US, Britain, and elsewhere were encouraged and subsidised to develop this new technology. In countries with few fossil fuel resources, the pursuit of new nuclear technologies to supply energy needs was vigorous.

Technologies focusing on the potential to harvest renewable energy remained largely underdeveloped after 1945, when fossil fuels and nuclear power were seen as more economic forms capable of meeting future needs. At present, the crisis in non-renewable energy resources, and the technologies based upon such sources, are not imminent, but can be effectively foreseen. It has become clear that our technological advances have had both global and local environmental consequences. Our over-riding faith in progress through technology is increasingly questioned, as can be seen if we look at nuclear power.

Fossil fuel resources are inevitably finite; conservation represents our best available energy source. Indeed, most of our new sources of energy in the last 25 years have come from improved efficiency, and there remains a great deal of scope for improvement in this regard. An important aspect in moving towards greater energy efficiency is to ensure that the appropriate kind of energy is used for a particular task. For example, the costs of electricity production, once loss in translation and through supply lines is taken into account, are far higher than other forms. The energy wasted in the process each year would provide enough power to heat all the homes in the US. In the longer term, it is by tackling the deeper roots of wasteful patterns of production and consumption that we will resolve the energy crisis, not by creating more energy. It is important that we recognise the importance of changing our values, attitudes, and life-styles in this regard. There must also be a parallel shift in energy production from non-renewable to renewable sources, and from so-called hard technologies — based upon rigid and centralised use of fossil fuels — to softer technologies — those which are environmentally benign and ecologically balanced. The technology to utilise the vast resources of direct solar energy which this planet receives each day already exists and will be a central component in this essential transition back to technology's alignment with nature.

Human history is the history of energy transformation. Every era is marked by its own techniques of energy generation. We are now entering a new solar age.

Urban Hotspots
In cities, heat islands reveal themselves as white, red, and yellow areas. These thermograms are a tool to heighten awareness of conservation and to give advice for insulating buildings (1).

1

Energy Evaluation

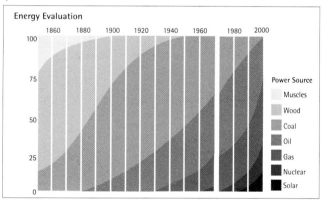

Power Source
- Muscles
- Wood
- Coal
- Oil
- Gas
- Nuclear
- Solar

2

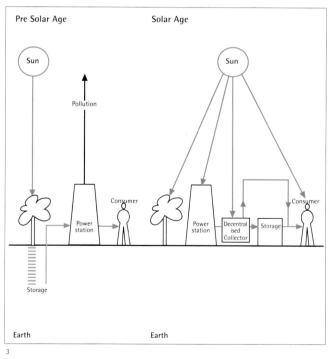

Old and New Solar Energy
The cycle of solar energies on Earth can be divided into solar energy that has been stored underground for thousands of years — old solar energy — and the energy that comes from the sun daily and that can be used directly by passive and active means. We need to develop technologies that use 'fresh' solar energy efficiently.

Architecture and Architects
Renewable energies in architecture and design

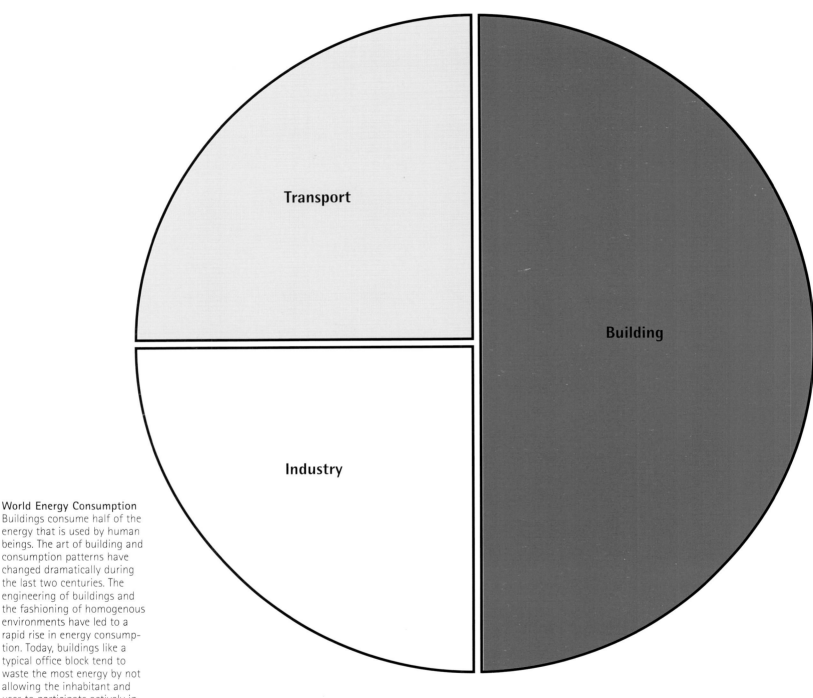

World Energy Consumption
Buildings consume half of the energy that is used by human beings. The art of building and consumption patterns have changed dramatically during the last two centuries. The engineering of buildings and the fashioning of homogenous environments have led to a rapid rise in energy consumption. Today, buildings like a typical office block tend to waste the most energy by not allowing the inhabitant and user to participate actively in conservation.

The world's energy consumption can be broken down into three major areas: industrial, commercial, and residential. Most energy is used in the commercial/industrial areas; less goes into residential use.

Architects, engineers, and urban planners are not directly responsible for our built environment, as an increasing number of buildings are built with no care for quality or efficiency and without any architect involved. Nevertheless, architects, engineers, and urban planners are responsible for the energy inefficiency of buildings they design.

Our built environment represents a particular manifestation of technological innovation. Buildings provide shelter, facilitate our activities and interactions, and represent our desires and provide cultural expression. The methods by which we apply technologies in the design and construction of buildings have direct implications for the amount of energy consumed. The enormous amount of energy consumed by buildings reflects a continuing increase in the demands placed upon energy resources and symbolises the problematic relationship between architecture and technology that has emerged during the industrial age. The two have become interdependent, and architectural innovation has increasingly necessitated technological and engineering expertise, coupled with higher energy demands in both construction and operation.

The Industrial Revolution heralded the pursuit of progress and innovation dictated by a human desire to do away with our dependence upon natural constraints and, in so doing, to overcome and dominate nature. Rather than working with particular environmental qualities, buildings have increasingly come to represent enclosed, isolated boxes in which the internal environment is artificially controlled. Structures are maintained at temperatures deemed comfortable according to the purpose of the building: whether the temperature outside is -20 degrees or 35 degrees Celsius, the internal temperature remains constant. Achieving this comfort necessitates considerable energy consumption.

Of course, the level of energy use is largely dependent upon the technologies applied in design and construction, and this may be considered at three levels. Technology determines how much energy is required to operate the services in a building; technology determines what kind of energy is utilised, and how efficiently; technology determines how this energy is generated or harvested. How technologies are employed in building design is the ultimate responsibility of the architect and engineer. They are responsible for dictating the energy requirements of their designs. For example, if structures are designed that use a lot of glazing, then the energy requirements of buildings will necessarily incorporate the costs of artificially maintaining internal conditions against extremes in external temperatures. Likewise, if a building has insufficient window space, energy requirements increase as a result of having to provide artificial lighting.

A number of goals and objectives for more efficient building design can be proposed:

a) Buildings should only need to use artificial mediators inside when the prevailing conditions externally make human activities uncomfortable. As such, buildings can provide a buffer against uncomfortable environmental conditions — for example, extremes in temperature or winds.
b) Buildings should avoid restricting natural conditions reaching their internal spaces that would be of positive benefit to their occupants. For example, buildings should be designed to maximise the use of daylight over artificial light; likewise, buildings should aim to be naturally ventilated with fresh air rather than be controlled through energy-consuming heating and ventilation systems.
c) Buildings should be designed to assist in the collection and storage of received energy sources, particularly solar energy, and then utilise this when and where required. By working with, rather than trying to overcome, the Earth's natural energy cycles, buildings can be designed that consume far less energy.
d) Buildings should also be environmentally responsive to their local surroundings. Not only should they minimise internal energy consumption; they should also aim not to create external demands or induce negative environmental effects. Local energy cycles can be utilised, but should not be altered or used in an unsustainable way.

To facilitate these goals, we need to learn from our preindustrial history to realise the fundamental importance of the relationship between human activity and nature. Our first building structures provided simple protection from uncomfortable temperature extremes, and until fairly recently a large majority of people spent much of their lives outside, rather than within, buildings. Although the cities of early civilisations altered these trends, lives remained very much dictated by solar and seasonal cycles, instead of trying to homogenise living conditions throughout the year, as modern internal building environments attempt to do.

Throughout the centuries, ingenious use of technology has enabled societies to create highly efficient structures utilising natural or renewable materials in their construction and similar energy sources to enhance their performance. All those who share interest, concern, and responsibility for the built and unbuilt environment should reflect upon successful historical examples and aim to revive and refine many of these forgotten and neglected principles. Recognising the dependency of human activity upon maintaining a sustainable relationship with the natural environment should stimulate greater understanding of constructions in nature. The sophistication and complexity of plant and animal structures — the importance of ordered chaos as seen in skins, shells, and cells — can provide many clues for contemporary research. Through a better understanding of such systems, our ability to adopt an holistic approach to building design, where both local and global environmental implications are taken into full consideration, will be facilitated.

Learning from Natural Systems

Solar Energy and the Environment
Basic facts

In order to understand the potential of solar energy, we would like to embark on a journey through the universe to the ultimate natural power source, the sun.

The energy available on Earth pales into insignificance beside the natural power of the sun. There is quite simply no greater energy source. The sun's energy output is some 2,000,000 million million times that of the largest nuclear reactor.

Like the stars, the sun is a spinning ball made up of layers of hot gases, predominantly hydrogen and helium. Its hydrogen fuel will be exhausted in five thousand million years, and it will then rely on helium. As a result, its appearance will change dramatically; the helium sun will be a thousand times brighter and a hundred times larger than the sun is now. At its core, the present sun's temperature is fourteen million degrees Celsius, at the surface six thousand degrees Celsius. Its energy is a product of nuclear fusion, a process by which nuclei of hydrogen combine to form helium, releasing a massive amount of energy. Energy moves from the sun's core to its surface by convection and radiation and is released as light and heat. It then takes more than eight minutes for the light to travel to the Earth.

While the sun provides the energy essential for life, it can also present danger. Luckily, the Earth is shielded from the sun's harshest rays by its own multi-layered cladding system. The atmosphere promotes living conditions on Earth and provides shelter for the biosphere against the unbearable conditions of outer space. Around half of the sun's energy output is simply scattered or absorbed in the Earth's atmosphere. More than 90% of the energy that does reach the Earth's surface is absorbed by the oceans, while a small percentage is absorbed by plants for photosynthesis. Human use of solar energy is negligible by comparison.

Forests on Earth create habitat for millions of creatures, but trees are the structures that use solar energy in the most efficient ways. The skin of a leaf is a permeable membrane, letting sunlight through and breathing carbon dioxide in and oxygen out in order to create the right comfort conditions for its cell. Each cell forms a membrane around a chlorophyll centre. Plants are, in fact, extremely efficient solar collectors. They trap the energy from sunlight to fuel the process of photosynthesis. Solar energy powers the chemical reactions that convert water and basic salts from the soil and carbon dioxide from the air into simple sugars such as glucose. Oxygen is a by-product of this process. By comparison with a simple photovoltaic cell, the process of photosynthesis is enormously complex, involving around a hundred chemical changes. Photosynthesis creates plants' food, simple sugars.

The plant growth fostered by solar energy in turn provides fuel for animals and humans. All organic matter can be defined as biomass and as such can provide energy. Plants are an important source of energy for a high proportion of the population. Most biomass energy exists in the form of firewood, but in treeless regions of the world, such as Bangladesh, crop residue and animal dung meet the bulk of domestic energy needs.

Nature's solar energy users have highly efficient and sophisticated ways of getting the most from their power source. Unlike humans, they cannot impose themselves on their environment and change it; they have had to evolve ways of fitting comfortably into their habitat. Within the animal kingdom there are countless examples of the way in which animals' bodies and the structures animals build use renewable energy efficiently. Humans are adaptable and have learned how to make themselves comfortable in widely varying climatic conditions with the aid of clothing and shelter. The first hominids flourished amidst the warm climate and rich resources of the African savanna. They had no need for shelter to protect them from adverse climatic conditions. It is not surprising, therefore, that throughout history and in many cultures in the world, this state of harmony with nature has become idealised as paradise.

Things are much more complicated today, of course. If humans — and with them their buildings — want to maintain a sustainable relationship with natural cycles, they will have to learn that all natural systems are subsystems of our ecosystem, which is itself a minuscule subsystem of our solar system. The sun is the central and only energy generator for all these billions and billions of systems.

The Sun and the Earth
A powerful relationship

The Milky Way is the Earth's own star city. The sun is only one of 500,000 million stars in our galaxy. The universe has 100,000 million galaxies, each one a mega-city of stars.

In our solar system, the Earth orbits the sun within a comfort zone, a narrow path in the solar system capable of sustaining life — not too cold and not too hot.

The sun is 150 million km from the Earth. The 1,392,000-km-diameter star is made up of layers of gas. At its core, the sun's temperature is fourteen million degrees Celsius, at its surface six thousand degrees Celsius. One m^2 of the sun's surface shines as brightly as six hundred thousand hundred-watt light bulbs.

The process of nuclear fusion by which solar energy is produced is well protected by several layers of gases. The amount of solar energy received by the Earth varies according to latitudinal effects and cloud cover, but the annual average is 15.3 x 10^8 cal/m^2, the equivalent of 40,000 kW of electrical energy for every human being.

The Earth orbits the sun on an axis of 23.5 degrees. The Earth's spin produces day-and-night cycles, and the tilted angle causes seasonal changes. Molten iron flowing in the Earth's outer core generates electric currents. These create the Earth's magnetic field, which stretches up to 60,000 km into space.

1

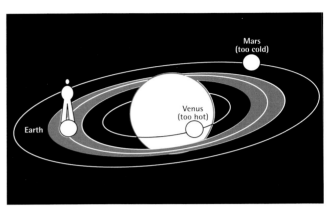

2

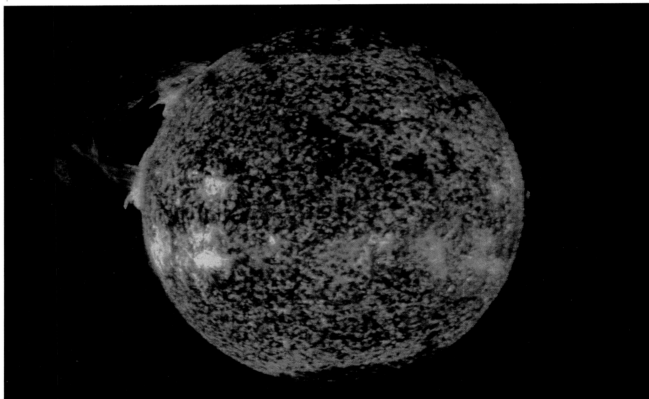

3

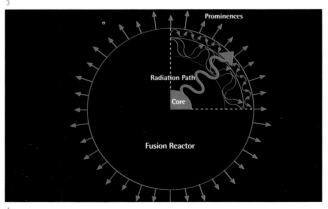

4

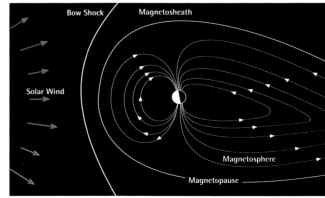

5

The sun is the Earth's only energy source. The Earth has its own cladding system (the atmosphere) thousands of kilometres above the ground, thus creating conditions that can support a wide range of animal and plant life — a true Open System.

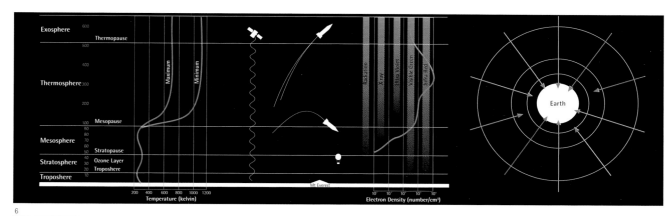

6

7

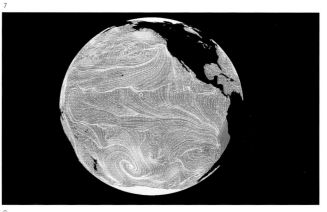

8

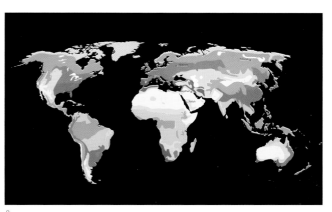

9

The atmosphere is part of the Earth's multi-layered, semi-permeable skin. It extends to an altitude of a thousand km and has five layers: troposphere, stratosphere, mesosphere, thermosphere, and exosphere. These filter the different wavelengths of solar radiation. The troposphere, which extends to an altitude of 20 km, is the only layer in which living creatures can breathe.

The biosphere stretches from the depth of the oceans to a height of about 15 km in the atmosphere. It is our living space and contains different ecosystems that interrelate with each other. Cycles of sustainability form the basis for life. Everything is constantly being recycled. Living things take in water, carbon, nitrogen, and oxygen, while plants release oxygen into the air as part of the process of photosynthesis. Through the decomposition of living things, substances are recycled back into the biosphere and used again for new life. Our biosphere is the only sphere known to us that can support life.

Regions vary in climate according to their position on the Earth's surface. Each type of climate is determined by how near a region is to the equator and by its distance from the sea. The Earth's radically different climates are always changing. Changes of weather occur because the heat from the sun keeps the air constantly moving.

Solar Energy
The sources of renewable power

Solar energy reaches the atmosphere in various forms. The sun is a non-polluting source of renewable energy and is essential in the formation of wind, clouds, thunderstorms, rain, and other weather conditions, some of which can be converted into usable energy.

The Earth's dynamic cladding system, the atmosphere, regulates energy flows by filtering through water vapour. Reflection and radiation are essential to the well-being of the planet, which would otherwise overheat.

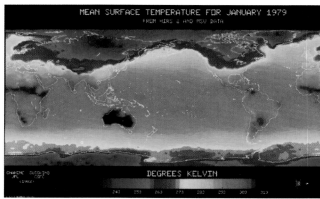

1

The first law of thermodynamics states that all energy in a closed system remains constant. The second law states that in any transformation of one form to another, some of it dissipates and is no longer available for use. The Earth and its atmosphere form an open system dependent on the sun. Any form of solar energy can be converted into heat. But heat energy can never be converted into other forms of energy. All radiation coming from the sun is transformed into different forms of energy on Earth.

2

Solar radiation controls our climate. Some radiation does not penetrate to the ground; some is reflected off the atmosphere back into space. The oxygen, ozone, and water vapour in the atmosphere absorb some of the radiation, which warms the atmosphere. Some of this energy reaches the Earth and supports life there (3).

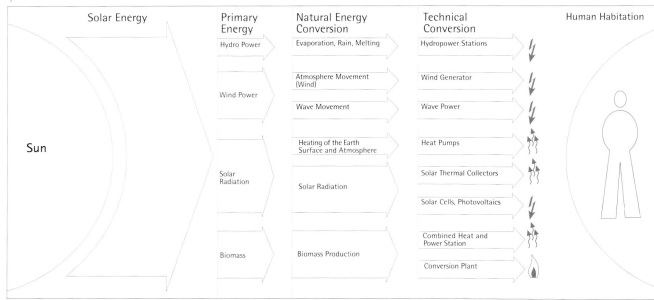

3

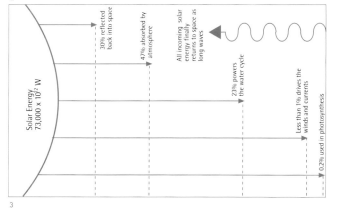

4

Solar energy is far more than just radiation. It is all around us and takes many different forms — clouds, waves, log fires, pieces of coal. These resources represent a massive energy potential greatly exceeding that of fossil fuels.

5

The chaotic behaviour of solar energies on Earth poses the greatest challenge in using renewable power efficiently in the future. In order to use them, we have to understand them.

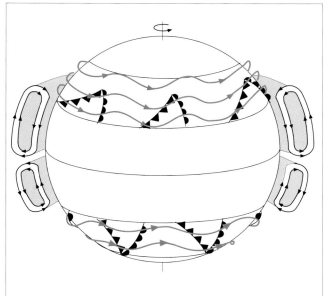

6

7

The Earth's wind patterns are complicated by the poles and by the rotation of the planet. This deflects the winds from a straight path to the right in the northern hemisphere and to the left in the southern hemisphere. North and south of the equator are the Hadley wind cells, in which warm air rises and flows away from the equator to sink again at the tropics. In the polar cells, air masses sink at high latitudes and flow away from the poles as cold air, eventually forming parts of the polar front.

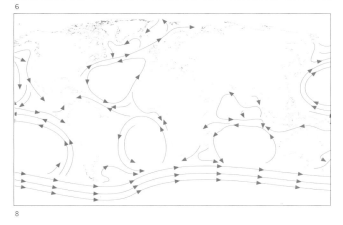

8

9

Ocean currents may warm or cool areas to a degree that is not typical of inland locations at the same latitude. The world's climatic belts do not show a regular and gradual decrease in temperature from the equator to the poles. Mountain ranges may block or divert the movement of air masses or change their nature as they rise and cool.

Plants and Cells
Complex energy transformation systems

For millennia, the biosphere has run on solar energy. Plants, blue-green algae, and certain bacteria are producers, capable of converting solar energy into stored chemical energy by the process of photosynthesis. Each year, these remarkable organisms produce more than two hundred billion tons of food. The chemical energy stored in this food fuels the metabolic reactions that sustain life.

Leaves are the plants' solar collectors, the interface with radiation. Chlorophyll and other pigments in chloroplasts (structures within a cell) capture the energy of the sunlight shining on a leaf and use it to power the amazingly complex set of chemical reactions known as photosynthesis. This is the most crucial process of transformation of energy on Earth. Through photosynthesis, solar energy is transformed into the air that creatures breathe. Chlorophyll absorbs light from the sun, soaking up red and blue, but reflecting green. Chlorophyll acts as a catalyst. Through respiration, plants take up carbon dioxide and release oxygen constantly.

Energy is distributed through a highly efficient network. Roots serve to anchor the plant and aid in absorption of materials from the soil. Leaves are integral to the process of photosynthesis. Water travels through the plant stem via xylem cells. Food substances travel through a different pipeline network, the phloem cells — a very efficient servicing system.

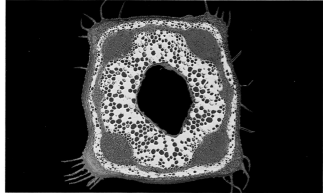

Plants are highly efficient solar collectors harvesting solar energy. They use solar energy to transform carbon dioxide from the air into chemical energy while enriching the atmosphere with oxygen. As biomass, they are an energy source in their own right and form the starting point for the food chain that sustains most living creatures on Earth.

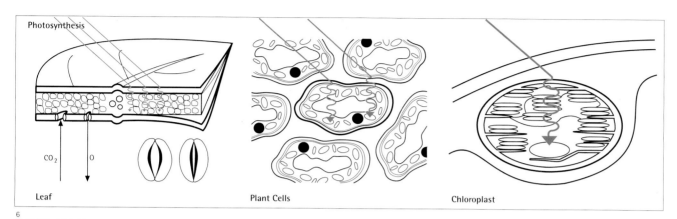

Photosynthesis

Leaf

CO_2

O

Plant Cells

Chloroplast

6

Photosynthesis means 'putting together by light'. Leaf cells are made of cellulose and have a stiff outer wall surrounded by a plasma membrane. Each cell contains dozens of chloroplasts to trap the sunlight. Air and carbon dioxide enter and leave the underside of the leaf via stomata, or pores. Cells are miniature solar cladding systems. These complex processes are based on membranes that are selectively permeable.

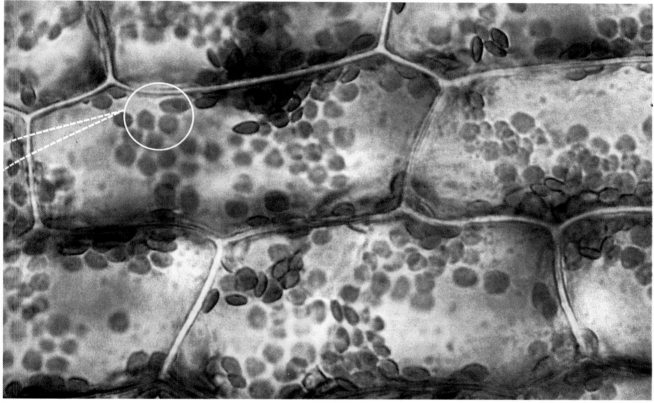

7

Phototropism is the growth of plants according to the direction of light. It is due to the unequal distribution of auxin. Auxin travels down one side of the stem away from the light, causing the cells on the darkened side to elongate. Therefore, the stem bends towards the light. This illustrates how plants respond to external stimuli. By dynamically responding to the sun, they achieve efficiency in converting energy.

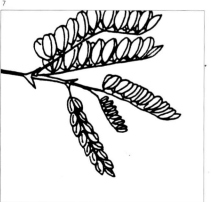

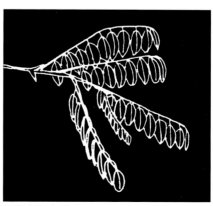

8   Strong Sunlight, Closed Position   Little Sunlight, Maximum Aperture   No Light, 'Sleeping' Position

Solar Tracking
The leaves of *Robina pseudoacacia* track the sun. With strong solar radiation, the small leaves turn upwards, so the leaf surface is reduced to the minimum. In diffuse daylight, the plant opens up its leaves to the light, so that the incoming light can be used to the optimum. At night, the leaves turn downwards.

Cycles of Solar Energy
Sustainable ecosystems

The three nutritional groups in our ecosystem are: producers such as plants, which synthesize organic food; consumers, mainly animals; and decomposers, bacteria and fungi. Activities of the producers make organic materials, which are fed on by the consumers. The decomposers free inorganic materials from the dead bodies of the producers and consumers, thereby ensuring a continuous supply of raw materials for the producers.

Plants, animals, and all forms of organic matter are part of the Earth's biomass. Plants are part of a sustainable cycle, as most have a positive carbon dioxide balance. This means that they absorb more carbon dioxide than they release when they rot. Coal and oil absorbed their carbon dioxide millions of years ago, but are releasing it now, creating an imbalance in the carbon cycle, the circulation of carbon in the biosphere.

The food chain is a nutritional sequence extending from the sun to humankind. Each organism in this sequence feeds on, and therefore derives energy from, the preceding one. The efficiency of the energy transformation when an animal eats a plant is generally less than 20%, so only 20% of the energy contained in the food material is incorporated into the body of the consumer.

Most organismes go through different levels of dependency on energy supplies. An embryo depends entirely on its mother's energy supply. As it develops, it becomes more independent.

Parasites are the only organisms that remain 100% dependant as they develop. They suck highly concentrated energy out of the hosts and ultimately destroy them.

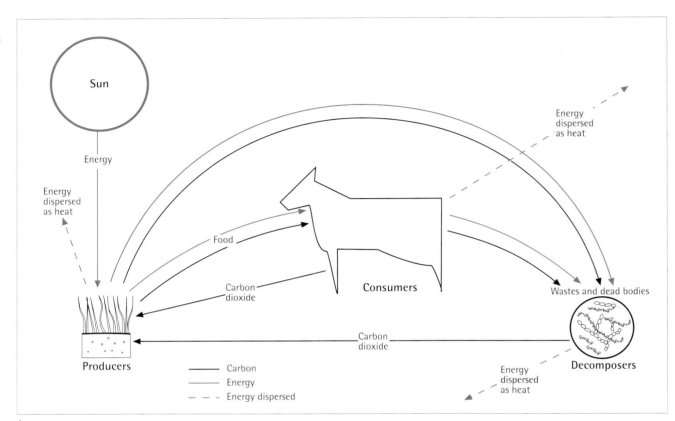

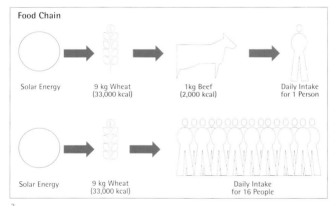

Food Chain

Solar Energy | 9 kg Wheat (33,000 kcal) | 1kg Beef (2,000 kcal) | Daily Intake for 1 Person

Solar Energy | 9 kg Wheat (33,000 kcal) | Daily Intake for 16 People

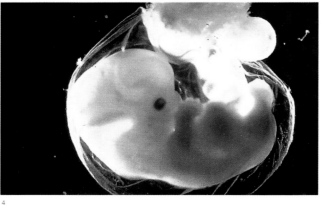

Solar energy is the beginning of the food chain. If we want to create sustainable systems, we need to learn from nature. Sustainability is a question of relationships. Our ecosphere demonstrates a wide range of relationships, which are parasitic, commensal, or symbiotic.

6

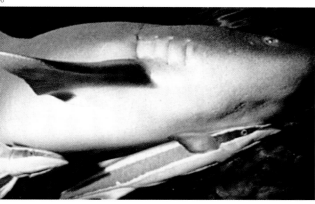

7

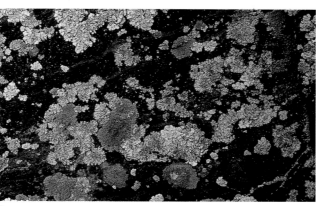

8

The complexity and productivity of a coral reef exceed those of any terrestrial environment. In many ways, a coral reef is the equivalent of the tropical rain-forest. This complex community contains many sub-communities and is itself part of the marine habitat. It can be seen as an example of a complex symbiotic structure and might trigger visions for urban planning and life in the future. Of course, associations between organisms vary. When species are closely associated and at least one can benefit from the other, this relationship is commensal. This means eating from the same table. In a symbiotic relationship, the association is mutually beneficial; both parties gain from the relationship. In a parasitic relationship, the parasite gains while the host suffers harm.

The shark and the pilot-fish have an association of commensalism. The pilot-fish cling to the body of the host, feeding on its scraps.

Lichen that grow on plants form entirely new symbiotic structures. Here, a mushroom forms the structure and the lichen produce organic substances on which the mushroom depends.

33

Animals
Body management systems and building skills

Animals have evolved to fit into their own ecosystem. The technologies developed in order to sustain life in various climates are elaborate. Energy and its efficient use are a matter of survival.

Living in hot and dry climates, camels store heat to minimise evaporative water loss during the day. At night, they lose heat but conserve water through conduction and radiation. Camels adapt to external temperature in order to minimise energy loss — i.e., they drop their internal temperature during the night to suit their environment.

The polar bear has thick black skin under its translucent white fur. The sun's rays enter the fur and warm the dark skin. The fur acts as an insulator, locking in the heat. Thus it is possible to keep a body temperature of 35 degrees Celsius in extremely cold environments.

A bird standing on the ice could die if the ice-cold blood in its feet returned to its heart. To avoid this, arteries act as heat exchangers, preheating the blood in the extremities as it returns from the feet.

The Albatross
Animals are not only efficient organisms in themselves; they have also developed technologies using renewable energies for their needs. Many birds use thermals to rise and stay in the sky just as a wind glider does. The albatross is an expert in aerodynamics. In order to be able to reduce its metabolic energy consumption, it makes use of varying windspeeds and turbulences over the sea. By this application of solar energy in flying, the albatross is capable of travelling up to 15,000 km nonstop. Other birds use thermals over land.

1

2

3

Polar Bear

Sun In

Heat Trapped

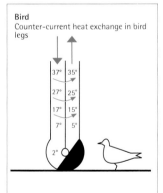

Bird
Counter-current heat exchange in bird legs

37° 35°
27° 25°
17° 15°
7° 5°
2°

4

5

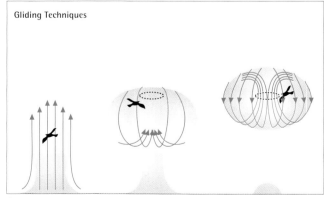

Gliding Techniques

6

Animals consume solar energy indirectly through biomass and are equipped with their own high-performance energy management systems to allow them to survive in environmental conditions that could be fatal. Animals are also impressive builders, especially those who live in large societies.

Termites' nests are among the most spectacular structures built by animals. Through orientation, the nests are protected from overheating in hot climate zones. The African termite, *Macrotermes bellicosus*, has become famous because of the excellent climatisation of its nests. Each nest is separated from the outer walls and stands on columns. Spaces are connected via bundles of vertical tubes. During the day, the outer walls are hotter than the inner walls. Warm air is exchanged through the porous walls, and cooler air is sucked up from the basement. During the night, the inner walls are warmer than the outer walls, so the direction of circulation changes (8). An illustration by Henry Smeathman given to the Royal Society in 1781 shows a nest that contains streets, bridges, canals, food stores, nurseries, guard rooms, and a royal palace (7).

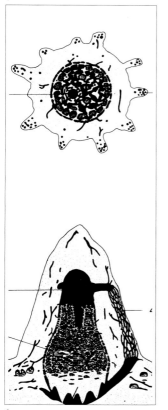

The dramatic forms of giant termitaries (9) are a common sight over large areas of West Africa. The principles on which their construction is based can also be applied to buildings.

Humans and Their Environment
Does human form follow environmental function?

Human Origins

In order to understand human beings, and particularly their relation to their environment, we have to go back to our roots. Humans are warm-blooded mammals that produce body hair and feed their children on milk. Apes and humans share a number of features and are collectively called humanoids.

The evolutionary line split 3.5 to 4 million years ago, but today humankind and chimpanzees still share 98% of their DNA.

The origins of modern humankind lie in the African savanna. The human organism is well suited to survive in this environment (4).

The brain sizes of apes and humans differ dramatically (5). A modern human has a brain size between 1,200 and 1,700 cm³. Homo erectus already had a brain size of between 750 and 1,250 cm³, but a chimpanzee has a brain size of between 320 and 480 cm³. Increasing brain size meant constantly rising energy demands. Even though the brain only accounts for 2% of overall body weight, it consumes 25% of total calorie intake in the case of an average adult.

The human skin's performance is tuned to life in the savanna. Sweat glands create moisture on the external body surface, which acts as an evaporative cooling system (6, 7).

1

2

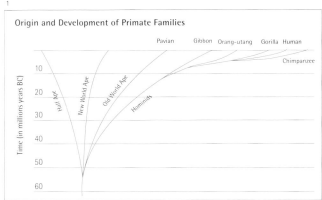

Origin and Development of Primate Families

Pavian Gibbon Orang-utang Gorilla Human

Chimpanzee

Time (in millions years BC)

10
20
30
40
50
60

Half Ape
New World Ape
Old World Ape
Hominids

3

4

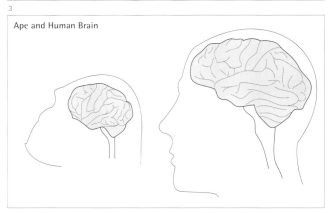

Ape and Human Brain

5

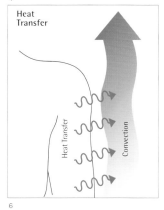

Heat Transfer

Heat Transfer
Convection

6

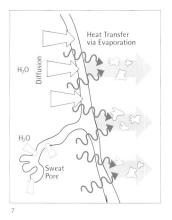

Heat Transfer via Evaporation

Diffusion

H_2O

H_2O

Sweat Pore

7

The human body is a highly sophisticated machine with certain basic requirements. As a warm-blooded creature, a human being has to keep the body at the right temperature for comfort in varying climates. Human skin performance is limited. Clothing and buildings are meant to compensate for these deficiencies.

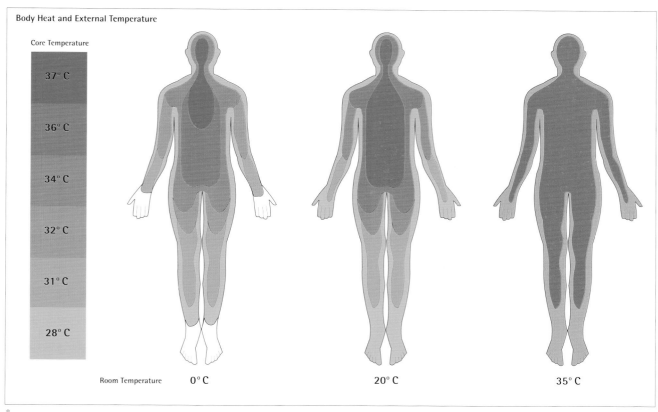

Body Heat and External Temperature

Core Temperature

37° C
36° C
34° C
32° C
31° C
28° C

Room Temperature   0° C   20° C   35° C

8

Body Heat and External Temperature
Humans are constantly faced with the problem of keeping their core body temperature even at approximately 35 degrees Celsius. This is a challenge for the human metabolism, as the outside temperature is in constant change, depending on climate and the time of day. To keep the body temperature as stable as possible, various techniques are employed. In order to keep the brain, heart, and other main organs in perfect condition, the body lets the extremities cool down first and creates temperature gradations throughout itself. As we shall see, some vernacular buildings work in a similar way.

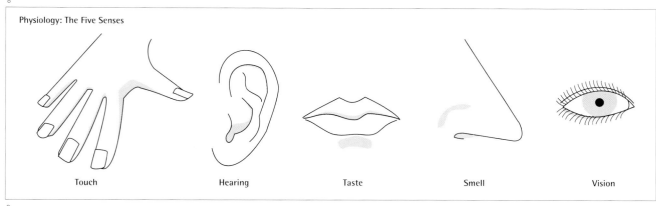

Physiology: The Five Senses

Touch   Hearing   Taste   Smell   Vision

9

The Human Senses
In the same way as metabolism has developed, human physiology, especially the senses, is the interactive tool with the environment. The senses perceive external stimulation and warn the brain if it is in danger, but are also the sensors for enjoyment. In this respect, it is interesting to think that the senses are ideally stimulated in the savanna environment.

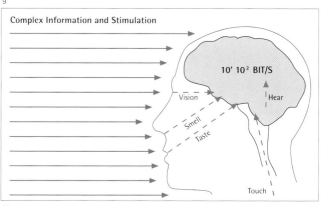

Complex Information and Stimulation

10' 10² BIT/S

Vision   Hear

Smell
Taste

Touch

10

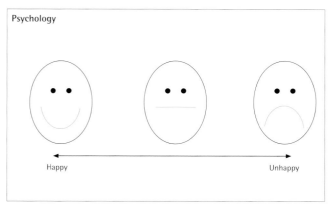

Psychology

Happy   Unhappy

11

Physiology and sensual perception
are directly linked to human psychology. The feeling of a person is not only generated by the senses; the psychology/mood of a person always influences his or her perception as well. This is crucial to keep in mind when one tries to design habitable space with the aim of creating comfort and the feeling of well-being.

Methods of Compensation
Fire, clothing, and shelter

Migration of Homo erectus from the savanna started as early as 1.8 million years B.C. These early humans moved up to Java, where remains of the Mojo Kerto child were discovered. Later, Homo erectus spread further into Europe and Asia, where he managed to survive for almost 1.5 million years before becoming extinct. Homo sapiens, modern man, only started his journey from Africa a hundred thousand years ago. It was Homo sapiens who developed techniques and technologies ranging from agriculture to photovoltaic cells, from caves to high-rise buildings.

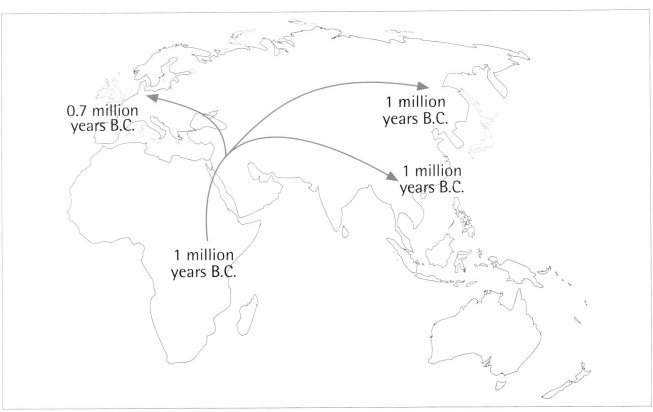

0.7 million years B.C.

1 million years B.C.

1 million years B.C.

1 million years B.C.

1

The discovery of fire approximately four hundred thousand years ago can be seen not only as the major invention that ultimately led humankind to become independent from natural conditions and cycles, through artificial light and heat, but also as the first major step of active energy conversion constantly requiring resources. (The demands for firewood still cause major environmental problems in most underdeveloped countries in the world). Even though the open fire created well-tempered spaces, these were still too limited. Humankind turned to other forms of compensation, like natural protected niches and microclimates (caves), and more flexible compensation, adding higher-performance animal skins to their own skins and by constructing portable shelters.

2

3

Human exploration of new territories/climatic zones made necessary the technological development of forms to provide for human survival and comfort.

4

Early Built Structures for Shelter
As humankind was confronted with more hostile climates, people tried to compensate for their bodies' deficiencies by creating second and third skins. Beginning with clothes, it was a logical step to create more spacious enclosures. Even though caves and natural land formations were probably the first forms of compensation, there is evidence of interesting built structures. One of the first built shelters found is a hut in Terra Amata, near Nice, France, which was built about 400,000 B.C. It was made of branches leaning against each other, fixed by heavy stones and possibly covered by animal skins. Its size was approximately six by twelve m; it could have given shelter to about fifteen hunters.

5

6

Certain African peoples have no need to compensate for the environment. As they live in a hot and humid climate, their only need is sufficient ventilation.

Human migration and travel have moved beyond Earth's climatic zones to outer space. The performance of clothing and shelter has had to increase as a result.

Responsive Solar Buildings

The Earth's Comfort Zones
Between heaven and hell

Ice Caps
Sub-zero temperatures are the norm. The only building material that is in plentiful supply here is ice. The only resource for clothing is animal skins. These are the basics of the polar survival kit.

Tundra/Taiga
Although the warm summers allow settlement, winters are too cold. The nomad's home must be designed for easy dismantling and portability. Yurts respond well to a whole variety of climatic conditions.

Mountains
Snow, avalanches, wind, and rain are obstacles to be overcome. Here, location and orientation become critical design factors. The structures produced are hard workers — efficient, self-sufficient, and sustainable.

Continental Climate with Cool or Warm Summers
Buildings must be robust to cope, and materials have to be chameleon-like to be able to create the ideal indoor environment. Balancing comfort conditions using mass to absorb heat or insulating with wood is the goal.

Marine West–coastal Climate
These are the industrial heartlands. The strong winds and rain that come with the winter cold make this a good environment for modern humans. Whatever the weather, people are likely to spend much of their time indoors.

Mediterranean Climate
This zone is the closest to an ideal climate, and millions of holidaymakers flock to the area every year to prove it. But human beings still must be protected from the intense heat of summer by shading and thermal mass.

Subtropical Climate
Most of the year, the climate is pleasant, but summers are humid, so ventilation is a must in order to avoid overheating. In return for summer comfort, people must accept some discomfort in the cold winter.

Rain-forests
It is hot and humid; people overheat as their evaporative cooling systems are overloaded. What people need is ventilation and protection against the sun and rain. Walls, floors, and roofs must be capable of drying quickly.

Savannas
Here, humans can live without the need for protection in the form of housing or clothing. Homes are fairly low in performance, for shading or shelter from rain. Walls are permeable with minimal insulation.

Steppes
Homes in this zone have to shade and cool and provide protection against sandstorms. Human ingenuity has developed cooling systems using renewable energy, evaporative cooling, earth cooling, thermal air movement, wind towers, and screens.

Deserts
The exact opposite of polar regions, but just as hostile in terms of temperatures and water supplies. Without water, the nomadic hunter-gatherer existence has had to continue. Peoples' homes in deserts are generally temporary.

The world's climatic regions offer different types of living environment, from the hell of extreme cold and heat to the heaven of the savanna.

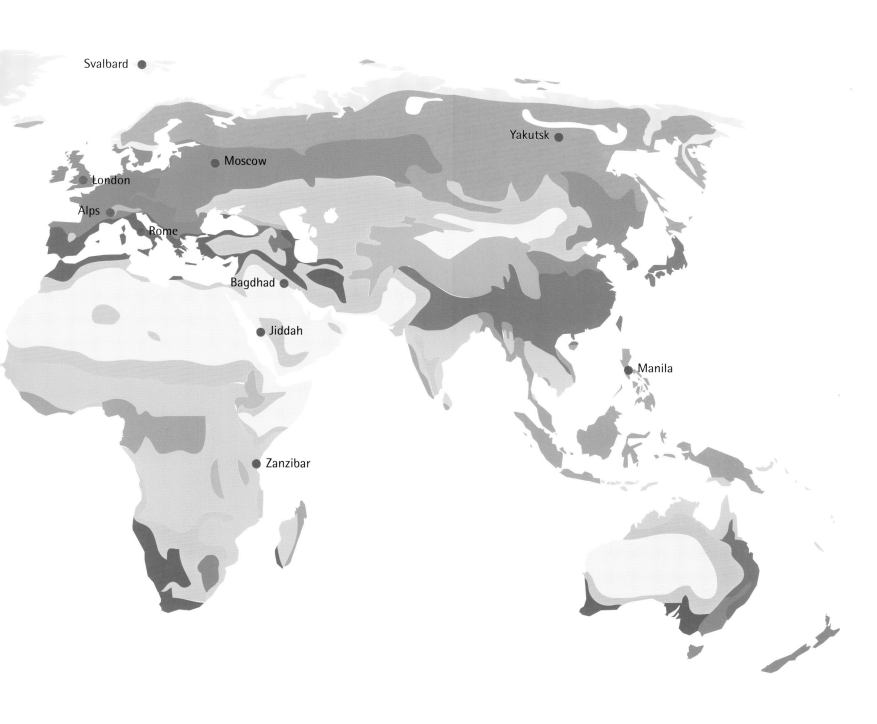

Svalbard

Yakutsk

Moscow

London

Alps

Rome

Bagdhad

Jiddah

Manila

Zanzibar

Architecture versus Vernacular
A matter of building principles

Vernacular builders have to make sure that their structures are highly efficient. They can only use local materials and construction techniques that make economic sense. The running costs of their structures, especially, energy consumption has to be low because of the limited resources available.

The Pyramids — high architecture — were not designed with energy efficiency in mind, although solar energy was considered in great detail when they were constructed.

The Earth provides the food, water, and oxygen that humans need to live, but survival cannot be taken for granted. The natural environment provides a wide range of challenges. Climate conditions can be extremely hostile and vary widely. For example, the temperature may go as low as -40 degrees Celsius in the polar regions, but in the desert cold weather is classed as 0 degrees Celsius. And an extremely arid desert may go without rain for as long as five years.

The human body has evolved to give some help in the struggle for survival, for instance by changing skin pigment. However, humans' primary means of providing themselves with comfort in the natural environment lies in creating their own protection using clothing and buildings. Around the world, people have developed energy-efficient building forms that are suited to the climatic conditions of their particular location — a sort of solar vernacular. They have developed simple yet cleverly built solutions to the environmental challenges set before them, whether by heat, cold, rain, or wind. These solutions have, of necessity, been developed using only a limited range of indigenous building materials, all of them renewable.

Everyone in the world has the same fundamental needs from their homes: shelter and comfort. The design of the basic house, however, varies greatly from region to region according to the natural resources available and the prevailing climate. In the polar regions, the igloo has evolved as the standard solution for sheltering from the extreme cold, while in the desert the tent traditionally has suited the mobile existence of nomads. However elegant and

successful these simply designed homes may appear, they are seldom considered to be architecture. Architecture is regarded as the preserve of the few, the wealthy elite. Only those in a position to afford architecture have also been able to ignore energy-efficient methods of building and maintenance. Architecture is designed by specialists and expresses the power and status of the owner. Vernacular, by contrast, is building for the masses, and the end result is inevitably less luxurious and often less comfortable.

Widely varying vernacular building designs have allowed people to live in harsh climates, but they have seldom succeeded in providing the very highest levels of comfort. The relationship between humans and their environment is finely balanced, and true comfort is often difficult to achieve.

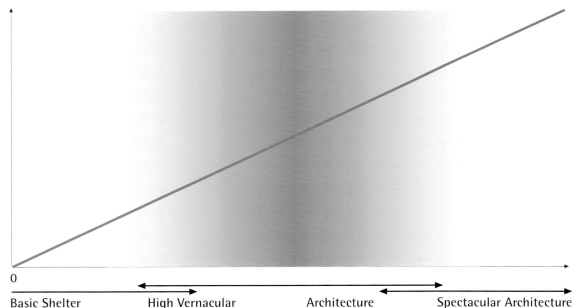

It is no coincidence that human groups from different continents, creeds, and cultures appear to have come to similar solutions independently in their struggle with similar environments. In this way, basic regional characteristics have been established.

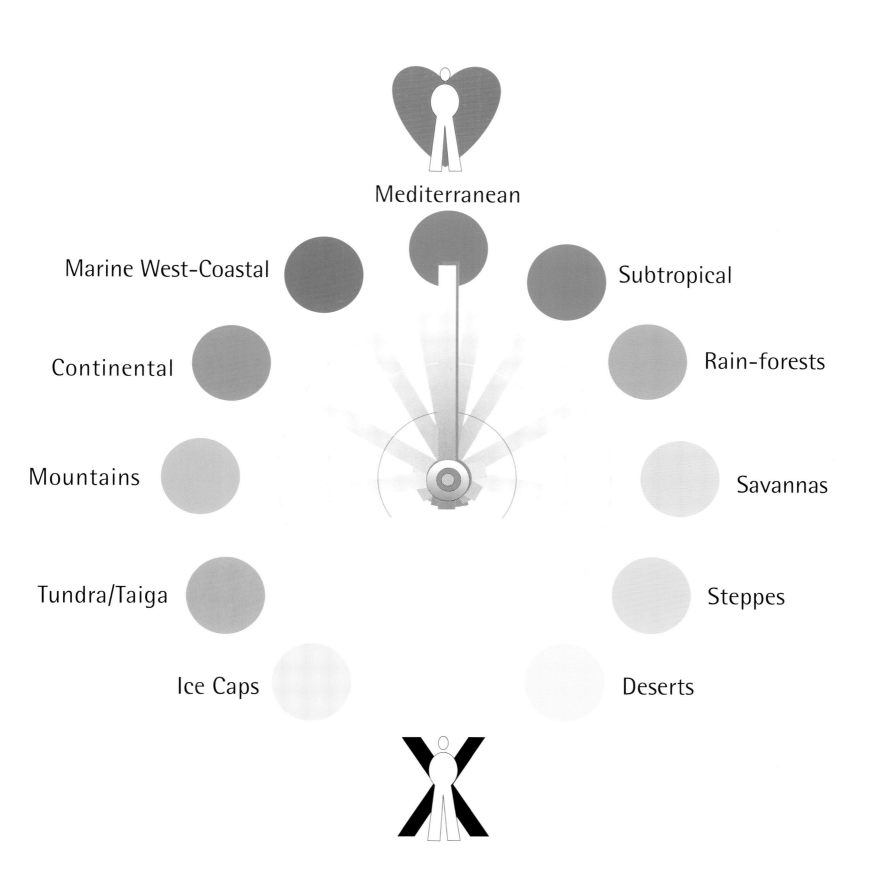

Mediterranean

Marine West-Coastal

Subtropical

Continental

Rain-forests

Mountains

Savannas

Tundra/Taiga

Steppes

Ice Caps

Deserts

Ice Caps
Polar climate

Ultimate Insulation
Creating a building for survival rather than comfort in a polar winter — without mechanical aid — would challenge the best designer. The igloo is the perfect solution.

The ice blocks used for igloo construction can be as large as 1 m long, 0.5 m wide, and 0.2 m thick. The Eskimo builder sets out a 5-m-diameter circle and lays the first layer. The following blocks are cut at an incline so that the dome rises in a continuous spiral. The door opening is cut into the completed dome (4). Sometimes several igloos are connected for more space (6).

Insulation
Some Eskimos line the inside of the roof of their igloos with animal hide for extra insulation. With the addition of blubber lamps and the body heat of the family, an igloo might have an internal temperature of up to 15.5 degrees Celsius, in an outdoor temperature of -40 degrees Celsius (3).

The Eskimo has not only applied his ingenuity to building. In Greenland, five-hundred-year-old mummified bodies were found clothed in sealskin garments sewn with sinew and waterproofed with seal oil. They also wore undergarments made from cormorant, duck, and goose feathers.

1

2

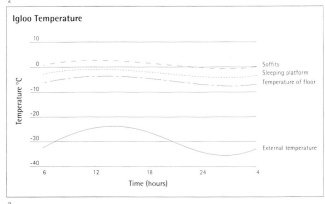

Igloo Temperature

3

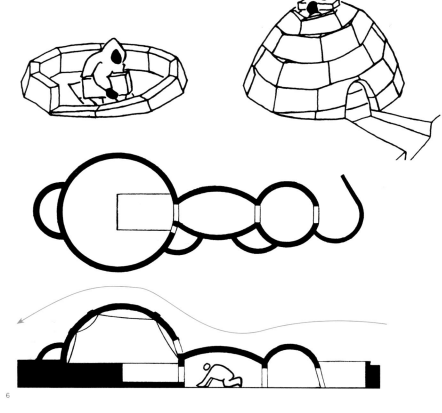

4

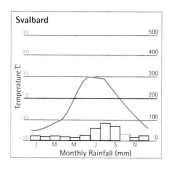

Svalbard

Monthly Rainfall (mm)

5

6

Sub-zero temperatures are the norm. Very few animal species can survive the extreme cold. The only building material is ice. The only resource for clothing is animal skins.

Tundra/Taiga
Arctic climate

Nomad Shelters
As building materials are very scarce on the steppes, builders frame their houses with whatever they can find. Most natives sink their houses into the ground or construct temporary tents in spring and autumn. Their covers are sewn from caribou or seal skins.

1

Thule Engineering
Inhabitants of the tundra and taiga build dug-in houses, where for heating reasons the entrance to the living area is recessed. As timber is readily available, sod-covered houses are wood-framed. Homes are ventilated by a section of hollow whale vertebra (3). The *kashim* serves as a gathering place where dances and feasts are held. It is usually framed with split wall timbers and pole rafters and roofed with sod (4).

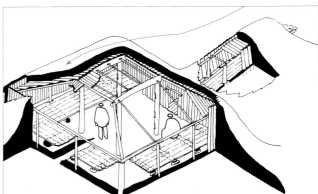

3

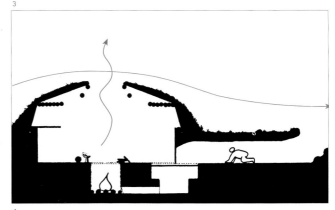

5   2   4

Although the warm summers allow settlement, winters are cold, with permanent frost on the ground. Agriculture and building activity were restricted until recent times, leaving these regions open to nomads, whose homes had to be designed for portability.

6

The yurt has proved its adaptability across the globe. Nomads are equally at home in their yurts on the steppes, in the gravel desert, or in mountainous regions. Yurts are to be found in Russia, Mongolia, Afghanistan, and elsewhere. Although the name, and the outer detailing, may differ from country to country, all yurts have the same underlying structure. Circular in plan, each has an open lattice frame of willow wands for the wall. This wall frame can be expanded and contracted for transportation from site to site (8). A typical dwelling is five m in diameter. A lattice comprises more than 30 wands, light, preformed poles lashed to the frame. The crown of the yurt is raised on poles and has a central opening that symbolises the eye of heaven and through which smoke disperses.

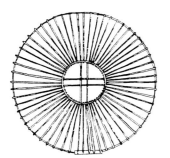 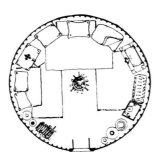

7

9

Lightweight, Adaptable Structures
The frame of the yurt is covered with woollen felt or reed mats. Sometimes decoration is added to the exterior. Space inside the yurt is strictly divided into quadrants (7). There is a separate space for the head of the family, women, and children, and for guests and the shrine. The hearth is at the centre.

8

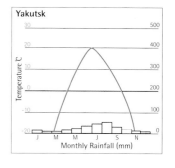

49

Mountains
Cold, wet or dry climate

Living with the Landscape
In the mountains, buildings cannot hope to fight against nature. They must be in harmony with this singularly unforgiving landscape and climate. Buildings may be dug into the ground, hugging it for protection, or raised up to minimise humidity. Few building materials are available on the mountainside, and transporting them can be difficult, so homes have to be built to last. The stone and wood used for building also produce an energy-efficient home. Buildings are commonly sited on south-facing slopes so that they get maximum sunlight. The south/east orientation of buildings maximises daylighting and passive solar gain through the long winter. Straw, stone, and wood are the most widely used materials. Roofs are pulled down to earth level on the weather side (1: stone building in Val Verzasca).

1

Granary structures in the Alps are mostly very small, one-room structures, to suit the basic storage needs of the farmer. This wood-block construction (2.2 by 2.6 m) in the Mongo in the Alps dates from 1561. Orientation, ventilation, and protection against thieves must all be considered when designing a granary — a well-protected treasury (2, 3).

2

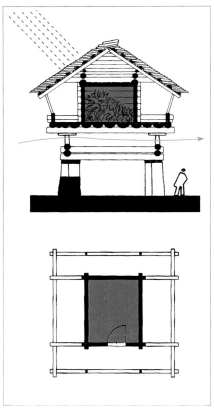

3

The obstacles to be contended with when building in the mountains include snow, avalanches, wind, and rain. Location and orientation are critical design factors. The structures produced must be hard working, efficient, self-sufficient, and sustainable.

4

5

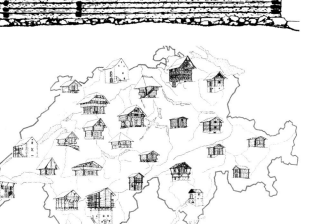

6

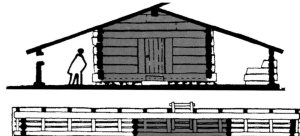

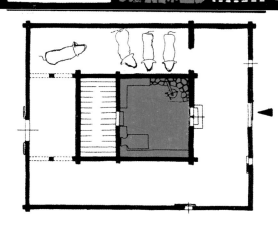

7

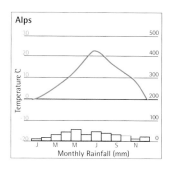

Nature's Storage
The buildings of the southern Alps are mostly south-facing. These open-sided barns, with cantilevered galleries enclosed by wooden lattices, are designed for drying grass in the warm summer months while providing basic protection from harsh winter weather (4: a *Walser* in Algna Valesisia, Italy). The log construction and wooden studs are burnt brown by the sun.

Granaries of the Swiss mountain regions (6) illustrate the various forms that have been developed over the centuries. They serve several purposes: in the cellar, wine and vegetables are stored; on the ground floor, wheat; the first floor is used to dry fruits, meat, vegetables, and other winter goods; on the second floor, general household goods like clothes and furniture are stored. The top floor can serve as an additional bedroom.

Symbiotic Structures for Humans and Animals
In the wraparound cheese-making dairy buildings of the Alps (5, 7) the farmer has everything he needs for his work. Living and working quarters are surrounded by a cow byre in a single building. The animals are sheltered, and as they are gathered around the living quarters, they give the farmer's home additional warmth. These houses are generally oriented south/south-west.

Continental Climate
Cold and warm summers

Cold Summer Climate
In Russia, Belarus, and Canada, buildings have to be designed to cope with summer cold rather than heat (1: Canadian village houses, 1920s). Wood and stone are the most readily available construction materials, and wood is the staple for buildings. As wood is also the primary home energy source, the full potential of the biomass is exploited. Timber also has energy benefits. It has a high resistance to the flow of heat and a low thermal capacity. The latter means that a timber building will warm up quickly when heated.

1

The block house in Russia has practically solid wooden walls. The use of entire tree trunks does create problems of draughts, however (2). The European *Fachwerk* house employs wood as a framing material (3). Infills are of clay and straw. In order to protect the clay from rain and snow, the storeys can be set back to create overhangs.

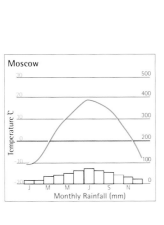

Moscow
Temperature °C
Monthly Rainfall (mm)

2

3

Temperatures can swing from -10 degrees Celsius in winter to 30 degrees Celsius in summer. Buildings have to be robust enough to cope; materials would have to be chameleon-like to be able to create the ideal indoor environment all year round. For building designers, it is a question of balancing comfort conditions using mass to absorb heat or insulating with wood.

4

Dwellings below Ground

The construction costs of cave dwellings (4: Xicun near Luo-yang, China; 5, 6: Tungkwan, China) can be one-fifth of the costs of conventional brick and timber houses in the same region. Earth is not only cheaper but is also a better insulation material for heat retention in winter and keeping cool in summer. The interior of a cave dwelling can be eight to fifteen degrees Celsius cooler in summer and up to ten degrees Celsius warmer in winter. The construction of such dwellings causes very little damage to the environment as the earth surface is generally untouched. Caves facing south are traditionally reserved for the head of the family and the elderly. Those facing west are occupied by children, and kitchen and utility areas generally face east. The north-facing caves usually serve as latrines and pigsties.

Warm Summer Climate

The choice is simple for buildings here: either they have to have a buffer between the inside and outside, or they have to be highly flexible. Comfort conditions can never be perfect all year round.

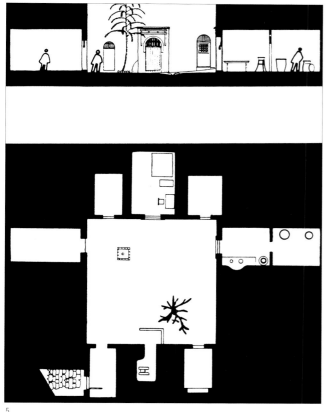

5

6

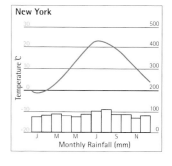

New York

Temperature °C

Monthly Rainfall (mm)

Marine West-coastal Climate
A warm, temperate environment

Roofs for Protection
When the weather gets rough at sea, sailors batten down the hatches. They make sure that the roofs of their buildings are just as secure. Norman sailors devised thatched roofs that resembled upside-down ships' hulls, with the bow to the wind and the stern sheltered to the east. Sailors brought to building their understanding of protecting the weather side (generally the west), of water- and wind-proofing. For protection from wind and rain, buildings need either to be carefully oriented or to have their roofs pulled down low, to offer minimum resistance. Thatched roofs offer excellent weather protection — the strands of thatch act like animal fur (1: English thatched country house, Longstock, Hampshire).

1

Farmhouses on the mainland in Donegal (2) are lime-washed and thatched with straw. These are the only materials that are readily available, and they form the walls of both house and enclosure.

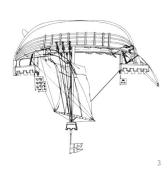

3

4   2

Not too hot, not too cold — the oceans have a calming influence on the temperatures on land. The strong winds and rain that come with the winter cold make this a good environment for modern people to work in, as long as they have warmth and protection.

5

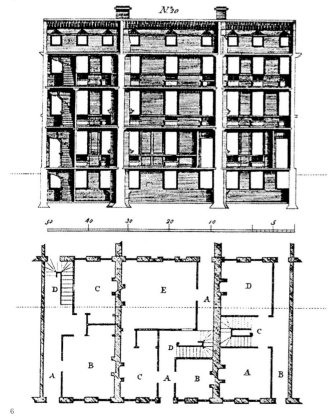

6

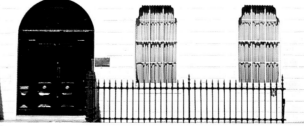

7

Dense urban structures allow little daylight to enter buildings. The less daylight there is, the larger windows need to be, so a balance must be struck between lighting and insulation. In this city street in San Sebastian, there is a buffer space for insulation behind the heavily glazed facades.

Through careful planning, different microclimates can be created within one building. These areas can serve different purposes in a climate that changes throughout the year.

Georgian houses in England (6, 7) get the lighting and insulation balance right and have provided people with comfortable refuges against the industrialising world outside. For more than two centuries, they have shown how adaptable they can be, for domestic or commercial use, and as a result they have kept their value. The durability of the stripped, classical combination of brick, wood, and glass and the low embodied energy content of these houses have proved successful.

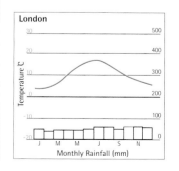

London
Monthly Rainfall (mm)

Mediterranean Climate
Close to ideal conditions

Habitable Shade
The builders of the Mediterranean are experts when it comes to shading. This region boasts a long history of shading devices and a rich variety of solutions. In this history, shutters are a relatively recent development. Long before them came comfortable microclimates made possible by the construction of arcades and verandahs where walls and columns merge the bright heat outside with the cold dark indoors (1, 2: the old arcade next to the cathedral of Ferrara).

Atrium House
In early times, living spaces were the protected zones around courtyards. Distinctions between inside and outside were blurred, with the real comfort climate existing in the shaded areas between the two.

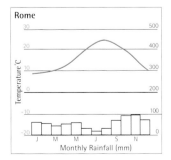

Rome

Temperature °C

Monthly Rainfall (mm)

The Mediterranean climate zone is the closest to an ideal climate. But people must be protected from the intense heat of summer by shading and thermal mass. Life slows down in summer, as cooling is not always affordable.

Density and Mass

The other way to stay cool in the Mediterranean is by using the bulk of the building itself. The close-set buildings of Genoa serve to create a micro-climate in the street outside. Buildings shade each other, so there is minimum heat penetration. The disadvantage is that interiors enjoy minimal daylight and ventilation.

6

7

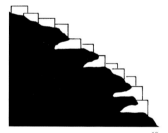

10

Thermal Mass

More successful is the use of the thermal mass of the building to even out the temperature variations of night and day. Mass is provided by thick, heavy walls or by burying the building in the ground so that the earth acts as a temperature balance. The principle works well in summer, but can make buildings too cold for comfort in the winter months (8: *truli* village in southern Italy). The principle of the *truli* is also apparent in the architecture of old greek villages such as Santorini, where built structures are combined with caves (9, 10).

8

9

Subtropical Climate
Warm, humid settings

Performance of the Japanese House

The screens and sliding doors of Japanese houses create buffer zones between inside and outside and allow maximum cross-ventilation. Traditionally, Japanese homes have been built to cope with the hot, humid summer months. Homes are constructed of timber, with clay walls reinforced with straw and bamboo lattices that offer greater thermal mass. They are generally single storey. Steep roofs with deep eaves on the south-facing facade allow winter sun into the house and keep summer sun out. Solar radiation is received by the roof's large surface area, keeping the temperature down. The thatched roof also benefits from the evaporative cooling of rainwater.

Japanese building standards require floors to be raised 45 cm above ground level, because the soil surface is wet and ventilation is needed to keep the crawl space dry. When the crawl space is ventilated, the soil surface is cooled by evaporation. The surface temperature of the floor of the house is therefore lowered by radiation exchange with the soil surface. Thus the underside of the tatami-mat floor is cooler than the top.

Japanese Men in Traditional Vegetable Raincoats

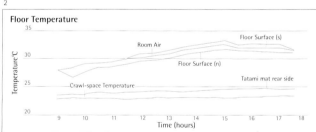

Floor Temperature

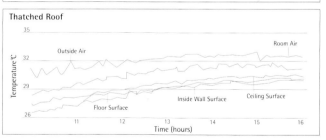

Thatched Roof

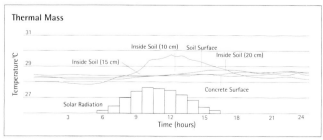

Thermal Mass

Most of the year, the climate is pleasant, but summers are humid so ventilation is a must. The Japanese and Chinese developed systems of dynamic walls to create buffer zones between inside and outside, providing comfortable summer spaces. Such spaces are, however, less comfortable in winter.

7

Early American settlers tended to create buildings that represented a compromise between their own cultures and construction applied to 'new' climatic zones. As the southern states of the US did not have settlements until comparatively recently, ventilation techniques for buildings are not as developed as those of Japan and China. However, there is an understanding of shading and of how to create well-ventilated spaces, as the design of this typical New Orleans house shows. Here, the porch is the buffer zone between inside and outside.

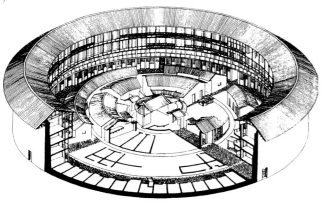

8

9

Chinese Roundhouses
The Chinese roundhouse is, in effect, a fortress. The 65-m-diameter building with its dense wall was designed to keep out marauders. The oldest roundhouse dates from 1680 and is in Chengqilou/Guzu. Most roundhouses are four storeys high and have nearly two hundred-fifty rooms. Only rooms on the second and third storeys are used for habitation. It is interesting how the form of this settlement reflects its performance. Within this wall is a fully sustainable community.

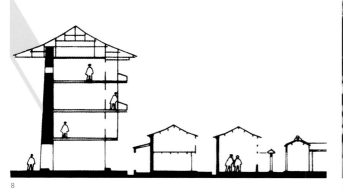

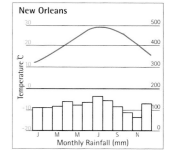

New Orleans

Temperature °C

Monthly Rainfall (mm)

Rain-forests
Tropical places

Aerodynamics for Survival

The homes of the Batak tribe of North Sumatra are designed for ventilation, with large saddle-back roofs and gracefully curving eaves (1: row of Toradja houses in Palawa, South Sulawesi). The deep, projecting, pointed roofs swing far over the gable fronts to give shade for the family at work inside. Homes are built of wood and thatch. Hardwood poles are placed in order of quality to reflect the importance of the space inside. Shorter posts are fastened with pin-and-hole fixings. These support a well-ventilated floor resting on longitudinal beams up to 10 m in length and on cross-members. Each house is occupied by several families, with occupants living on several levels (2: Batak village in Sumatra). Where you live in the house depends on your position in the family. The coolest parts are reserved for the most senior members.

Rice stores

were very important. As is often the case with vernacular building types, structures for securing the community's energy supply were technically the most advanced (3). Perfect conditions for the harvest of rice were felt to be more important than people's comfort.

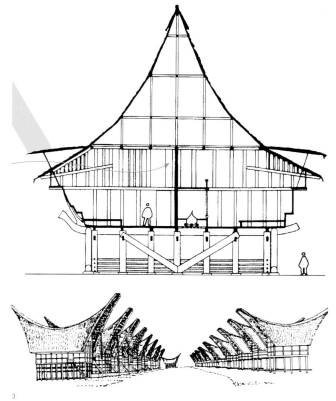

This is the perfect environment for plant life, but for humans the living is not so easy. The combination of heat and humidity can be hard to endure — humans overheat as their evaporative cooling system is overloaded. What they need is ventilation and protection against the sun and rain. Walls, floors, and roofs must be able to dry.

5

Thin, Permeable Walls
Thermal mass would not be any use in this climate, as the temperature does not change sufficiently from day to night. Buildings have to provide maximum shading and cross-ventilation, so walls are thin and the intensity of the sun through windows is obscured by blinds to let even the lightest breeze through (5: coffee plantation house in the Caribbean).

6

7

The layering of buildings' walls not only creates a sense of depth but also provides a wide variation of space that allows the occupants to adapt to various microclimates.

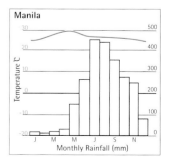

Savannas
Warm, wet environments

Basic Structures for a Basic Task

This is the nearest humans come to living under the sky. With long spells of hot weather, the prime environmental challenges in the savanna are creating shade and finding protection in the rainy season. All a building really needs is a roof, and many of the structures found in this climatic zone are little more than that (1: Bamileke house, Cameroon), acting almost like umbrellas. The quantity of grass needed for thatching a building is considerable, and every year a grass-gathering ceremony is organised. As structures are created from materials growing in the region, building can be seen as part of the natural cycle.

Even though life in Paradise is no longer perfect, it still seems possible to be comfortable with very few means.

Human origins lie at the edge of the rain-forest, the savanna. This is the climatic zone humankind was designed for, so people can live there without the need for protection in the form of housing or clothing. Homes are fairly low in performance; walls are permeable, with minimal insulation.

3

Maximising Air Flow
The walls that are constructed in housing for savanna-dwellers are thin and permeable to allow cross-ventilation. There is no need for mass here (3: Shinaka house in Madagascar).

4

5

Men socialise under a sunshade in Sadia Masli, Dogon (4). Its mass consists of dried millet stalks, and its carved pillars represent ancestors.

Movable Buildings
The tradition of the permanent house is quite alien to some cultures. When they move, they tend like nomads to take their houses or parts of them with them (5: moving day in Guinea). Such basic shelters are as portable as clothes.

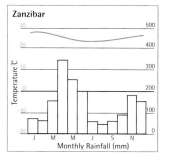

Zanzibar

Steppes
Hot, dry climates

Thermal Mass
In their quest to cool down in the steppes, builders have resorted to heavyweight solutions. Structures are massive, with dense walls to absorb heat. Buildings may be dug into the ground to use the earth mass for cooling.

Within the building, there can be clever technology to increase ventilation. In Hyderabad, Pakistan, the cool afternoon winds mostly come from the same direction. Therefore most buildings are equipped with enormous wind catchers which redirect the airflow down into the living quarters (1). Traditional homes in Baghdad may contain a *badgir*, an air scoop that takes in the north-westerly air stream. A *badgir* is a flue in the wall of a house which rises to the highest point of the roof parapet. It is typically 50 by 20 cm in cross section. *Badgirs* are at their most effective when built into walls transverse to the prevailing wind, with wide openings. Once the air is taken in, it sinks as it takes on moisture and cools in the channel. This is an example of an air conditioning system in its truest, most sophisticated, and most energy-efficient form (2, 3). All these principles need strong temperature variations to function properly.

The principle of ventilation
through badgirs is also applied in buildings without courtyards (3). The air is taken in as before but rises through a central space which has openings at the top.

Courtyards for Cooling
Courtyards can also help to lower the temperature. They act as a vertical vent through the storeys of a building and create a comfortable microclimate. The temperature differential between ground floor and roof can be as much as 20 degrees Celsius (4).

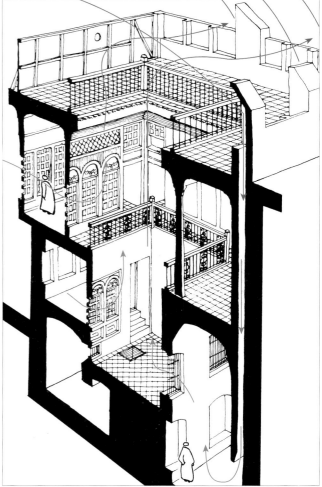

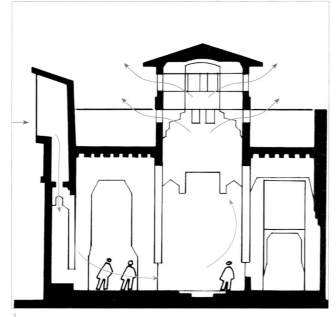

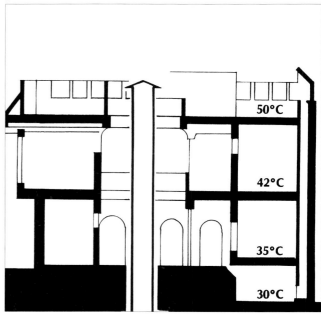

As the desert nears, only irrigated land can support agriculture. Homes are introverted, turning their backs on the harsh climate. They have to shade and cool and provide protection against sandstorms.

5

With wide variations in temperature and comfort within a building during the day, its occupants may live on different levels at different times of the day or year. In summertime, occupants may sleep on the roof where it is coolest, while in the afternoons they will seek refuge from the heat of the day by moving into the lowest levels. In September, a family might move to the winter quarters at the south-facing side of the house, while in April the north-facing rooms will provide greatest comfort. The occupants use buildings like this in a manner similar to the way the albatross uses the winds.

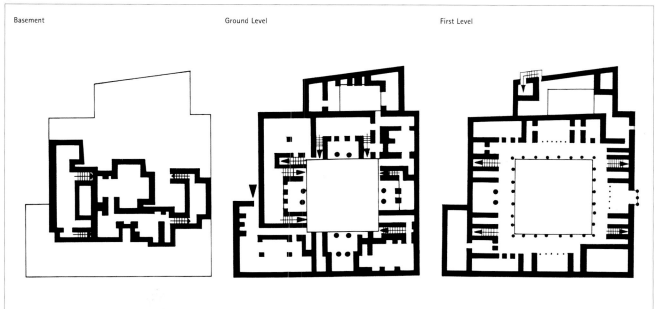

Basement   Ground Level   First Level

6

Courtyards and loggias are muilti-functional spaces. They are not only highly efficient for air conditioning and for comfort generation but also form the main communication link through the house. Japanese pavilions and the Renaissance loggias provide interesting parallels from the realm of spectacular architecture..

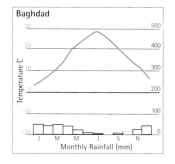

Baghdad

Monthly Rainfall (mm)

Deserts
The hottest and driest of places

Thermal Mass and Earth Materials

This is not most people's idea of comfort. Those permanent structures found in the desert are made with heavy walls of earth material and dug into the ground to keep cool (1: Kash-bah, Draa Valley, Morocco). Walls and roofs are of double thickness for maximum heat absorption. As rainfall is minimal, waterproofing is not an issue. If heavy desert rains hit the building, most parts of it are easily destroyed and have to be rebuilt.

1

Narrow streets with their ranks of tall buildings keep out the sunlight and the fierce, sand-laden winds, and stripes of shadow cool shoppers in a Moroccan bazaar. Roof screens filter the sun's rays, and the contrast is extremely welcome (2).

Mud masonry in the American Southwest (3) is built for daytime shade, using houses for storage and cold-weather sleeping. Rooftops are used for sleeping in summer (5). These constructions have a high heat capacity with thick adobe walls and mud roofs that act to flatten out the stressful thermal curve of the desert climate.

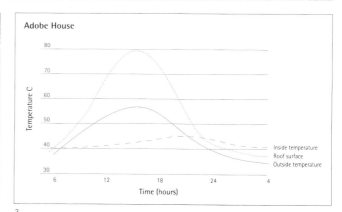

Adobe House

(graph) Temperature C vs Time (hours)

Inside temperature
Roof surface
Outside temperature

3

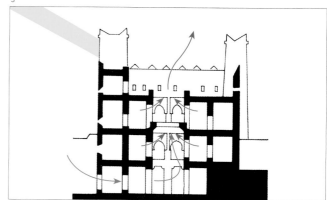

5   2   4

The exact opposite of the polar region, the desert is just as hostile, with life-threatening temperatures and little or no water supply. Without water, human beings have had to continue to live as nomadic hunter-gatherers, so homes are generally temporary and portable.

6

Temporary Shelter
The only way to live in an area with such a harsh climate and so little food supply is to adopt a nomadic way of life. Tents create their own microclimates, keeping out excessive heat during the day and excessive cold at night.

Nomads in arid zones commonly live in black tents (6, 7: black tents of the Qashgasi, Iran). These tents are made from strips of cloth made from goat's hair which are sewn edge to edge to form a large cover. The tent cloth is basically a membrane, stretched over poles and held in tension by guy ropes. Tent cloth may be stretched over a curved ridge to create a humped effect. This provides protection for the tent, stopping the poles from piercing the cloth.

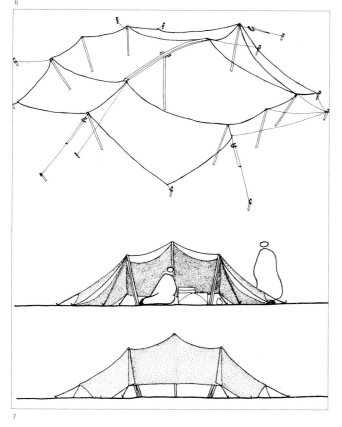

7

8

Tents of the Tuareg, Nigeria
Although it is hot in the daytime, night-time temperatures drop sharply in the mountains. So to catch the first warming rays of the day, tents are pitched with the open front facing eastward. A Tuareg family can transport its home and possessions on two camels (8).

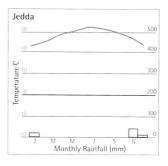

Jedda

Monthly Rainfall (mm)

67

The First Solar Structures

The Neolithic Revolution
The first energy revolution

The sun and its energy supply have been a fundamental influence since the very origin of the human species.

Our birthplace is to be found in the grasslands of Africa, where nature and climate combined to create ideal conditions for human development. Charting each of the stages in the evolution of the species is, however, an extremely difficult task. Hard factual evidence can only be gathered from the fossilised remains discovered from archaeological excavations around the world.

Human ancestors, the hominids, developed an upright stance. Once the bipeds' hands were freed, they could begin to perform a host of tasks, such as making tools. As their brain grew and their manual skills developed, humans were able to journey outside their natural comfort zone — the savanna — to more hostile environments. Once they stepped outside their ideal environment, they had to provide their own protection against adverse climate by making clothing and finding shelter in caves. The life of these early hunter-gatherers was a life of risk and chance in terms of both survival and food supply.

By the time of the first ice age 1,500,000 years ago, human abilities in finding food, clothing, and shelter were sufficiently well developed to guarantee survival. Ice ages alternated with warmer temperatures until 10,000 B.C. Homo sapiens, modern man, emerged 100,000 years ago and within only 70,000 years had spread to almost all corners of the globe. As in Africa some five million years earlier, climate was the catalyst for human development, providing the conditions in which people could thrive. With the ending of the ice ages, climatic extremes diminished and land was unlocked for habitation by animals and plants. Where animals and plants went, humans followed. Temperatures rose, melting the ice sheets that had covered as much as a quarter of the Earth's land surface. Water from the ice sheets fell as rain, causing the deserts to recede and blossom into lush, fertile lands. As in the oil boom that was to follow many thousands of years later, the desert became a vital source of energy.

In areas of the world where food sources were abundant, people relied upon nature to look after their needs. People made their homes in village settlements while continuing to live the life of the hunter-gatherer. But energy supply for the rapidly growing population was uncertain. In parts of the world, food was far from plentiful, and people had to look early on for ways of protecting and increasing their food supplies. The world has always faced the basic problem of matching food supply to demand, preventing famine in the face of population explosion. This fundamental need to feed was to lead to domestication of both plants and animals in the practice of agriculture — the Neolithic revolution.

The transformation from hunter-gatherer to farmer marked a massive step in the progress of human development and in the use of solar energy. The process of hunting and gathering depended on the productivity of the natural environment. When human beings began to farm plants, they increased their productivity by realising the potential of solar energy. With the passage of time, farmers were to develop ever more sophisticated means of maximising the solar-energy-gathering power of crops.

Plants and animals were first domesticated in the Fertile Crescent, a stretch of hilly land running from the Zagros Mountains in present-day Iran to southern Israel and Jordan. To begin with, cereals were planted in areas outside their natural habitat. The sheer hard labour involved in the agricultural way of life meant that people only turned to it when they had to — as a settlement's population increased. Agriculture meant that people could establish permanent settlements, villages with substantial homes and structures. The seeds were sown for the development of construction technology.

By 8000 B.C., major settlements were firmly established, such as Jericho in the Jordan Valley, which spread across one and a half hectares and is believed to have supported around a thousand inhabitants. Around the world, native plants and animals were being farmed. The farming of natural solar collectors led human populations into a vigorous phase of technological development. By 4000 B.C., agriculture had become the basis of life. Across the continents, early farmers were developing tools and equipment to ease such arduous work as ploughing and harvesting. The protection of the energy harvest throughout the winter months became of paramount concern. Biomass storehouses were built at the heart of settlements, and farmers made sure the harvest would be kept in the best possible condition by creating optimum temperature and humidity conditions within their energy stores.

Many types of cereals and vegetables, such as peas and lentils, were cultivated, and farmers also developed their skill in animal husbandry. Levantine communities relied on both goat and gazelle for meat, but had progressed to herding goats by 7000 B.C. Goats grazed on a wide range of plants and could provide milk as well as meat. In various parts of the world, pigs, cattle, and sheep were also domesticated. In many areas, people could only hope to maximise crop yields by the use of irrigation systems, and in each region the right solution had to be found. In Africa, for example, village dwellers in the Nile Valley had to build dykes to contain the river's floodwaters. In Mesopotamia, canal networks had to be constructed as the floods of the Tigris and Euphrates rivers did not provide enough water.

Solar Design for Plants
High efficiency for biomass

Plants, natural solar collectors, were at the heart of the Neolithic revolution (1).

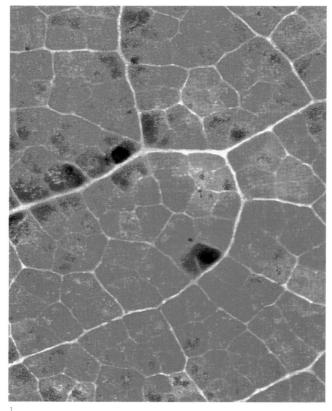

Terraces in China protect hills from erosion and irrigate plants. The watered rice plantations south of Honan are complicated irrigation systems on elaborate gradients. Fields are created on hillsides as a series of shelves, using stone retaining walls and, often, irrigation systems with spillways carry water downwards from shelf to shelf. This keeps the precious rice plants wet throughout the time of growth.

Ingenious ways of maximising plants' yield increased the efficiency of these natural solar collectors. The agricultural age changed the face of the Earth dramatically. Vast areas of forest were eradicated to make way for fields and plantations.

5

6

The agricultural landscape of parts of the American Midwest is fallow or planted with sugar beet. The direction and size of the strips are influenced by the terrain and by the direction of the prevailing winds (5).

The Star of Eserune, near Beziers, France, was constructed in the 13th century (6). The rays of the pattern of fields, which resulted from reclamation work, are drainage ditches. The star does not radiate, however; it collects. Drainage water flows down the gentle gradient of the ditches into a collecting sump at the centre; from there, a canal cuts through the hill in an underground conduit that feeds into a neighbouring pool.

7

8

The human impact on Earth that began with the Neolithic revolution is clearly visible in photographs taken from space.

The intensive cultivation of land in the fertile north of Italy expresses the ancient Roman planning grid and also shows the scale of more recent human activity on the landscape (8).

Building for Agriculture
Complex irrigation systems

Early irrigation systems improved the efficiency of land use and increased crop yield to sustain larger communities.

For rice plantation in China, irrigation was the most crucial factor. Rice needs most water during the growing period, but is also the most efficient plant as far as food production is concerned. In old Chinese books on irrigation, drawings clearly illustrate the techniques employed (1). Irrigation techniques were already in use from around 4000 B.C. on the Huangho River.

The water-wheel designed by the architect Vitruvius (2), was commonly used in the Roman Empire. It could only be used in rivers with a constant flow, however.

Windmills which were an essential feature of the landscape in some parts of medieval Europe, were used to irrigate land, but also as mills to grind grain. Waterwheels using hydropower were also used for this purpose (3). Today, vast areas of the Netherlands can only be used for agriculture and habitation because they are constantly irrigated, using renewable power based on the principle of the Archimedean screw (4).

1

2

3

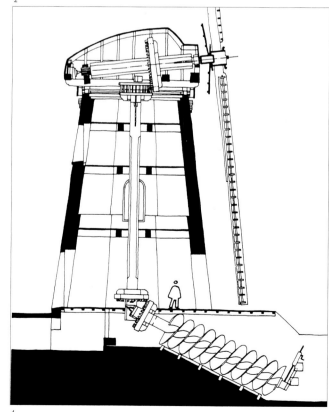

4

To irrigate fields, humankind has come up with some high-tech solutions.

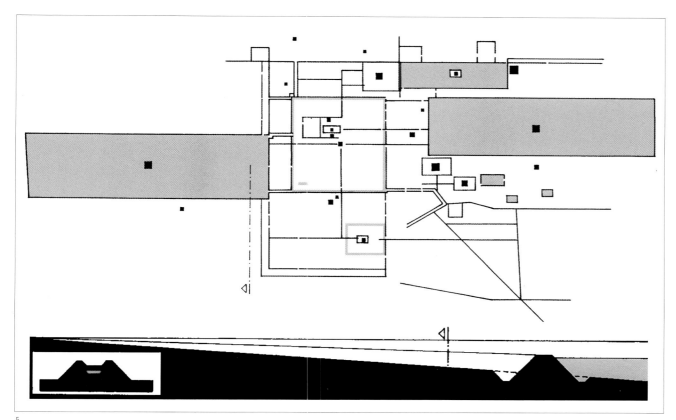

5

6

7

Angkor Wat

In the Fu-nan dynasty, agriculture was totally ruled by the monsoon. Only the rulers of Angkor in present-day Cambodia were able to break this dependency on natural cycles. The rice harvest was tripled by constructing huge artificial lakes, in which water was collected during the rainy season (5: plan of Angkor and Roulos). Angkor became one of the major rice factories between the 9th and the 13th centuries B.C. (6: temple of Angkor Wat as depicted by Louis Delaporte in 1868).

The Khmer probably used up to half of their total grounds for rice plantation, approximately 60,000 hectares. Each hectare produced 2.5 tons of rice twice a year. This was the basis for the power of Angkor in the 12th and 13th centuries.

Solar Cities

Early Urban Planning
The city as accumulator of solar-derived resources

The rise of the first cities between five and six thousand years ago reflected the culmination of a gradual process of proto-urbanisation which had been taking place for many thousands of years prior to the formation of urban concentrations. By this period, a series of important technological innovations had begun to transform human activities: the cultivation of grain; the development of the plough; the potter's wheel and the draw loom; and primitive metallurgy, enabling greater use of copper and other metals for tools. Evidence of intellectual activity — for example, abstract mathematics — could be found. Unlike technological advances since the Industrial Revolution, which have typically stimulated a diffusion of urban form and function, the innovations initiating change within these early civilisations led to an implosion, a packing together, of human activities. The city therefore brought together and concentrated activities that had until that time been unorganised and scattered over a dispersed area. This concentration facilitated greater interaction and enabled components of community life to exist in a dynamic, yet more stable and comfortable, environment.

Central to the formation of the earliest cities, of course, was the development of agriculture, and the location of the oldest civilisations are evidence of this. First, they all emerged in regions experiencing comparable climatic influences that lay between the Tropic of Cancer and a latitude of 30 degrees north. Second, proximity to a large river was important, providing a means of irrigation, transport, and the use of its fertile floodplain for agriculture. A strong dependency upon the natural environment in the provision of energy was therefore apparent. Solar energy, assisted by irrigation techniques, provided the necessary conditions for crop growth and the continuing supply of fuel woods. The river valleys of the Tigris and Euphrates (Mesopotamia), Nile (Egypt), Indus (India), and Wei-Huang (China) provided ideal conditions for the early civilisations to establish cities.

The development of cities in Mesopotamia and Egypt corresponded with a period of climatic change in which marsh- and grassland areas dried up and a steppe/desert environment became increasingly dominant. Exposure of the floodplain enabled more concentrated forms of cultivation and increased food production. In Mesopotamia, the need to collaborate in building and maintaining irrigation systems provided a catalyst for the creation of larger communities. The canal systems not only assisted in the production of crops, aiding the conversion of solar energy to food energy, but also in time were incorporated into the city structures themselves. As the wealth and sophistication of city residents grew, water was also utilised to increase comfort and pleasure. In Babylon, the famous Hanging Gardens were created on a series of elevated terraces irrigated from the Euphrates and assisted by a

pump system. The gardens managed to combine nature and architecture successfully to produce one of the first examples of spectacular solar design. Babylon also clearly illustrated the importance of sun orientation in its city form. The streets were arranged so that they enabled residents to derive the benefits of the climate, such as light, warmth, and favourable breezes, whilst protecting them against the less favourable aspects, providing shelter from harsh south-westerly winds and appropriate ventilation and shading.

The solutions for protection against harsher elements in the ancient Egyptian city of Kahun demonstrated the social divisions that were becoming apparent as a result of the division of labour and practices of enslavement. The slaves in Kahun were housed in the windy western quarter of the city to act as a human buffer, protecting the wealthier residents living in the east. A further example can be seen in Baghdad in Iraq, where servants and animals were condemned to the least favourable parts of the city.

At the height of its development, the Indus Valley supported large settlements, the largest being Harappa and Mohenjo Daro. The cities were defined by a high level of administration and a strictly defined social order. They were constructed to a high density based upon a gridlike structure, with the street pattern taking its orientation from the sun. An interesting feature of the citadels at the centres of urban areas was that they housed not only sacred and civic spaces but also the granary stores. The security of the city's energy source, its food supply, was clearly paramount.

Similar processes of city formation began to take place in the Wei-Huang Valley of China and the forests of the Mayan civilisation in Central America between 1000 and 2000 B.C. The key to success in all city-based societies was a common one — a secure political order. There were other common features. The influence of mysticism is recognised in the city form of both Mayan civilisations and China's Shang dynasty. In China, the dynastic leaders traced a line of descent from Shang Ti, the supreme ruler and controller of the sun, moon, stars, wind, and thunder. Oracles would be consulted before any work began on building a city, and their answer would dictate its development. In the Mayan city of Teotihuacan, the influence of mysticism is reflected in the domination of public spaces by sacred structures. The Pyramid of the Sun, the Pyramid of the Moon, and a host of other religious buildings were laid out among the secular structures within the city grid.

The use of regular grid patterns and the importance of solar orientation are characteristic of city forms of subsequent civilisations. The rigid framework offered by the

Farming and trade were important factors in the development of early cities. The sun, wind, and water were guiding principles of urban planning.

grid reflected the desire to create an ordered community that functioned efficiently. The grid provided a high level of syntactic logic, which was obviously important in allowing the inhabitants to find their way around on foot. This city form also assisted in creating strict urban divisions and provided a spatial representation of increasingly stratified societies. In ancient Greece, Hippodamos applied similarly rigid frameworks in the planning of cities. Hippodamos is also credited with the formalisation of the agora from a market square to a more formal civic space, thus providing a focus for urban life. Other components — for example, public baths, theatres, and stadia — symbolise the importance of health and hygiene, as well as leisure, in the Greek city. As a result, the standard of comfort and intellectual stimulation was high; however, the social stratification ensured that the urban experiences of many were rather more differentiated. The Romans inherited many of the cities developed by the Greeks, and the grid remained a central component of urban structure, as did the social and intellectual activities central to the Greek cities. Once again, the grid was aligned according to solar orientation, to maximise the benefits of this direct energy source, as well as minimise its detrimental effects by providing ventilation and shade.

All of these early cities shared a dependence upon a clear interaction between human activity and nature. Whilst the concentration of population and activities in urban structures enabled people to escape environmental uncertainty to a degree, the crucial balance between human development and the environment always had to be carefully maintained. Since the energy of ancient city civilisations was derived from solar energy through crop production, the need to maintain appropriate conditions for agriculture was paramount.

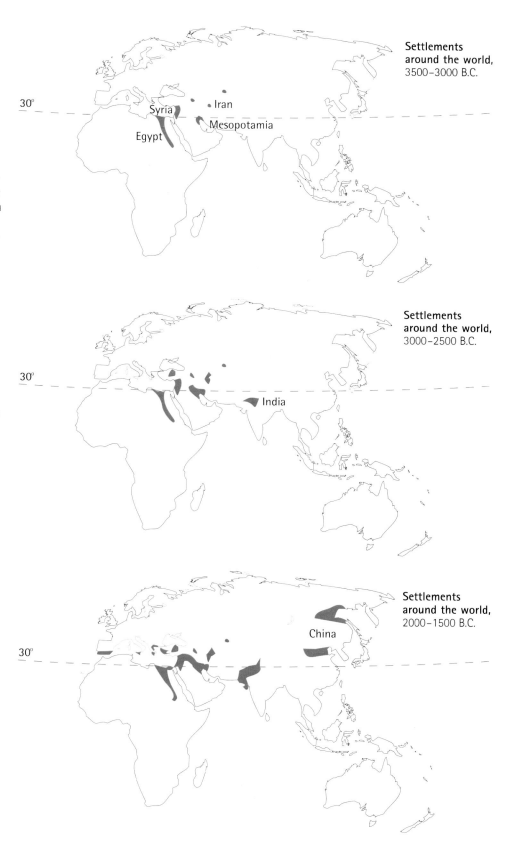

Settlements around the world, 3500–3000 B.C.

Settlements around the world, 3000–2500 B.C.

Settlements around the world, 2000–1500 B.C.

Ancient Egypt

Ancient Egyptian civilisation is remembered for its cities of the dead — the complexes of tombs and pyramids that run from the Nile Delta to Upper Egypt.

Calendar Buildings
The well-being and productivity of natural solar collection was one of the main concerns of early civilisations. In order to secure life-style and reproduction, questions of when it would rain and how much the sun would shine were crucial to survival. Some calendar buildings are astrological structures, others are temples to shelter the gods. Temples were economic as well as religious institutions.

Sun Worship
The sun was at the heart of ancient Egyptian belief. Sun worship was a manifestation of a universal principle (3).

El Lahun (1800 B.C.) was an ancient Egyptian city of barracks to house the army of people responsible for constructing the pyramid complex (4: city plan; 5: plan of typical house).

1

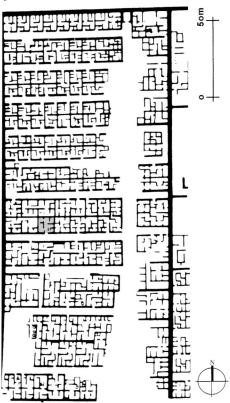

2

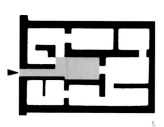

5

3

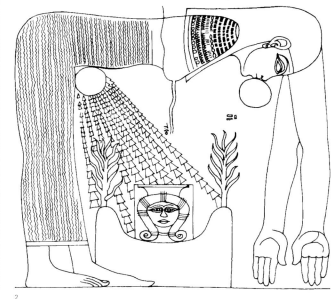

4

Babylon in Mesopotamia

SPECTACVLA BABYLONICA.

Agriculture is the basis for a sustainable community. Around 3500 B.C., the first cities began to emerge along the Tigris and Euphrates rivers as good harvests sustained increasing populations. New Babylon, the city famed for its Hanging Gardens (6: an 18th-century reconstruction), is believed to have been created in 4000 B.C. Its golden age occurred during the reign of Nebuchadnezzar in 600 B.C., when the king embarked on an ambitious plan to rebuild his city in some splendour. The Hanging Gardens were part of this plan, a celebration of agriculture, the technology to control nature and harvest solar energy. The town centre of Babylon (7) consisted mainly of the palace and the gardens. Typical Babylonian houses were arranged around courtyards (9).

6

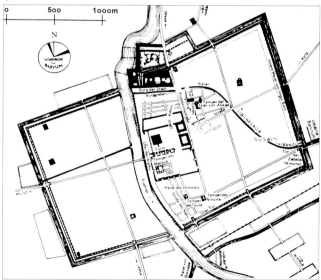

7

8

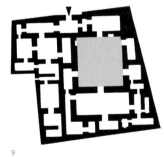

9

The town of Arbella (8), a very early settlement in Mesopotamia, has been inhabited for more than five thousand years. It is probably one of the most sustainable cities ever.

81

Mohenjo Daro in the Indus Valley

Mohenjo Daro (3000 B.C.)
Mohenjo Daro shows a clear north-south orientation and a tightly packed citadel, which like some of today's city centres provided a religious and ceremonial focus (2: Mohenjo Daro citadel). By 2500 B.C., the city's social organisation had been established. The wealthy lived in two-storey homes which had a series of rooms around a courtyard. The poor lived in one-room tenements. Throughout Mohenjo Daro, homes were built of standard-sized baked bricks. But this was not the only form of standardi-sation. Within the city, uni-formity extended to such areas as weights and script.

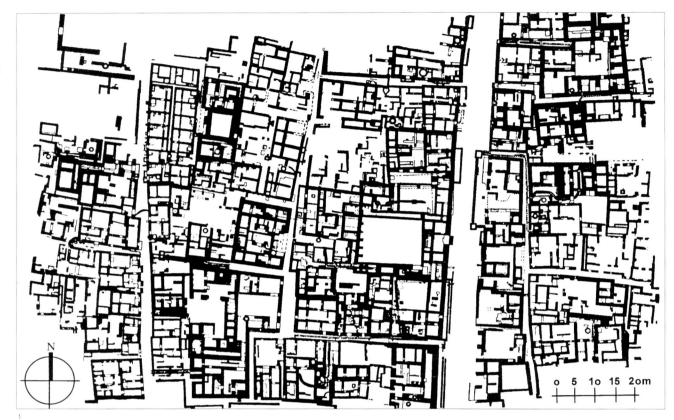

Homes in Mohenjo Daro had all modern conveniences, inclu-ding a public sewage system. Much of the housing was linked to a main drainage system (3). Within the citadel there was a great bath, possibly for ritual bathing. The citadel is also believed to have had a home for priests, an assembly hall, a temple, and a 45-m-long granary building, the latter showing just how much emphasis was placed on ensur-ing that the vital energy supply was secured.

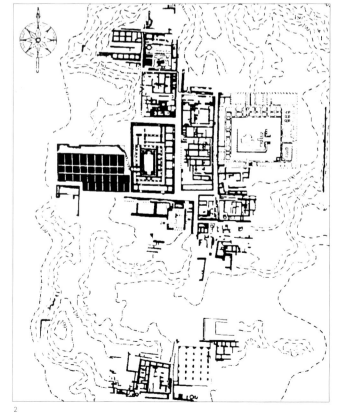

Chinese Cities

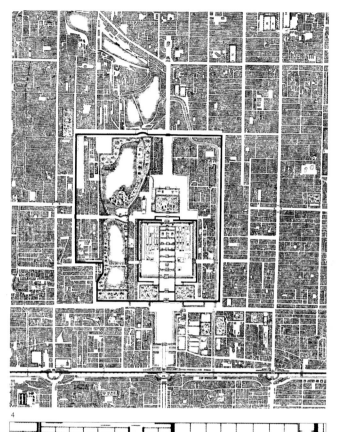

4

5

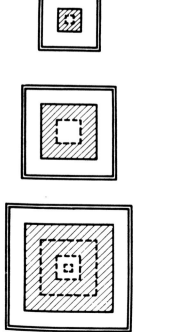

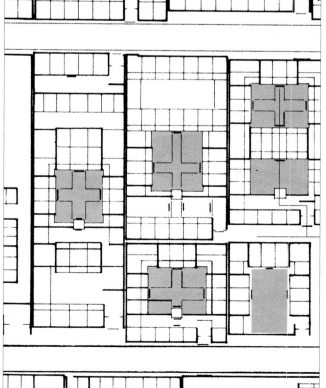

6

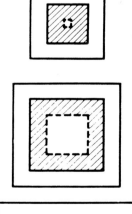

7

Most ancient Chinese cities were based on an orthogonal grid with a north–south orientation. The Chinese have always sought to ensure that their buildings and cities started their life with the best possible omens (5). During the Shang dynasty, oracles would be consulted before any work began on building a city, and their answer would dictate the community's development. Today, *feng shui* still exerts a strong influence on where, when, and how buildings are constructed, notably in dictating that they should face south. Beijing and the Forbidden City and Gardens (4) are examples of the traditional Chinese planning method.

The Chinese courtyard house (6) had its entrance at the south side. All rooms had access to the courtyard. Traditional Chinese town planning stipulated that there be no more than a hundred inhabitants per hectare, all accommodated in one-storey buildings. This was thought to be a well-balanced density.

The Shang dynasty of 1600 B.C. to 1027 B.C. established principles of harmony and social hierarchy in urban development. The square was considered the ideal layout and was used as the basis for both houses and urban plans (7). The city itself was divided into clearly defined social areas for residents of different occupations and status.

South American Civilisations

Teotihuacan (500 A.D.)

Urbanisation on a massive scale was the spur for development of Teotihuacan's remarkable plan. Urbanisation began in 100 A.D., and over the following six hundred years the city became home to a large population. Teotihuacan was developed on a grid layout over more than 20 km², with a basic modular unit of approximately 57 m. Main avenues of the city ran parallel at regular intervals from north to south. Most important of these was the Avenue of the Dead. To the east was the citadel and to the west the great compound — the sacred and political structures that formed the heart of the city. At the northern end of the avenue was the Pyramid of the Moon, and close to that the 70-m-high Pyramid of the Sun, one of the largest man-made structures in Pre-Columbian America. Apart from the many ritual structures, there were some four thousand lesser buildings in the city. Most of these were apartment buildings that housed tradesmen, farmers, and other city workers. Each apartment had several rooms and was sited around a central patio with kitchens and workshops. But not all apartment occupants worked within the building. Some, like the farmers who worked land outside the city, would have to travel to work — they might have been the first commuters.

1

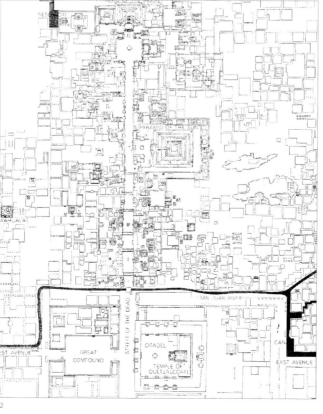

2

3

North American Civilisations

Pueblo Bonito (900 A.D.)

Irrigation of the desert created agricultural riches that formed the foundations for a thriving city. Pueblo Bonito is one of nine great houses whose ruins are to be found in Chaco Canyon in New Mexico. From the grandeur of the houses, Chaco is judged to have been a prosperous and significant city with a population in the thousands. The largest of the nine houses had more than six hundred-fifty rooms. The D-shaped complex is believed to have been five storeys high. The houses were built in stages, Pueblo Bonito starting as a semicircle of rooms, with further suites being added over the course of half a century. Rooms and ceremonial chambers were arranged in a grid pattern. The same standardised approach was applied to the siting of doorways and to the air vents that were all-important in the desert climate.

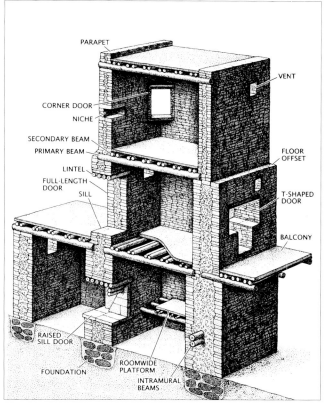

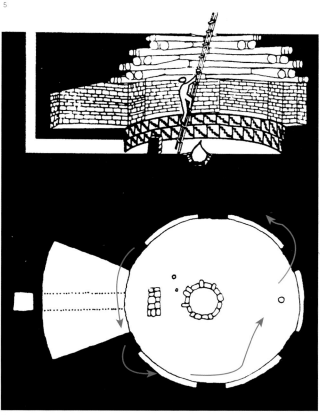

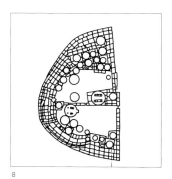

The Anasazi cliff palace from 1200 housed 250 people. They made use of the thermal upwinds that exist at the cliff in summer.

House-building the Hard Way

The great houses were made to last — they were built from sandstone blocks laid in walls up to one m thick at ground level. The sandstone was cut by hand from the surrounding cliffs. For floor and roof beams, trees had to be brought from forests up to 80 km from the city.

Greek Cities

A Solar City

Priene was developed in western Asia Minor in 400 B.C. as a new, entirely Hellenistic city. At the centre of the city grid are the expected municipal buildings and the marketplace (1: reconstruction). The southern section of the city was designed for recreational activities, with a *stadion*, or racetrack, and a *gymnasion*, an open court for sports.

Recent excavations have shown that almost all buildings at Priene were the same, with almost identical plans, sections, and elevations and similar orientation. The plans and axiometrics show this simple structure (2, 3). Every unit was organised around a courtyard. The buildings to the north were used for living. The main room had a shaded porch facing south (4).

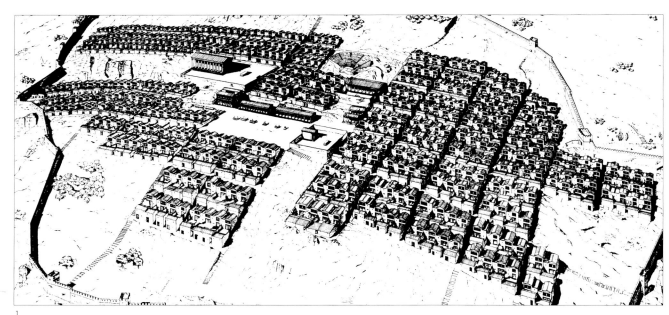

1

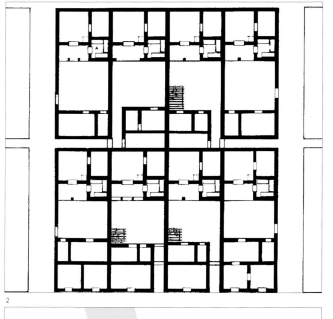

2

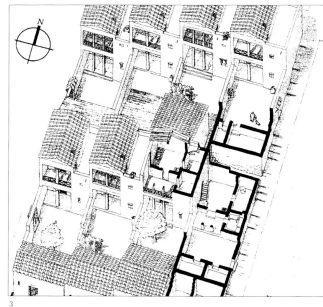

3

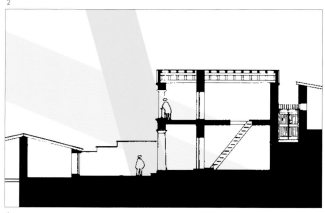

4

5

Based on the principles of solar orientation and ventilation ancient Greek cities represent the ideal solar city for a true democratic society. Apart from communal facilities, all buildings are laid out equally and solar.

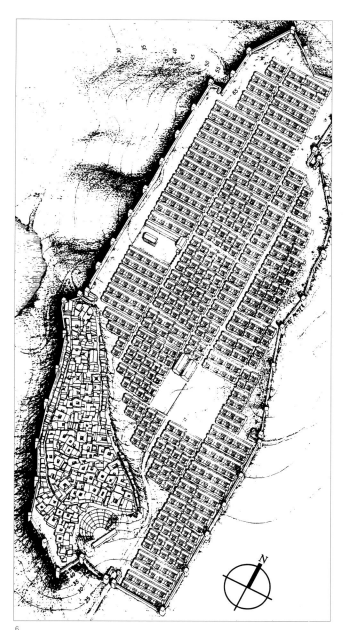

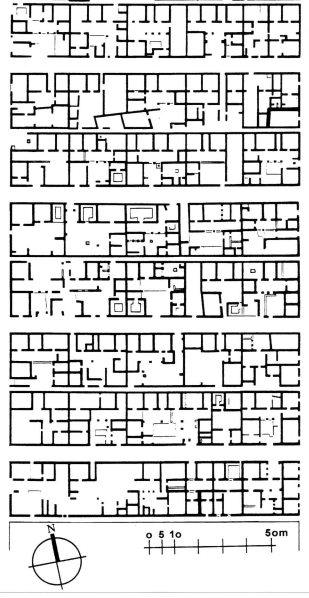

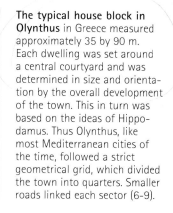

The typical house block in Olynthus in Greece measured approximately 35 by 90 m. Each dwelling was set around a central courtyard and was determined in size and orientation by the overall development of the town. This in turn was based on the ideas of Hippodamus. Thus Olynthus, like most Mediterranean cities of the time, followed a strict geometrical grid, which divided the town into quarters. Smaller roads linked each sector (6-9).

6

7

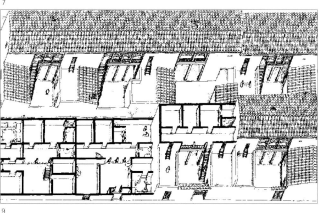

8

9

Architecture for the Agricultural Age

Spectacular Architecture
From Greek antiquity to the Industrial Revolution

Unlike vernacular, which is building for the masses, spectacular architecture has been created by elites for centuries. In ancient Egypt, the pharaohs built their pyramids as part of their religious ritual, taking the orientation of their grand structures from the sun. In 16th-century Isfahan, the Persian princes built their magnificent palaces with perfumed gardens to display their wealth and power to their people and provide themselves with the ultimate in pleasurable, comfortable living environments. In the 20th century, designers have come up with ways of combining modern materials to create new models for living in environmental harmony.

Examples of the spectacular can be found in religious structures from very early times. These structures were not created to provide shelter for members of the community, but to please and glorify the gods. They took their inspiration from the sun and the forces of nature; some of the earliest religious buildings took the form of calendar structures, which gave people an understanding of the passage of time through solar orientation. Glorification and appeasement of the gods were crucial to these communities to ensure that their prime means of survival, the harvest, would be protected from the harmful influences of nature, such as floods and adverse weather.

Spectacular architecture was also prominent in the secular built environment of the ancient world. Markets, forums, amphitheatres, and baths were designed to attract the public to gather and so had to offer high levels of environmental comfort, keeping the public cool in summer and providing protection in winter. At the same time, the wealthy found that they were able to surround themselves with luxury within their private palaces and villas, creating perfect indoor climate using passive ventilation, sunlight, and solar shading.

As we travel through time, spectacular architecture shows its ability to use solar energy for the twin purposes of comfort and celebration, the latter often in a religious context. In the Middle Ages, for example, solar energy continued to have a strong influence on Christian architecture, inspiring the orientation of churches and being used to create fantastic effects to give worshippers a glimpse of heavenly light. The sacred architecture of Islam, on the other hand, took its orientation from Mecca rather than the sun. The mosques and palaces of the Islamic world were designed with a concern for solar shading rather than lighting and with an emphasis on comfort rather than a pure expression of grandeur. The use of solar energy to provide comfort found its clearest expression in the Ottoman Empire and in the courts of the Persian princes in Isfahan in the 16th century. The built environment with its baths, gardens, and naturally ventilated, cool interior spaces was designed to give comfort and pleasure.

This was not, however, an experience that all levels of society could share.

The wealthier the owner of a building, the more aspects of solar energy he or she was able to exploit. For example, the 17th-century Moslem ruler Shah Jahan, builder of the Taj Mahal, had a magnificent palace that was cooled in summer and heated in winter by a small stream running through it. Although such buildings display a sophisticated understanding of the use of solar energy, the owners of these great palaces did not need to pay any attention to saving energy. Their sole objective was to get the maximum comfort and luxury from their surroundings, the state of total environmental well-being. They had sufficient wealth and power to be able to achieve their goal, and few modern buildings have equalled these levels of environmental quality.

The Renaissance brought the light, openness, and solar sophistication of Classical architecture to European building. As Europe progressed to the Baroque age, its style of architecture was to become increasingly ornate and theatrical, and the use of solar energy became more dramatic.

Luxury and comfort were, however, not made available to a broader section of the population of Europe and America until the advent of the Industrial Revolution. It was only then that mass production turned comfort into a marketable commodity.

The Shaded Porch
Architecture of the Antiquity

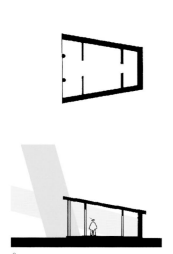

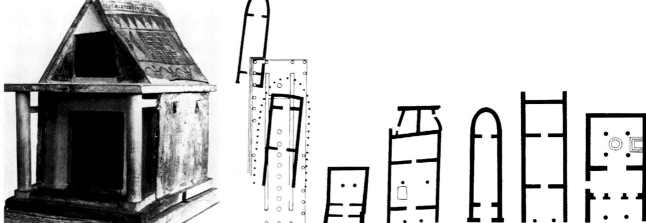

The **megaron** is one of the most basic building types (1, 2). Its simple room and porch unit formed the basis for the evolution of generations of more sophisticated structures. In ancient Greece, the megaron took the form of a rectangular room with axial colonnades that led out onto a porch. Some have credited Socrates with the invention of the first solar house, but it is more likely that what he was really describing in his writings was a well-oriented megaron (3). Megarons were used for worship and provided the plan for the first Greek temples in 800 B.C.

The **Greek courtyard** house was set around a colonnaded space that offered shade and comfort during the hot summer months. The courtyard was laid out so that it also would trap the sunlight in winter (5).

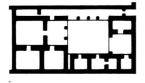

The need for shade in summer and sunshine in winter dominated life in ancient Greece. The monumental temple architecture for which Classical civilisation is revered grew from the modest origins of the megaron with its simple porch.

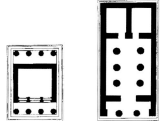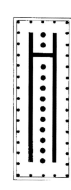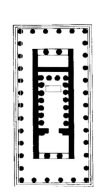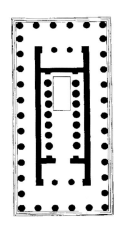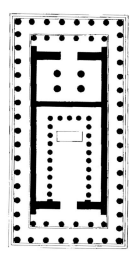

6

Later temple plans clearly show their megaron origins. In the early megarons, shade was only provided at the building's entrance. Over the centuries, the shading was extended around the whole building. This created a comfortable environment around the temple and added to its grandeur (6).

7

Greek temples like the Parthenon represent a magnificent cultural and artistic achievement, but in solar design terms they are still basically shaded colonnades for worshippers to stroll through on their way to the statues of the gods (7-9). These temples used various shade and lighting techniques. By manipulating size (scale), multiples, repetition (column order), and refinement of the proportions, structures were created that ultimately represented the deities and priests in the city and magnified their power.

8   9

Shade in the Greek Temple
According to solar design principles, the columns form a giant brise-soleil.

Stimulation and Comfort
Architecture of the Caesars

The striving for comfort and leisure led to the building of beautiful villas and gardens in Rome. Hadrians Villa could be described as the ideal house – surrounded by circular ponds allowing a fresh breeze through cross-ventilation (1, 3).

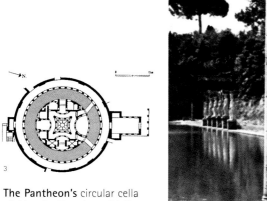

3

The Pantheon's circular cella of 44 m in diameter, with its niches and dome, created drama using sunlight (4, 7). At the dome's apex, an oculus nearly 9 m in diameter allowed a beam of light to stream down. The oculus also served a practical purpose as a sundial.

Trajan's Market in Rome (2, 5, 6) had much in common with a modern shopping precinct. This cultural and commercial centre contained 150 shops, libraries, meeting places, and offices spread over five levels. Its semi-circular arcade created light, while at other levels roof lights and openings let maximum daylight and cross-ventilation down to the lowest level. These intelligent daylight guiding systems were highly sophisticated and could serve as inspiration for buildings today.

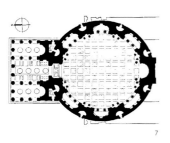

7

1

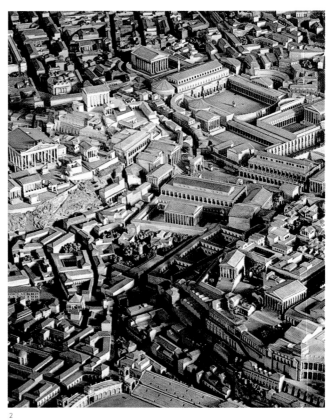

2

4

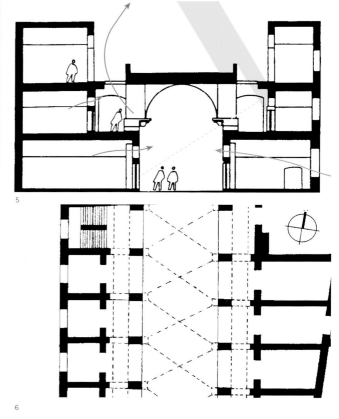

5

6

Solar design reached new levels of sophistication in ancient Rome as comfort became a key concern. The Romans created monumental surroundings blending space, shade, and cooling breezes. Recreation played an important role in Roman society. Baths and heating systems marked the emergence of active comfort systems.

The Via Triumphalis was the main shopping street of the new Roman cities. Multiple rows of colonnades formed shaded spaces in front of shops and stalls. The colonnades had awnings that could be fitted across the streets for shade.

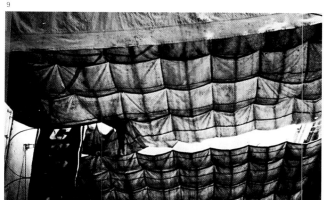

Side Streets
Spaces leading off the Via Triumphalis were used for gatherings and festivities. They also provided sites for the first court sessions and, later, for Christian gatherings.

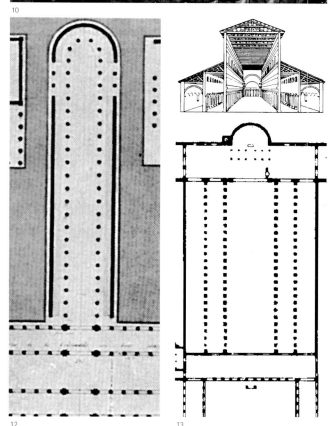

Roman basilicas (14) make clear reference to the shaded colonnaded street (12), as do Christian basilicas such as Old Saint Peter's in Rome (13).

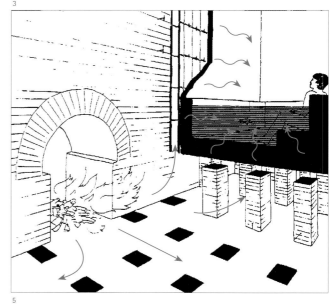

The Baths of Caracalla (3) could accommodate 1,600 bathers in its frigidarium (cold-water pool), tepidarium (warm-water pool), and calidarium (hot-water pool). Pool buildings were supplied with water by a purpose-built aqueduct, and with heat by a hot-air system located in cellars. Inside the recreational complex there were also lecture halls, exercise rooms, dressing rooms, lounges, and secondary buildings containing shops, restaurants, libraries, and gymnasiums (1: reconstruction of Baths of Diocletian by E. Paulin). These complexes were set in land-scaped gardens and oriented to the south-west. The admission fee charged to Roman citizens to use these facilities for a day was minimal. The size of Roman bath complexes can be gauged from the plan of the Baths of Diocletian, which were larger than those of Caracalla. The main bath building was 240 by 144 m. The hot bath faced towards the winter sun to gain as much solar heat as possible. In some of the more elaborate bath buildings, the sweat room had enormous windows facing south and south-west and a sand floor that absorbed solar heat during the day and released it in the evening.

The hypocaust system was the Romans' prime means of raising the temperature inside buildings to comfortable levels (4, 5). Wood was thrown into the heating system through openings on the side; the elevated floor enabled the hot air to move freely underneath the floor and up the chimneys. Fresh air entered through special wall inlets.

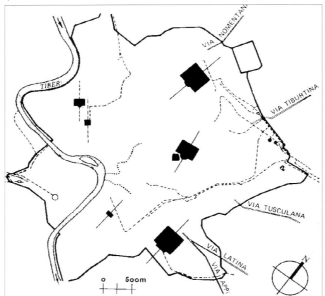

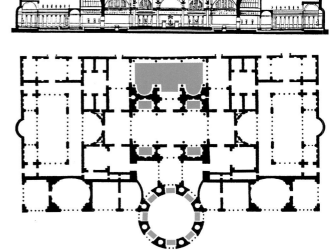

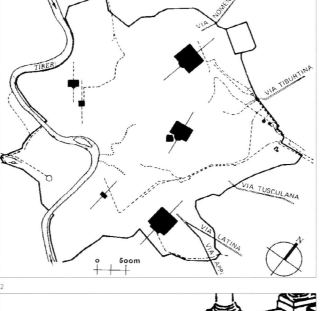

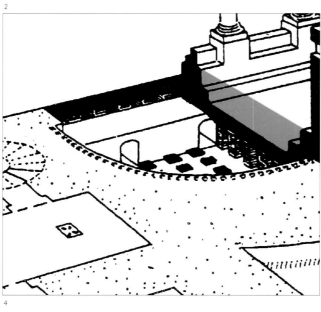

96

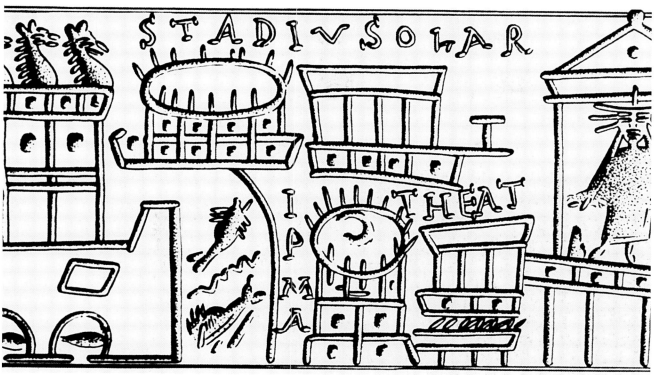

6

The Colosseum
The ancient Romans also found recreation in spectacle, and in the city's amphitheatres and circuses the comfort of visitors was crucial. In the Colosseum, fierce battles would be staged and thousands of animals and many gladiators killed for the public's pleasure (12).

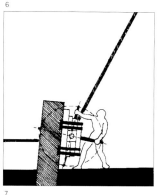

7

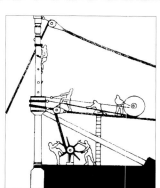

8

9

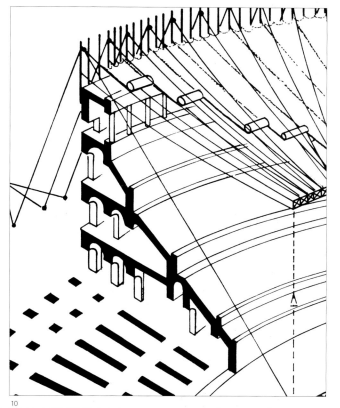

10

To enable the Colosseum's 50,000 spectators to sit comfortably in their seats all day long, a sophisticated device for creating shade was incorporated into the structure and could be put into position during the spectacle (7-10). Around the top of the arena there were long poles supporting ropes along which awnings could be spread. A special task force of two hundred sailors was stationed next to the Colosseum and would rush into action to operate the mechanism. The shading was called *vela*, meaning 'sails.' Spectators described how the pleasure of being shaded would be enhanced by a cascade of flower petals and sweets raining down from the awnings as they were unrolled (11: mural from Pompeii).

11

12

Heavenly Light
Christian architecture in the early Middle Ages

The Hagia Sophia in Constantinople (538 A.D.) gave Byzantine worshippers a lasting image of the heavenly light that would be their reward if they lived suitably devout lives. Built by the emperor Justinian, the church was described as 'full of light and reflections of the sun.' Mosaics and rows of windows set throughout the church, most notably around the dome, give the massive interior an ethereal quality (1-3, 5, 6).

Clerestory lighting and large alabaster-paned windows created a diffuse light in the more modest Church of San Vitale in Ravenna. The plan shows the octagonal form of the church, with its light-reflecting colonnades (4).

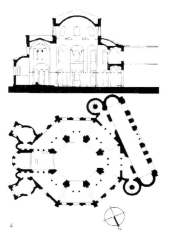

4

Mosaics were applied to surfaces in Byzantine churches to act as tiny light reflectors, adding to the impression of dissolving walls (2).

1

2

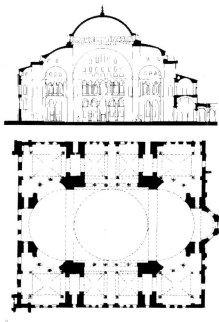

3

For Christians, the heavenly light becomes a symbol of their saviour. The psychological power of solar energy was used to provide drama in new churches.

When the Hagia Sophia was consecrated, Justinian is reported to have made the proud boast: 'Solomon, I have surpassed you.' No matter what the season or the time of day, the interior is bathed in light. To accomplish this, innovative design was called for. Two architects led the big-budget project. The building is rectangular in plan, 77 by 72 m. The 30-m-diameter, 65-m-high brick dome structure rests on four arches carried by pillars. Leading to the central dome is a series of graded vaults culminating in four enormous pendentives.

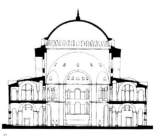

5

6

Sophisticated Shade
Islamic architecture of the Middle Ages

The forbidding walls of early desert mosques did not only keep out intruders; they also provided shade from the sun. In contrast to Christian architects, Islamic builders developed the subtle qualities of shade.

The solar influence on Islamic design can be seen clearly in the plans of mosques at Samarra, Kairouan, Cairo, and Kufa. All have long shaded arcades extending around the courtyard. Islamic buildings are introverted so that the facade is on the inside of buildings. No matter how individual mosques are oriented in relation to Mecca, they always follow the basic principle of providing maximum shade.

1

2

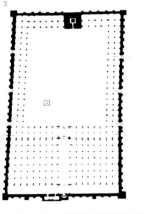

3

4

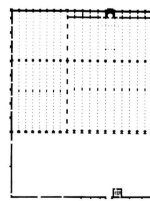

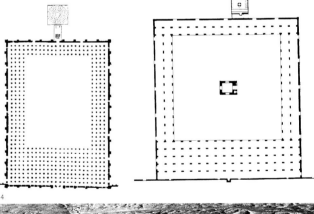

5

6

The dense, often blank exteriors of the buildings of the Islamic world conceal rich interiors and show evidence of a sophisticated knowledge of shade and ventilation.

7

8

Interior detailing was designed to play subtly with light and shade. Shiny surfaces such as marble, tiles, and mirrors were used to reflect light. The screens that allowed cooling breezes to pass through rooms were intricately detailed to create patterned light effects, with designs often based on symmetry and complex geometry.

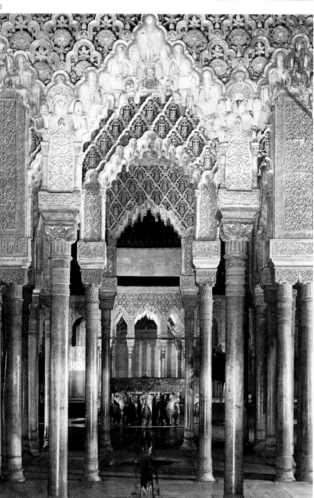

9

10

Desert techniques of cross-ventilation and shade were taken to Spain by the Moslem conquerors. The Great Mosque in Cordoba has a series of arcades within its high-walled enclosure (9). Light reflectors range from the marble columns to the gold and glass mosaics of the central dome.

At the palace of the Alhambra in Granada, the Court of the Lions is an outstanding example of the virtuosity of Islamic architecture (10). A crucifix pattern of water channels divides the garden into four parterres. The scents of the garden and the splash of running water are integrated aspects of the architecture, which reflects the splendid life-style of the last years of Islamic Spain.

Coloured Light in the Occident
The medieval Christian solar boom

The Gothic style, with its light, transparency, and drama, was a complete contrast to the Romanesque. Two people played a key role in developing the Gothic style: the Cistercian Bernard of Clairvaux and the Benedictine Abbot Suger. Bernard brought purer outlines and refined vaulting to allow more light into buildings, but he believed in simplicity. It was Suger who added the element of theatre. His abbey of St Denis would, in his own words, 'shine with the wonderful and uninterrupted light of most luminous windows.'

Abbot Suger took his belief in God as 'the superessential light' from the writings of Duns Scotus and a fifth-century mystic called 'Pseudo-Dionysius the Areopagite.' The first architectural representation of Suger's belief in celestial light was in the abbey of St Denis, near Paris. Suger wrote of this early Gothic work, 'The church shines with its middle part brightened. For bright is that which is brightly coupled with the bright, and bright is the noble edifice which is pervaded by the new light.' This desire to create more dynamic, lighter architecture manifested itself at a time when construction techniques were developing rapidly. Ways of cutting, lifting, and bonding stone were being improved significantly. Structural engineering skills were being stretched, sometimes beyond the limit, by the challenges of the new Gothic designs. In France between 1180 and 1270, some 80 cathedrals and 500 abbeys were constructed. From there, the Gothic spectacle spread to England, Germany, Spain, and Belgium.

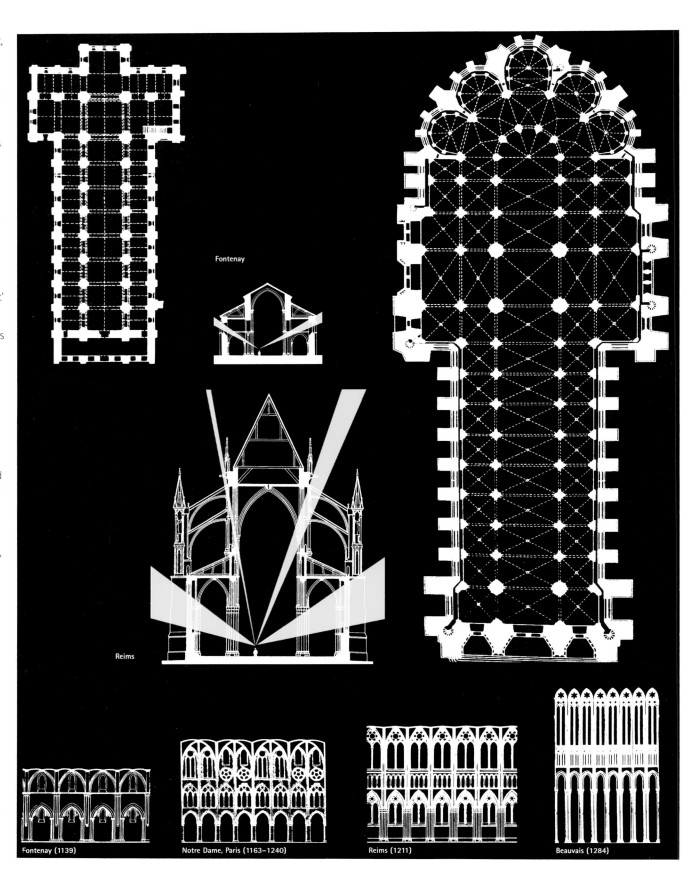

Fontenay

Reims

Fontenay (1139)

Notre Dame, Paris (1163–1240)

Reims (1211)

Beauvais (1284)

New building technology and prefabrication let Gothic churches and
cathedrals shine with 'the new light.'

Shaded Pavilions of the Orient
Architecture in medieval China and Japan

Pavilions were constructed as measures of wealth, luxury, and comfort from earliest times in China. Emperors competed with one another over the beauty and sophistication of their pavilions and pergolas (2: architectural sketch on bronze bowl from 475–221 B.C.). The large roofs provided protection from sun and rain, while walls were permeable for cross-ventilation. The painting of a water mill from 950 A.D. (1) illustrates the architecture of the time.

Pagodas have had many purposes in Chinese society, as shrines, watchtowers, or funerary buildings. They are based on the logic of the single storey repeated four or five times. It is interesting to compare the simple repetition of the 11th-century Sakyamuni Pagoda (4) of the Fogong Temple with the repetition in modern high-rise buildings in China.

The Sakyamuni Pagoda dates from 1056 A.D. Its base is 30 m wide, and its height is 67 m. It is the oldest preserved wooden pagoda in China and the highest wooden building in the world.

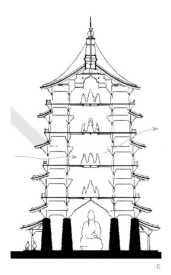

In medieval China and Japan, structures were made from renewable materials.

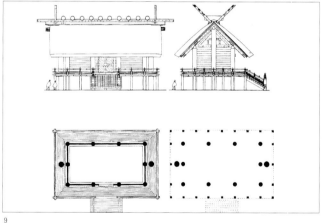

7

8

The **Golden Pavilion** in Kyoto, Japan, can be seen as a highly sophisticated light-and-comfort modulator (7). Gold-plated surfaces and the reflecting water create special effects.

The gate to Todaiji Temple in Nara is one of the oldest wooden structures in the world (8). It is evidence of the durability of such renewable materials as wood and thatch.

9

10

Wooden Shinto shrines were built to honour the Japanese sun gods. To retain the shrines' purity, they are rebuilt every 20 years. However, the design principles on which they are based date back to the sixth century, when Shinto was Japan's only national religion. With its posts standing away from the side walls outside the building to support the ridge purlin, its thatched roof, and its original beam work, this shrine probably preserves the architectural techniques of prehistoric Japan.

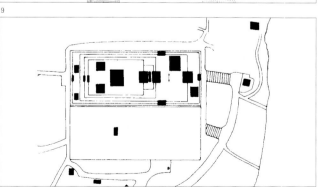

11

12

In Praise of Shade
Late medieval architecture of the Far East

The interior of the Taihe Hall in the Forbidden City, Beijing (1), was rebuilt in the 34th Year of the Kang Xi dynasty. It is one of the three main buildings in the Forbidden City and, with a height of 35 m, the biggest. The elegance of the interior, shaded by sophisticated wooden screens and columns along the exterior colonnade, illustrates the Chinese approach to comfort. Techniques for creating shade in China and Japan are still more advanced than heating technologies for buildings. Very cold winters in most Japanese and Chinese regions make the interiors of these buildings almost unbearable during winter.

The Northern Gallery of Bei-Hai Park, on the island of Qionghua (2), is part of a garden of the emperors' summer residence. It is one of 60 shaded galleries that connect the various pavilions on the island.

Chang-Ling Hall is the mausoleum for the emperor Yong Le (3). With a width of 67 m and a depth of 30 m, it is the biggest of the Ming-dynasty mausolea. The 60 columns that support the roof are entire tree-trunks. Four of them have a diameter of 1.2 m.

The Ching-dynasty arcade in the Forbidden City (4) shows the delicate craftsmanship of traditional Chinese architecture.

While Christian architects were fascinated by shining light, builders in China and Japan were creating centres of shade and calm.

5

6

7

8

The Japanese are masters of the use of diffuse daylight and refined the relationship between inside and outside using screens and verandas. The shoji, or translucent screens, are only one of many examples of the ways in which the Japanese control light within buildings. Shoji screens of the Katzura Palace in Kyoto are the main design element in well-tempered interior environments (5).

Devices for creating shade at the Nishi-Hongan-ji Temple allow a play of patterns at the windows (6).

The relationship between building and nature is a carefully considered one that has been established over centuries in Japan. The careful directing of views and the quality of space were important aspects of design philosophy in early Buddhist cultures.

9

Luxurious Comfort for the Ottomans
The early modern age in the Near East

Ottoman architecture found its greatest expression in the work of the architect Sinan. He was a contemporary of Michelangelo and, like Michelangelo, undertook a prodigious amount of work in his lifetime. Sinan built around 350 mosques, working throughout the Ottoman Empire. The Hagia Sophia influenced Ottoman builders from around 1500, but it was Sinan who refined the principles into a model of elegance. His Mihrimah Mosque has an interior that is very different from that of the Hagia Sophia. Light enters the building on all sides, reflecting off the cool surfaces of the brightly coloured tile panels on the lower walls (1).

1

The balance between open and closed spaces which allow light inside but which remain shaded, created luxurious architecture. In the Ottoman Empire, solar energy was devoted to the principle of pleasure.

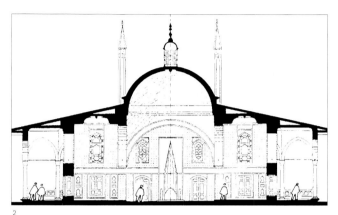

The plans of palaces and houses were based on rooms grouped around central loggias. The Ottoman Turks also built waterfront pavilions. With their large, openable windows catching the cooling breeze from the water, the environment was extremely pleasant. People could relax on raised divans around the edge of the room.

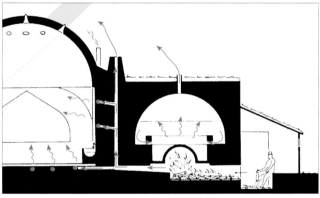

The Turkish bath was central to the Ottoman way of life (4). It was a prime source of comfort and pleasure, and considerable ingenuity went into developing the services systems to allow the baths to operate efficiently.

The harem, or women's quarters (6: harem bedroom of Mustafa II), were the most private areas of any house, to which women were confined. The rooms had cool, tiled walls and maximum cross-ventilation.

The mosque and market-square in Gelibolu (7: reconstruction by Fossati) show the dynamic shading devices and colonnades characteristic of Ottoman exteriors and recall Italian Renaissance architecture.

Perfumed Gardens for Princes
Luxury and light in Persia

Persian palaces traditionally consisted of a series of buildings, usually in a garden setting. The pavilions would be used for different purposes and at different times of the year. The palace expressed both the ruler's public and private life, providing a mix of formal ceremonial space and comfortable private quarters where he could relax.

Ali Qapu Palace in Isfahan overlooks a park that served as both the main market square and the ruler's polo ground (1–3). He would watch proceedings from the shaded loggia on the right. The cross-section shows the heavy mass of the building behind the light, airy porch with its distinctly modern appearance. This porch is a masterpiece of solar design. Cooling spaces abound inside Ali Qapu Palace.

Chihil Sutun is one of the garden pavilions of the Ali Qapu Palace complex (4, 5). Its name means '40 columns' and comes from the 20 wooden columns supporting its portico roof, seen in reflection in the water surrounding the pavilion.

The new sector of Isfahan designed and build by Shah Abbas included the most sophisticated solar designs of its time: A) the Ali Qapu Palace; B) the Chihil Suturn; and C) the Hasht Bihiht (5).

1

2

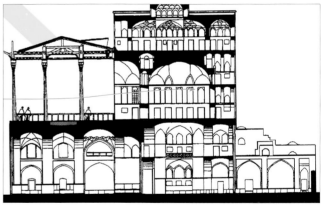

3

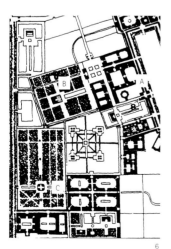

6

4

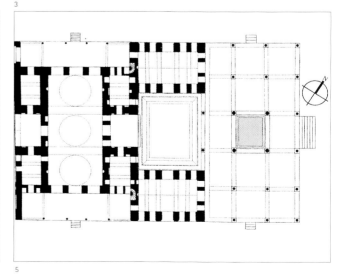

5

For the lucky few, life in Persia provided an admirable mix of entertainment and comfort. There was cooling water, abundant shade, and the bliss of the perfumed garden.

Perfumed gardens represented the height of luxury in Persian culture and were represented throughout art and literature as the ultimate human delight.

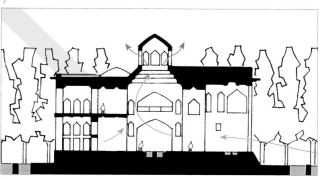

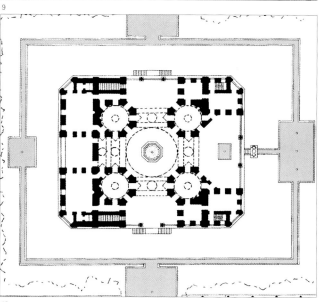

The garden pavilion of Hasht Bihisht (10, 11) was built in Isfahan in 1669–70. The plan is symmetrical and consists of four domed octagonal apartments that are two storeys high. In desert areas where water shortage is a major problem, the luxury of a flowering garden provides a glimpse of paradise. Gardens were built purely for pleasure, to enjoy nature, the heavens above, and the breeze. Their spaces are intended to increase people's sense of well-being and enjoyment.

Building Technologies of the Moguls
Early modern architecture in India

The Moslem ruler Shah Jahan had water flowing through the private quarters of his palace for cooling (1). In summer the water would be cooled with ice, and in winter hot water would be added to it. A clever combination of grilles and water supplied the rooms with a water-cooled airflow during the hottest summer months. Rows of columns allowed the building's users to enjoy comfortable shaded spaces.

The palaces of Fatehpur Sikri, near Agra (2), built by the emperor Akbar in 1570 at the age of 28, employed every known technique. It was designed for maximum cooling. The section shows how the palace was built around an artificial earth mound to create more mass for cooling. Rulers would build palaces which expressed their wealth and indulged their desires.

Delicate mirrors on the complex vaulting of the palace of Jaipur (4) act as light reflectors during the day. Palace builders had to be careful to keep heat out during the day, but let light in.

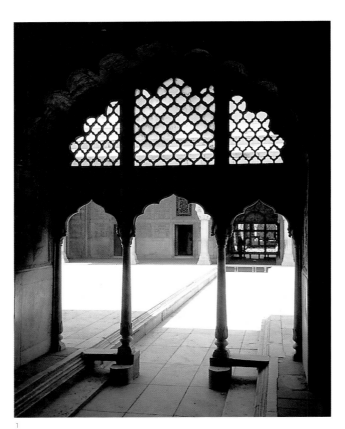

1

2

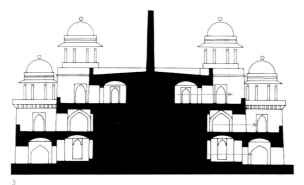

3

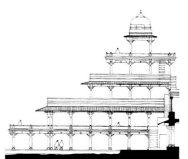

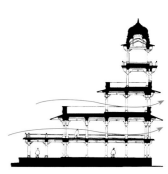

4

5

The dream of Mogul architects was to create the ultimate diaphanous wall. Powerful rulers spared no expense in creating their palaces. The multi-functional membrane/screen carved out of white marble allowed the greatest comfort in inside/outside spaces.

6

Mogul screens are far more sophisticated than modern devices for creating shade. The filigree designs and the dramatic play of light and shadow create virtual spaces within rooms.

7

Screens inside the Red Fort in Delhi (7) are made of white marble with colourful inlaid stones. The marble surfaces and the screens that filter the light and allow cross-ventilation all provide comfort even in the heat of the day. The marble structure shines in the brilliant sunshine, its elevations punctuated by voids that create shadows.

The Wall Becomes Habitable Shade
Renaissance architecture in Italy

The arcades of the Procuratie Vecchie on the Piazzetta di San Marco in Venice has multi-layered elevations with loggias and arcades (1). While earlier buildings had relatively flat elevations punctuated by simple openings, this new architecture is characterised by deeper facades and the adaptation of the ancient architectural orders. Architects enthusiastically took on Classical principles, notably those of Vitruvius, whose *De Architectura* was the only ancient architectural text to survive in its entirety.

1

Temporary shade in the arcades took the form of curtains, which could be rolled down or up according to the time of day. With this simple device for varying shade, the arcade became a comfortable and highly adaptable space (2). Palladio's Loggia del Capitano in Vicenza appears cool and inviting in the intense heat of the summer (3).

2

3

The Palazzo Piccolini in Pienza, designed by Bernardo Rosellino, shows perfectly how a building facade could almost be dissolved by the use of loggias and arcades (4). The barrier between inside and outside was reduced to the bare minimum.

4

5

It was the rediscovery of Classical texts and the love of life and luxury that brought the loggia and atrium back to buildings. Later, the loggia was to become a symbol of the harmony between architecture and nature, adding a third dimension to the wall with new qualities of light and comfort.

6

In his **Villa Rotonda**, Palladio made dramatic use of the loggia as an architectural element. The villa, which was constructed in 1566 in Vicenza, has porticoes on all four sides (6, 7). The loggia, a shaded porch, had its origins in the megaron of ancient Greece. Palladio said of the design: 'It is upon a small hill with easy access ... And it is encompassed with most pleasant hills, which look like a very great theatre, and are all cultivated ... and therefore, as it enjoys from every part most beautiful views, some of which are limited, some more extended, and others that terminate the horizon, there are loggias made at all four fronts.'

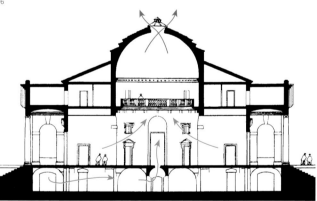

7

8

The **Villa Rotonda** draws cool air from the cellar below. This cool air is then channelled through the building's core distributing itself evenly throughout the building (7).

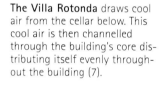

11

9

10

The **Costozza villas**, near Vicenza, benefited from an unusual cooling system (8–10). They were built above natural caves, and the cool air from the caves was used to ventilate the villas via marble grilles. Palladio wrote of his fascination for the system and tried to apply it in his own work.

Virtual Lighting
Baroque churches to thrill the masses

As European architects sought to create more dramatic effects in churches, they moved away from direct sunlight. Instead, they designed light-guiding systems to create illusions of space and light, carefully concealing the windows. Two of the leading exponents of this approach were Cosmas Damian Asam and his brother Egid Quirin Asam. One of their major works is the church of Weltenburg, near Kelheim in Germany. This church clearly illustrates the goals of Baroque builders.

1

2

4

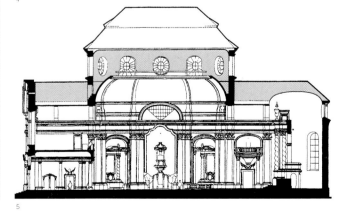

3

5

In Baroque churches, light sources are hidden, so that the congregation is dazzled by light. These special effects were created using complex light-guiding systems.

6

7

8

9

In Italy, the drama of Baroque lighting effects can be seen in the dome of Santa Chiara. The dome is multi-layered — the skin is penetrated and allows views into a brightly lit virtual sky painted on the layer behind it. The only lighting is through hidden windows (6).

In Guarini's Cappella della Santa Sindone in Turin, white light pours through the dome's tiers of riblike arches. The chapel below is decorated in contrasting black marble. A central shrine surrounds the altar, which contains the Shroud of Turin (7).

The dome of Guarini's San Lorenzo in Turin has a similar multi-layered, kaleidoscopic effect. Light and shade are accentuated in the ribbed dome with its lantern and light boxes (8, 9).

Changing Concepts of Solar Power
Political strength versus sensual comfort

Louis XIV styled himself the **Sun King**, but his understanding of solar energy was relatively unsophisticated. Versailles was an expression more of the monarch's power than of the ability to use solar energy to provide comfort. Louis XIV's knowledge of the sun was confined to geometry and orientation; he offered no shade for strollers in his magnificent gardens. There was some use of renewable energy in the gardens there, with massive water-wheels powering a pumping system to supply water to the fountains and water features. It was Louis XVI who brought comfort to the life of the French monarchy. He differentiated between the ceremony of public life and the private life of the king, surrounding himself with every device for comfort — furniture that he could relax in and new mechanical systems for heating, water supply, and sanitation.

Sophisticated lever systems supplied the palace with running water. The waterworks in the gardens of Versailles played an important role as mirrors of light and made the palace appear to sink into a sea of shimmering gold.

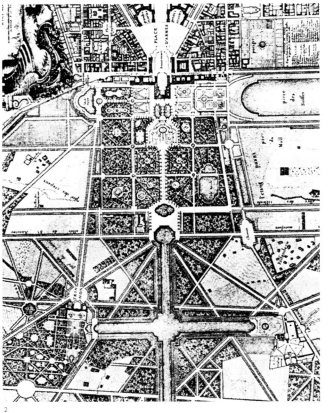

124

For the French king Louis XIV, the sun was a symbol for political power. In contrast, at Sans Souci, solar energy is a clear symbol of sensual comfort and pure luxury.

5

Sans Souci was built in Potsdam by Frederick the Great on a mountain of glasshouses. Potsdam has a cool continental climate, but by stacking the glasshouses on a south-facing slope Frederick was able to plant vineyards and ensure that he was well supplied with wine. Here, he was following the concept of solar energy for comfort and luxury. The gardens of Sans Souci were full of luxurious pleasure places. The boy adoring the sun is the symbol of comfort with solar energy.

7

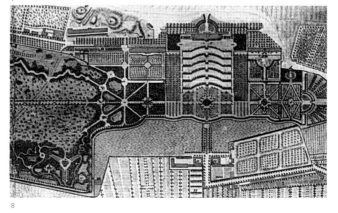

6

8

Architecture for an Industrial Age

The Industrial Revolution
The second energy revolution

Philosophers such as Goethe, Kant, Voltaire, and others initiated an upheaval in thinking around the time of the Industrial Revolution. The back-to-nature movement, which found its strongest expressions in the writings of Rousseau, expressed another powerful current of the time.

Social upheaval found its expression in revolutions, in Europe, beginning in the 1780s. Liberty, equality, and fraternity were the goals of the revolutionaries.

The Industrial Revolution marked a significant transition in world history, as a number of societies began to shift from predominantly agrarian to industrial economies. Although industrial manufacturing had expanded gradually prior to the latter half of the 18th century, it was at this time that the scale and nature of the forces of production underwent a transformation, with increasing circuits of capital and associated new forms of spatial organisation. In parallel with this transition, Enlightenment thought reflected a desire to break with history and tradition in the pursuit of progress, modernisation, and human emancipation. Reason, based upon objective, demystified, and desacralised science, provided a new logic for the project of modernity. The separation of religion from the realm of objective science enabled the Enlightenment thinkers to embrace rational forms of social organisation and justify the scientific domination of nature. The removal of natural limits from human progress promised freedom from scarcity and want and supported the goal of the greatest possible happiness and comfort for the greatest number of people.

The Industrial Revolution and the project of modernity clearly held a complementary and dialectical relationship. New technologies based upon the use of fossil fuels provided the pivotal factor in this regard. Coal and coke provided a more economical form of energy than charcoal, and the development of more compact steam engines based upon this new energy source opened up whole new vistas for industrial production. This power source enabled the replacement of small workshops by large, mechanised factories. New forms of industrial production and capital organisation necessitated new forms of spatial organisation. A heterogeneous industrial and social landscape evolved: towns and cities grew rapidly in locations with close proximity to raw materials, concentrating upon coalfields; transportation links, by inland canal, toll road, and railways, developed between regions to facilitate movement of raw materials and finished products; and communications continued to improve through technological advances such as the Morse telegraph and the telephone.

The new technologies of the Industrial Revolution enabled architects and builders to transcend the limitations of human scale: indeed, buildings came increasingly to represent a submittance to the control of technology itself rather than the use of technology as a tool for architecture. Therefore many of the great architectural achievements of this period — for example, Paxton's Crystal Palace built for the Great Exhibition of 1851 — represented and inspired pieces of technological engineering rather than feats of architecture. A preoccupation with progress, personal comfort, and convenience obscured the growing evidence of negative repercussions. The costs of progress did lead to a rise in living standards for a greater number

of people, although as descriptive studies of life in industrial towns and cities of this time illustrate, high levels of deprivation through poverty, overcrowding, and disease were more common experiences of urban living.

Not only were housing conditions improved with open green spaces, but new settlements also promoted reform through education and hygiene, providing schools, hospitals, and almshouses. As a means of combating alcoholism, there was a notable absence of bars and public houses. Such settlements symbolised growing concerns regarding the quality of urban environments and an increasing desire to escape the city and live in cleaner and more open countryside — the birth of 'green' living. Also influential were such social reformers as William Morris and John Ruskin, who advocated a return to more rural ways of life and who proposed settlements based upon values espoused by the Arts and Crafts Movement. The construction of electric tramlines and railways in the larger cities of Europe and North America, which commenced during the 1880s and 1890s enabled the middle classes to move further away from the squalor associated with inner cities.

Such trends were clearly recognised in Ebenezer Howard's highly influential proposals for the creation of slumless, smokeless Garden Cities, which aimed to combine both town and country, enjoying each of their benefits as well as avoiding each of their disadvantages, and therefore providing the best of both worlds. Influenced by the City Beautiful and Arts and Crafts movements, Howard envisaged a group of social cities, each with a population of 32,000, linked to one another by rail. Whilst Howard's cities were based upon a radial structure and concentric rings, the garden city proposal provided by the Spaniard Soria y Mata followed a linear structure. Soria y Mata envisaged a single street that would act as a 'locomotion vertebra', incorporating all transport and other services for the city, which could be developed to link existing urban centres. In Britain at the turn of the 20th century, the ideals set out by the Garden City movement gained wide acceptance, although development took place in suburbs on the peripheries of large towns and cities in a manner with which Howard would not wholly have agreed. A return to healthy, solar living away from the slums became the preference among those who could afford it.

Across political ideologies, modernism acted during the interwar period to define the fundamental belief in the explicit relation between human progress and new forms of social organisation. Architecture, urban planning, and all other arenas of culture aimed to symbolise this new age. Some favoured a return to nature and disurbanisation whilst others rejected individuality and romanticism and favoured scientific rationality. In the case of the latter, technological innovation was to be employed to enable

The last two centuries have witnessed profound changes through advances in industry and technology. Dramatic societal changes have taken place that both reflect and respond to the introduction of new technologies and the power associated with their control.

social reform, and architectural determinism received new impetus. Modern architecture was not simply an expression of a new aesthetic image, but the very substance and representation of the new social conditions that were to be created. Notions of less being more and form following function, as well as a vision of buildings as 'agents of redemption' and 'machines for living', represented the rationality and objectivity structuring the dominant architectural design canon at the time. The modern movement is commonly associated with such figures as Le Corbusier, Mies, Gropius, and the Bauhaus and, from 1928, the collective represented by CIAM (Congrès Internationaux d'Architecture Moderne). Urban charters introduced by CIAM led to many of the features that dominate contemporary urban landscapes: for example, functional zoning through segregation and specialisation.

A return to healthy solar living through deurbanisation provided a competing school of thought. In the UK, the influence of the Garden City movement remained strong, and suburbanisation based upon public transit routes predominated in the creation of 'Metroland'. In the US, innovative ideas for suburban design were proposed — for example, the plan for Radburn, New Jersey, which emphasised a segregation of street and vehicular traffic, the provision of connecting green spaces, and the clustering of housing units around cul-de-sacs. Frank Lloyd Wright's Broadacre City Project, which was dispersed and anti-urban by definition, was initiated during this period. In Russia, principles from both the modern movement and the dispersal school can be recognised: architecture was modern in influence, whereas urban planning represented a preference for lower density and deurbanisation. As communal living arrangements, which had been favoured during the 1920s, lost favour, lower-density, linear-based urban expansions based upon Soria y Mata's proposals gained increasing acceptance. The most abstract and theoretically consistent representation of this was provided in 1930 by N.A. Milyutin, whose proposal comprised a linear city functionally zoned into six parallel strips. Moisei Ginzburg and Mikhail Barshch's outline for the green city extension to Moscow illustrated similar principles in a rather more specific configuration.

The rational architecture of the modern movement and its practice through the Bauhaus were instantly eclipsed in Germany following the National Socialist seizure of power in 1933. Demonstrative of the confused ideologies of the Third Reich, while the Nazis wished to represent the aims of utilitarian, universal standards of industrial production, they also evidenced a desire to meet the psychological needs of the people and supported a return to the rooted values of the agrarian economy. A gradual transition away from the cubism of the Weimar Republic towards pitched-roof structures increasingly came to

symbolise natural, ecological objectives as central to the Third Reich.

Following World War Two, a similar dichotomisation of solar living arrangements was apparent. On the one hand, the construction of high-density, modernist blocks based upon CIAM principles and surrounded by green open spaces gained favour in both inner-city regeneration and peripheral city housing estates; on the other hand, population dispersal and movement to suburbs gathered pace. In the UK, lower densities were encouraged through the New Towns programme, which maintained many of the guiding principles proposed almost 50 years earlier by the Garden City movement. In the US, productive capacities and innovative technologies could be redirected into creating new living and working patterns — a spatial manifestation of the switching of capital. In downtown areas, glass tower constructions were facilitated by continually improving technologies in lift design and operation; heating, ventilation, and cooling systems; internal restructuring — for example, open-floor planning; and novel architectural and engineering techniques.

By improving our living environments through lower-density living and our working environments through climatically controlled office and factory spaces, we have increased our energy consumption requirements dramatically. In the Industrial Age, technological advances have brought about a continually growing dependency upon both those technologies and their energy requirements. Furthermore, the two world wars demonstrated the potential to use technology for devastation, and the dehumanisation of killing through increased mechanisation. Nevertheless, it should be recognised that innovation has provided innumerable advantages. Mass production has brought about increased food production, medical advances have increased average life expectancies, and living standards have greatly improved for a large number of people. In the industrialised countries at least, many homes now have heating, lighting, and a plethora of labour-saving devices that are considered essential.

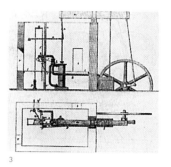
3

Machines and Technologies
Energy transformation of existing resources via the steam engine led to a dramatic increase in productivity, which — as with the agricultural revolution — led to a dramatic change in life style. The main difference was that the agricultural revolution was based on natural resources that are renewable, while the Industrial Revolution was based on natural resources that are non-renewable.

Enlightenment and Revolution
Technology and building technology 1760–1815

Indicators of progress include Cartwright's weaving machine of 1786, the first mechanised equipment of its kind, Horrock's weaving machine of 1803, and Watt's steam engine of 1769 (1–3). Thomas Cook went on his second voyage around the globe in 1773.

When James Watt took Thomas Newcomen's steam-pumping engine for draining mines, patented his invention, and went into manufacture with Matthew Boulton, he set European society on course for full-scale industrialisation. Engineer Sir John Rennie had two Boulton and Watt engines installed at the new Albion Flour Mills in London, to drive millstones and work hoists, cranes, and other mill equipment. The modern factory was born. The steam engine allowed production methods to be mechanised to produce materials. The workforce moved from the field to the city to operate the machinery of new industries.

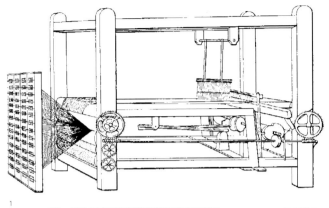

1

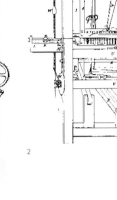

2

3

1760

1760 - First mountaineering
1761 - First chronometer
1764 - Voltaire
1767 - First spinning machine
1769 - Watt patent for steam engine
1769 - Goethe's plant drawings
1770 - Caspar David Friedrich

1770

1773 - Boston Tea Party
1776 - Declaration of Independence
1771 - Ecole de Médecine
1783 - Montgolfier Balloon
1783 - Boullée Library and Museum
1784 - Kant, *Aesthetik*
1789 - French Revolution

17

The machinery in this mill in Bedford in England was powered by water steam (4). These so-called water frames were situated on the first storey and in the basement.

The panoramic view, first experienced by ballooning, lifted human beings' view of the world (5, 6). A wider audience was able to appreciate this change once the diorama had been invented.

4

5

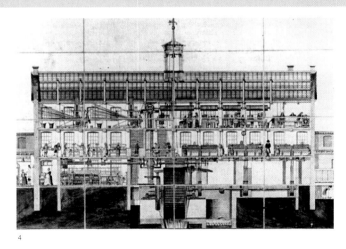

6

After the Thirty Years' War Europe entered a period of rapid philosophical and scientific development, the Age of Reason. The possibility to transform energy into movement as well as heat began to change the world. It was now possible to produce materials quickly and efficiently, but the price for progress had to be paid in fossil fuels.

7

8

Working conditions in coal mining in the UK were appalling. South Wales became one of the most important coal-mining areas in Europe. Penydarren had its own steam-powered railway by 1812.

| 90 | 1792 - Sir John Soane, Bank of England
1792 - Palais Municipal, Paris
1795 - Palais Bourbon, Paris
1797 - Workhouses
1797 - English factory system
1804 - Napoleon named Emperor | 1800 | 1808 - Belanger, Halle du Blé
1805 - Battle of Trafalgar
1809 - Durant, Prison
1809 - Poyet, Hospital
1811 - Glyptothek, Munich
1812 - Napoleon in Moscow
1815 - Battle of Waterloo | 1815 |

A PEEP AT THE GAS LIGHTS IN PALL-MALL.

9

When gaslight was first installed in public spaces, citizens reacted with suspicion. This cartoon from 1809 shows people's scepticism regarding progress.

Abstract Light of the Enlightenment
Panoramic views without windows

The rational thinking of the Enlightenment philosophers filtered through to architecture, and Baroque lighting effects were abandoned in favour of functional daylighting. In Paris, Jacques Gondoin's Ecole de Médecine receives clear, neutral light from a semicircular sky-light in the coffered half-dome (1). Light comes from above, so there is no logical reason to incorporate windows in the facade; this served as the model for many parliament buildings.

Etienne-Louis Boullée's design for the Bibliothèque du Roi in Paris filled the walls of the library with bookshelves rather than windows (2).

In London, Sir John Soane's additions to the Bank of England evoked a similar sense of forbidding grandeur. The bank's stock office (3) is typical of the windowless halls created by its architect between 1788 and 1823. Daylight sources placed high up in the walls. Across Europe, business, study, and the process of government were being conducted in these strictly controlled environments, cut off from the outside world.

A design for a museum by Boullée shows a monumental, but almost entirely windowless building flooded with daylight from a huge central hole in the dome (4)

When François-Joseph Belanger added a dome to the Halle du Blé in Paris, he used a combination of materials which was to reappear in buildings throughout the 19th century (5, 6). The open courtyard was originally covered by a wooden dome. When that was destroyed by fire, Belanger proposed an iron and glass replacement, and this became one of the first structures to use that combination of materials on a large scale.

2

1

3

4

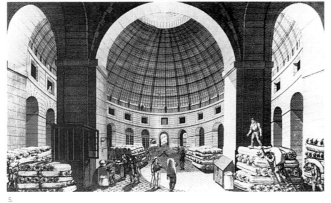

5

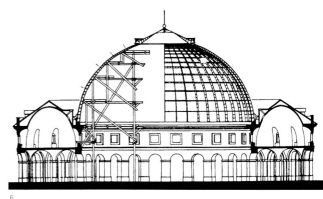

6

Rational thinking is expressed by direct light and strict order in introverted spaces. In the Enlightenment, the panoramic view became popular — from a balloon or a mountaintop.

Human perspective on the world changed through the 18th century. The wealthy built themselves belvederes, observation platforms from which women could watch men display their skills in falconry. A new exploratory pursuit, mountaineering, allowed people to look down on their surroundings — the writer and philosopher Goethe was among those to write a description of this new experience. Flight, first experienced by ballooning, also lifted the human view of the world. This new view was brought to a wider public by the diorama, a darkened room housing a 360-degree panoramic painting. Visitors would pay to enter dioramas and experience these new views. Such structures, with their panoramic windows, anticipated the feeling of fully glazed modernist buildings.

Spectators (9) stare out a 'panoramic window' onto an artificial landscape.

Rational Use of Sunlight and Structure
Similar principles used for humans and machines

An Early Hospital Building by Durand

Rigid geometry is apparent in the hospital and prison designs of Durand (1). This plan, dating from 1809 was produced in response to the appalling conditions of many existing hospitals and adopts a logical approach to the treatment of the sick. The rigid functional layout was designed for maximum efficiency of treatment, with good daylighting and cross-ventilation in the building the only concessions to human well-being. This hospital was designed to allow people to be processed efficiently, as if they were on a factory production line.

Durand's design for a prison is in the same precise geometrical style (2). Like the Roman legionnaires' camps, these buildings are clearly oriented to the sun.

Tenon and Poyet carried out tests on the ventilation scheme of their hospital project and employed various concepts in their design process. Before general acceptance of the germ theory of disease, hospitals were designed to provide the best ventilation possible. Flues conducted air from beneath the floor to grilles beside the beds. Air entering at the eaves cooled the ceiling in summer (3, 4).

The workhouse of 1797 designed by Samuel Bentham and Samuel Bunce has a distinctly modern-looking facade made from iron and glass (5).

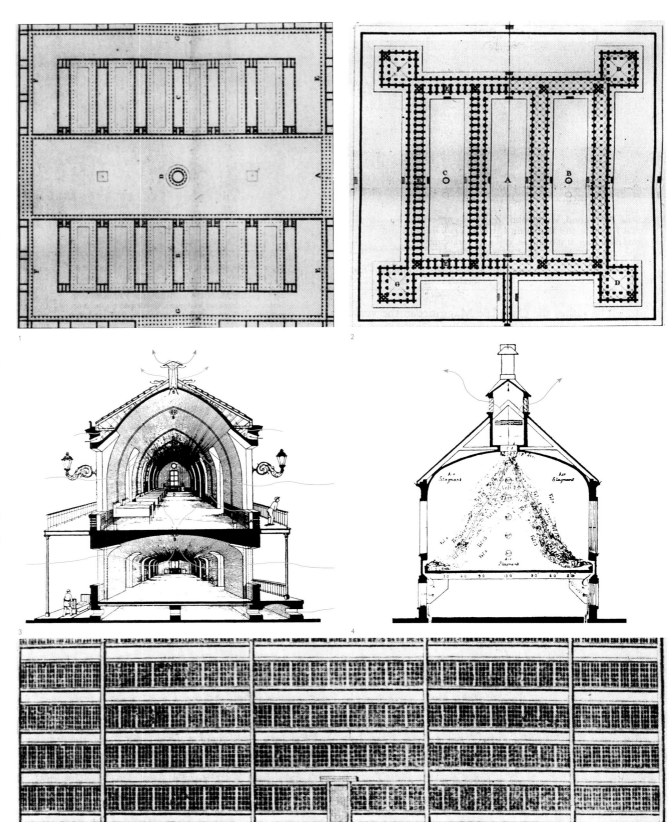

The rational approach to light, space, and structure influenced the development of modern building types — prisons, workhouses, hospitals, and especially factories — and resulted in new geometries and technologies.

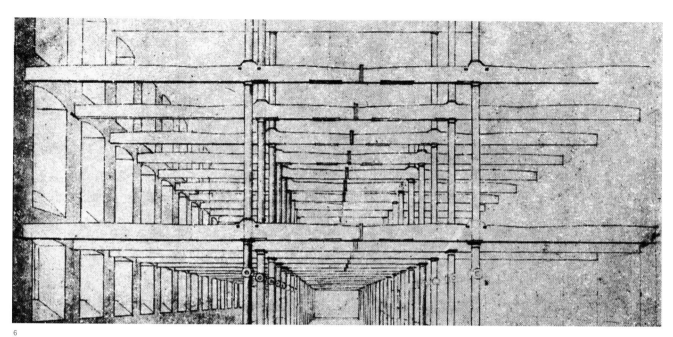

6

The new production processes were carried out in factories, purely functional buildings that were little more than the casing for the machinery of mass production, with an absence of ornament and maximum clear space for production lines. Like the equipment inside the building, the factory itself was built using modern materials and construction techniques. Walls were still masonry, with cast iron used initially for columns and only later for beams as well. The move from timber to a cast iron structure was driven by the need for fireproofing. As the building type evolved, the masonry wall dissolved increasingly into the columns and beams. The structural frame, or skeleton, was born.

The first iron-framed building was Marshall, Benyon, and Bage's flour mill at Ditherington near Shrewsbury, constructed in 1796 (6). The English factory established a pattern that was to be taken up by steel-frame buildings just over a century later. However, its initial flexibility was restricted by the energy systems used. The whole factory was literally driven by one machine that transformed all energy into mechanical movement.

7

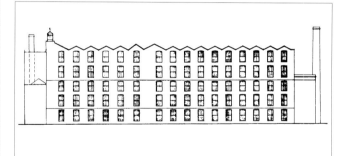

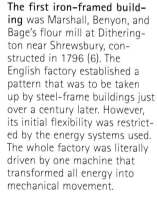

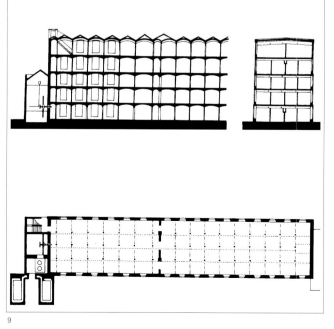

8

9

British Supremacy
Technology and building technology 1820–1870

Indicators of progress include Stephenson's Puffing Billy; Turner's painting, *Rain, Steam and Speed* of 1844; the Hobby Horse bicycle of 1818; and a more developed model of 1839 by Scottish blacksmith Kirkpatrick McMillan (1-4).

Fossil-energy conversion could not only make parts of a machine move, but could also move the entire machine — thus the invention of the loco-motive. The railway system took off following the success of engineer George Stephenson on the Stockton-to-Darlington line in 1821. By 1835, England was in the grip of the first rail-way boom. In addition to high fossil-fuel consumers like the locomotive and the steamship (5), the 19th century witnessed the development of another less environmentally damaging form of transport, the bicycle. This relied purely on biomass energy, human muscle power.

1

2

3

4

5

| 1820 | 1820 – Locomotives
1820 – Invention of the bicycle
1824 – Conservatory movement
1830 – Cast-Iron stoves at home
1830 – Paxton, Glass-house
1834 – Ice-machine patent | 1835 | 1838 – Bicton Garden Conservatory
1839 – Becquerel, photovoltaics
1840 – Kew Gardens
1842 – Great Western Railway
1845 – Thomas Cook Travel Agency
1847 – Jardin d'Hiver, Paris
1849 – Gold Rush in America | 18 |

Consumer culture came into being with the development of mass-produced goods for the home. These goods were de-signed to make life more com-fortable. Gas lighting began to be installed in homes — the examples shown here date from the 1850s (6).

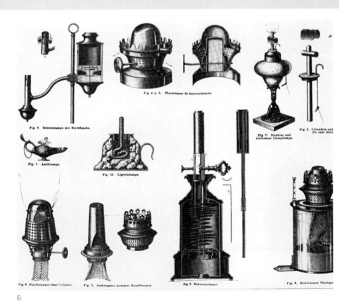

6

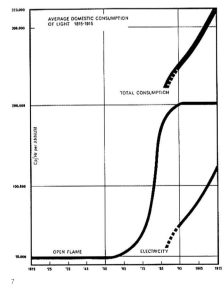

7

As industry in Britain boomed, demand for transport increased, and factory owners created heavy traffic on the country's network of canals in their efforts to transport their goods to port. New forms of travel using steam and human muscle power were developed.

8

9

10

11

By the end of the 18th century, iron had become a popular construction material, especially for bridges in England. Technical developments were also improving the quality of glass, and when the glass tax was abolished in England in 1845, architects were free to use glazing as an everyday, rather than a luxury, material. When architect Matthew Digby Wyatt saw London's Crystal Palace, he predicted that its combination of iron and glass would herald a new era in architecture. By 1855, Henry Bessemer had developed a steel production process that drastically cut the cost of steel.

The fashioning of glass for London's Crystal Palace, the Great Western steamship of 1854, and further advances in the evolution of the bicycle — a pedal model and the Safety Bicycle of 1875 — were signs of the fast-moving progress in the mid-19th century.

50

1851 - Crystal Palace, London
1852 - Kings Cross, London
1853 - First elevator
1854 - Patent for reinforced concrete, UK
1855 - Turkish bath revival
1857 - Gas ovens at home
1859 - First drilling for oil

1860

1860 - Mouchot, solar inventions
1863 - London Underground system
1864 - Peter Ellis, glass facade
1865 - Glasgow, glass facades
1867 - Gallerial, Milan
1868 - Brooklyn Bridge, New York

1870

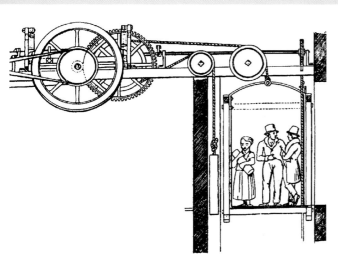

12

13

Engineering and technology were to have an equally radical effect upon non-domestic buildings. The first elevator was displayed at the New York World's Fair of 1853 by the Otis Elevator Company. Around the same time, bathrooms were becoming more common in the US.

From Greenhouse to Crystal Palace
The beauty of solar engineering

Fascination with the exotic plants and cultures of their colonies grew as Europeans began to experience foreign lands for themselves for the first time with the advent of tourism. This fascination was to manifest itself in the construction of countless glass-houses to recreate the ambience of the jungle. The practice of enhancing plant growth in glass-houses had existed for centuries. But the 19th century saw that glass-houses could have another purpose: to allow climatic zones to be manipulated to turn parts of a city like London into a tropical rainforest. The spectacle of the huge glass-house caught the imagination of people to such an extent that these buildings soon progressed from being the playthings of kings and emperors to being places for the enjoyment of the general public.

The Great Conservatory for the Duke of Devonshire at Chatsworth House was designed by Joseph Paxton and Decimus Burton in 1836-40 (1). The structure was made from wood, with cast iron used for the pillars and gallery. The same type of ridge and furrow glazing was used later in the Crystal Palace. This design made a considerable impact at the time of its construction, with a local newspaper, the *Derbyshire Courier*, publishing a lengthy description of the building and its contents.

Paxton's Bicton Gardens Palm House in Devon (2, 3) also had flowing curves, perhaps following the advice of Sir George Mackenzie to make the surface of a greenhouse roof parallel to the vaulted surface of the heavens, or to the plane of the sun's orbit.

1

2

3

The experience of being able to capture sunlight in greenhouses fired people's imagination. Soon it became possible to control vast areas of artificial environment.

4

The Great Palm House at Kew Gardens in London was designed by Decimus Burton and Richard Turner in 1844 (4, 5). The 100-m-long structure is made from cast and wrought iron. The services/heating system had 12 boilers supplying hot water to an underfloor pipe network, which could keep the inside of the hot house at a temperature of 27 degrees Celsius throughout the winter. The conservatory had become a high-energy-consuming climate machine, but at the same time the illusions of the exotic world had to be maintained. Designers took elaborate steps to conceal the services from public view.

The Vinery at Hampton Court Palace (7) still produces a good harvest, currently around eight hundred pounds of Black Hamburg grapes each year. The vine was planted in 1768 by Capability Brown.

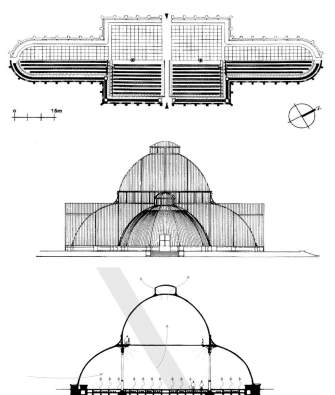

5

6

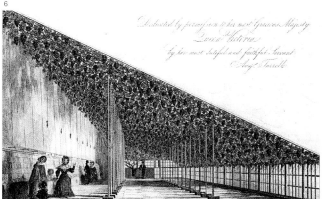

7

8

A royal fascination now spread to private homes. Early in the century, conservatories were only found in grand homes, such as The Grange in Hampshire (6). But later in the century, prefabrication of glasshouses allowed far more modest homes to join in the trend. A late 19th-century example in Paris is an architect-designed version with a surfeit of fanciful detailing (8).

London's Crystal Palace, home of the Great Exhibition of 1851, provided a breathtaking example to the world of what could be achieved. The best products of British industry were displayed in Joseph Paxton's 600-m-long exhibition hall. The structure was built from cast iron, wrought iron, timber, and sheet glass. Ventilation of the vast building was by adjustable louvres in the walls; a raised slatted floor also helped to maximise air flow. To combat solar gain, canvas awnings were installed in the roof, and exhibitors erected their own sun canopies over their displays. The huge glass cover created an artificial Mediterranean microclimate in the middle of London.

Construction of the Crystal Palace was completed in just 22 weeks, by standardising components to make assembly a relatively simple, repetitive process. A basic 2.44-m cladding module was assembled in spans of up to 22 m. Roof-glazing installation is shown at the right. To streamline the assembly process, glass was installed from special glazing wagons designed by Paxton. The smooth-running, well-organised construction of the Crystal Palace set a model for industrialised building around the world.

Dismantling the Crystal Palace proved just as easy. The exhibition hall stood in Hyde Park for 18 months. It was then reassembled in south London, with a slightly altered design. In its new incarnation, it housed tropical plants, educational displays, and concerts. The Crystal Palace was finally destroyed by fire in 1936.

1

2

3

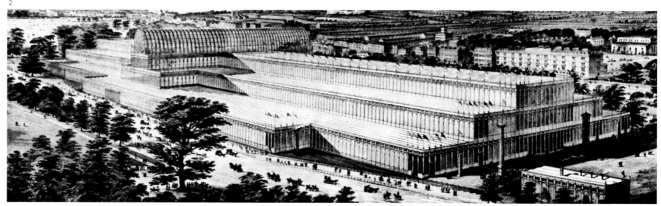

4

Munich's Crystal Palace was similar to London's but on a much smaller scale (5, 6). It was designed by A. von Voit and constructed in 1853. London had started a fashion for crystal palaces that spread as far as New York, where a glass-house was a feature of the World's Fair of 1853.

5

6

7

Flights of fancy in the artificial world of the conservatory became increasingly grandiose. The roofgarden on the Königs-bau in Munich, Germany (7), was created for Ludwig II of Bavaria in 1867. It was extravagantly furnished and contained a panoramic painting of the Himalayas, a bamboo and silk pavilion, and a pond with rowing boats. There were special lighting effects to create moonlight or sunset. A desire to create artificial worlds has since been expressed in such environments as Disneyland and the gamblers' paradise of Las Vegas. Today, entering an artificial world is not the exclusive pursuit of kings.

8

9

Designers of the main railway stations of the 19th century adopted the architectural fashion of the Crystal Palace to create cathedrals of transport. Examples include London's St Pancras, the work of E.M. Barry (9). St Pancras' roof boasted the largest span anywhere in the world.

The Beginning of the Energy Race
Technology and building technology 1870–1914

A boom of solar inventions started at the end of the 19th century. In France, Augustin Mouchot, a professor of mathematics at the Lycée de Tours, developed solar collectors and motors, ovens, and even a still to make brandy. In the US, engineer John Ericsson predicted as early as 1868 that the world's consumption of fossil fuels would lead to crisis and worked on refining solar motors. The sunny states of the US were to be the natural testing ground for solar power, and engineers H.E. Sillsie and John Boyle established full-size solar power plants there in the early 1900s.

Travel and Transport
By the end of the 19th century, comfort and elegance had been incorporated into travel and transport. Shown is a drawing-room car of 1897 belonging to the South Eastern Railway (5). The London Underground transport system came into operation around 1863 (6).

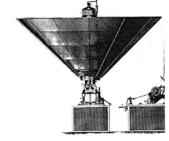

1870	1880	18
1870 - Rockefeller Centre 1874 - Flora, Berlin 1874 - Mouchot Solar Engine 1875 - Krupp Housing 1876 - Bon Marché, Paris 1879 - Solar printing press	1880 - Hotels and winter-gardens 1884 - Gaudí 1885 - Le Printemps, Paris 1885 - Home Insurance, Chicago 1888 - Wright, Rookery Building 1889 - Galerie des Machines, Paris 1889 - Eiffel Tower, Paris	

Indicators of progress include a solar-powered printing press developed by Mouchot's assistant Abel Pifre in 1880, Mouchot's portable solar oven developed in 1877 for use by French troops in Africa, his solar motor impressing the crowds by powering an ice maker at the Paris Exposition of 1878, and a hot air engine developed by Ericsson in 1872 (1-4).

Building technology was advancing hand in hand with industry and transport. Machines and monuments were constructed that tested design skill, construction technology, and new materials.

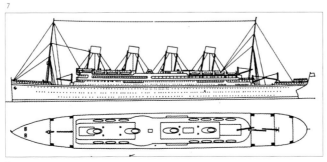

Throughout the 19th century, engineers were engaged in the pursuit of power, in finding ways of providing enough energy to feed the seemingly insatiable machinery of heavy industry. Most innovations were in fossil-fuel power, electricity, and gas, but in Europe and the US, solar energy had many proponents.

11

12

Combustion Engine
People's ideas about transport were to be changed irrevocably by the development of the internal combustion engine. Germany, Britain, and the US were the centres for development of the motor car. In 1896, Daimler began to manufacture cars in Coventry — the model shown below (13) dates from the following year. By 1904, there were already 17,000 motor vehicles on UK roads; by 1914, that figure had risen to just over 265,000.

13

90

1893 - GUM, Moscow
1895 - Reliance Building, Chicago
1901 - Horta
1902 - Ebenezer Howard
1903 - Garnier, Cité Industrielle
1905 - Unwin, Garden City
1905 - Einstein

1905

1906 - Wagner, Post Office
1909 - Wright, Robie House
1910 - Gaudí, Casa Mila
1912 - Atkinson, Sun House
1914 - Taut, Glass House
1914 - World War One begins

1914

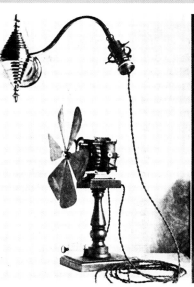

14

THE WEATHER IS ALWAYS PLEASANT IN WESTINGHOUSE FANLAND. CURRENT FROM LIGHTING CIRCUIT FOR THE FAN COSTS ONLY 1/4¢ AN HOUR.

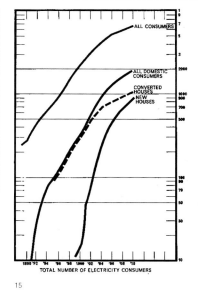

ALL CONSUMERS
ALL DOMESTIC CONSUMERS
CONVERTED HOUSES
NEW HOUSES

TOTAL NUMBER OF ELECTRICITY CONSUMERS

15

Electric Energy Consumption
The number of electricity consumers grew exponentially as machinery was installed to save labour and increase comfort. One of the first pieces of electrical equipment for domestic use was the fan.

Glass Buildings for Work and Play
Daylight in covered streets, piazzas, and factories

Glazing was used to bring comfort to the process of shopping. Like those of the ancient Romans, the great shopping centres of the 19th century were designed to allow people to shop in the comfortable environment of the covered street. Elements of the glass-house were incorporated into commercial buildings in order to entice shoppers to spend. Shopping arcades were constructed around the world, from Naples to Moscow, in widely differing climates.

Two examples of the shopping arcade are Milan's Galleria Vittorio Emanuele II (2-4) and Moscow's GUM (1). The cruciform plan of the Galleria is topped by glass tunnel vaults meeting at a glass dome. The section shows how air is pulled through the Galleria's cool basement to ventilate the arcade. As solar gain could overheat the building in summer, the ends of the arcade were left open to maximise air flow. To keep out the icy winds of Moscow's harsh climate, the ends of the GUM centre were closed in. Designed by A.N. Pomeranzev to replace an entire district of small shops and stalls, the centre was a network of 16 blocks with joining covered streets — a bazaar for a cool climate.

Floor grating in the Galleria in Milan

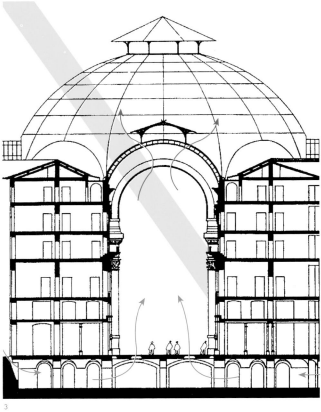

As retailers competed to sell their goods, shops became more comfortable and attractive, using greenhouse technologies until they attained the luxury of the department store — a modern cathedral dedicated to industry and commerce. The structural steel frame extended out to the facade removed the requirement for any structural load to be taken by external walls.

6

7

The large store windows were not for looking out of or for letting daylight into the building, but to allow passers-by to see what was on sale inside. The shop window soon developed into a complete facade. The Halladie Building in San Francisco was designed and built in 1893 with one of the first curtain walls (6).

8

9

In the competition to sell the wealth of consumer goods to shoppers, the covered marketplace developed as an environment of comfort and sophistication, another artificial world. France's *grands magasins* were huge buildings with halls filled with luxury goods, atrium spaces with magnificent staircases leading from floor to floor, and glass roofs. The first true department store was Paris' Bon Marché. The Bon Marché was followed by the Grand Magasin du Louvre, the Belle Jardinière, the Magasins Réunis, Printemps (7, 9), and the Galeries Lafayette (8).

The new principle of the
structural steel frame that
extends into the facade had
its origins in the English factory
building system of the 18th
century. When the wall became
independent of the structure,
cladding was released from
the constraint of structural
performance, and new, lighter
materials could be used. The
efficiency of the building itself
allowed it to climb higher and
higher.

The skyscraper was made
possible by a combination of
two technologies — steel framing and the passenger elevator.
The potential of high-rise construction was first explored in
Chicago. The Reliance Building
was designed by Daniel H.
Burnham and John W. Root (1,
2). The completed building has
heavily glazed facades — a
foretaste of the curtain wall —
while a photograph of the
building under construction
shows its skeleton.

A key innovation in construction technology was the development of reinforced concrete
at the end of the 19th century,
notably through the work of
François Hennebique. In the US,
Albert Kahn used concrete
extensively in the design of
factories for the Pierce Arrow
Motor Car Company in 1906
and the Ford Motor Company
in 1905 (3, 4). These factories
were completely different from
the 19th-century sweatshops
of England's Industrial
Revolution. Large windows
allowed the assembly-line workers to spend their days in
naturally daylit, airy spaces.

1

2

3

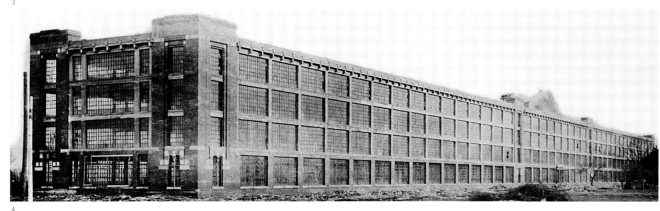

4

The glazed wall became high architecture. As cladding no longer had to perform a structural role, it could take the lightest possible form, and the best way of making the external wall dissolve was to build it in glass. The division between inside and outside space was once again removed. This can be seen in the open staircase of the office building of the Werkbund Exhibition in Cologne, designed by Walter Gropius and Adolf Meyer and constructed in 1914 (5), and in the Fagus Works, also by Gropius and Meyer, which were constructed in 1911 (6). The minimisation of the wall to a new glass skin allowed maximum external awareness, daylight, and transparency.

5

6

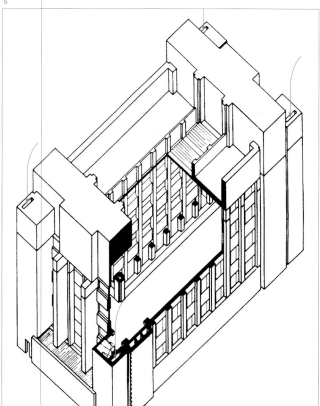

The Larkin Building in Buffalo, New York, built by Frank Lloyd Wright in 1904, while not one of the most advanced air-conditioned buildings of its time, did use a large atrium similar to the *grands magasins* (7). Paul Christophe's text on the Hennebique system directly influenced the course of Auguste Perret's career. The first of Perret's concrete structures was an apartment block in the rue Franklin, Paris, constructed in 1903 (8, 9).

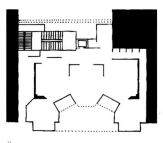

7

8

9

A House in the Sun
Healthy solar living for the middle class

Appalling living conditions were one of the consequences of rapid industrial and urban development. Slums were to be found in the world's major industrial cities, from the Meyers Hof housing blocks in Berlin in the late 19th century (1) to the tenements of New York City, shown in a photograph taken by Jacob Riis (2). To maximise profit, housing developments were high in density, and homes received little direct sunlight and were poorly ventilated. The poor quality of housing and over-crowded living conditions fostered ill health and disease.

Gustave Doré's etchings of 1872 show the horror of life in the London slums, including a typical terrace of houses in London tightly packed between railway bridges (3).

Desire for exposure to the sun for pleasure grew in popularity, so that by 1911 there were sunbathing areas all over northern Europe. These areas were screened from public view (4).

New transport networks emerged as a result of the electrification of urban rail and tram lines. Employees no longer had to live within walking distance of their workplace and could move out to the more favourable surroundings of the developing suburbs. At first, migration was essentially a middle-class phenomenon, but with time working-class sub-urbanisation, often assisted through council housing pro-grammes, followed. Dependence upon these networks was illustrated by the importance of the proximity of the underground or subway to suburban construction and to the stimulation of speculative development.

1

2

3

4

UNDERGROUND

Ruislip Village
and all around lie the
quiet fields and lanes.

BOOK TO
RUISLIP.

Cheap Return Tickets
on Sundays.

5

As industrial cities became overcrowded and overwhelmed by poverty, poor health, and crime, rail and tram lines into the surrounding countryside enabled the middle classes to escape. Recognising the links between poor urban environments and workers' mental and physical health, industrial philanthropists proposed new model settlements where healthier living could go hand in hand with social reform.

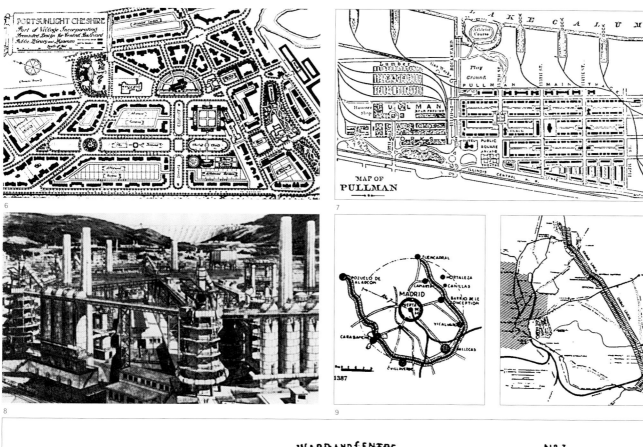

6

7

8

9

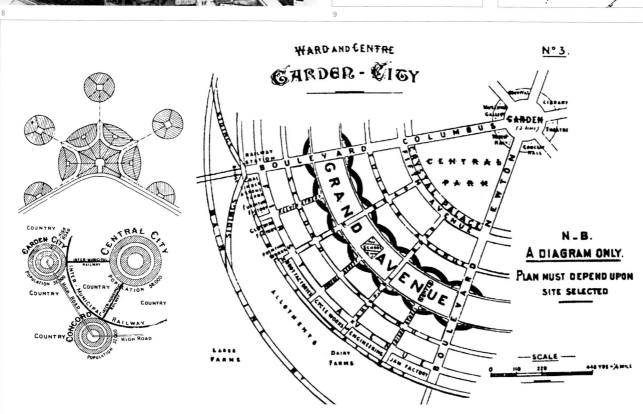

10

Industrial philanthropists pursued their ideals relating to social reform through the development of healthy living and working environments. The links between workers' housing and mental and physical health (and therefore productivity) were clearly recognised. Port Sunlight was established in 1888 by Lord Lever, adjoining his chemicals factory complex (6). George Pullman established his ideal town of Pullman to the south of Chicago during the 1880s. The settlement comprised workers' housing in close proximity to the factory and provided a number of communal facilities (7).

Garnier's proposals outlined plans for a socialist city of 35,000 inhabitants which was sensitively related to its local environment (8). A varied housing typology, in accordance with strict standards for the provision of light, ventilation, and green space, provided tree-lined residential areas and low-density urban form.

Soria y Mata's proposal for a linear garden city surrounding Madrid like a necklace was partially constructed beginning in the 1880s (9). In their more abstract form, the linear cities were envisaged as acting as 'locomotion vertebrae' linking existing urban networks together along transport corridors.

Ebenezer Howard's proposals for a ring of Garden Cities, which married the benefits of urban and country living, may have been the most influential in stimulating a return to healthy solar living surrounded by the countryside. Each one was intended to comprise a central city of fifty-eight thousand people and six satellite towns of thirty-two thousand inhabitants (10).

World War One
The mechanisation of killing

The process of killing and being killed became mechanised. No longer did soldiers have to face each other in hand-to-hand combat. The killer did not have to see his victim at close quarters; he could fire a gun or release poison gas canisters from far away. The new weapons of this war were poison gas, tanks, and above all, machine-guns. Sophistication in the use of steel reached new levels, in the production of armaments. Prior to the war, Germany and America had taken the international lead in technological innovation. Britain's wartime response was to encourage industrial development through a special Government office, the Department of Scientific and Industrial Research. War was to become a contest of high technology: the country that could produce the most efficient weapons would win. The cost in human lives was enormous. The Industrial Revolution had shown the full force of its negative power.

1

2

3

4

People Killed in the First World War in Millions		
Germany		1.8
Austria and Hungary		1.2
Russia		1.7
France		1.38
Britain		0.94
Total		10

7

5

6

152

The successful operation of the 20th-century war machine depends on technology and industry. In World War One, industry turned its energy to the production of explosives, motor engines, guns, and ships.

Depression and Hope
Technology and building technology 1918–1945

Indicators of progress include the Zeppelin airship (1, 2, 4).

In the building sector, the introduction of reinforced concrete caught the imagination of avant-garde architects. Le Corbusier's sketch for the Maison Dom-Ino with its Hennebique frame introduced the idea of design freedom for plans and facades (5).

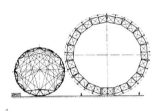

4

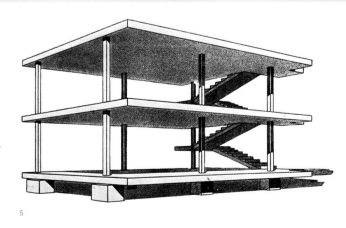

1

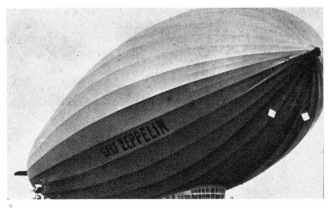

2

3

1918

1922 - Le Corbusier, Ville Contemporaine
1922 - Mies, Glass Tower design
1923 - 20,000 fridges
1925 - Le Corbusier, L'Esprit Nouveau
1926 - The Bauhaus, Dessau
1926 - Schindler, Beach House
1926 - Hannes Meyer, School

1926

1927 - Weissenhof Siedlung, Germany
1928 - Zeppelin flight around the world
1928 - Klein, Solar Housing
1928 - Melnikov
1929 - Neubühl master plan
1929 - Mies, Barcelona Pavilion

19

Developments in energy technology ranged from Adolf Hitler's state-owned utilities system in Germany to the USA's Boulder Canyon Project of 1930, the centrepiece of which was the Hoover Dam (6). The largest hydroelectric scheme in the US at this time was the Tennessee Valley Authority programme. This programme saw the construction of 16 major dams and was responsible for producing 5% of the national generating supply.

5

6

When World War One ended, people were able to reap the benefit of the technological developments of the war machine. Air travel became commercially viable. The interwar years saw the growth of electricity as a centralised energy supply.

7

8

9

10

The US was coming to dominate the international industrial scene. By 1937, the country was accountable for more than 60% of the world's oil consumption. The US was the world's leading car-producing nation, with Britain second and Germany third. American industry was developing a new area of expertise, production engineering, which brought management and efficiency to the production process.

30

1931 - Le Corbusier, Soviet Palace
1931 - RIBA solar publication
1932 - Owen Williams, Boots Factory
1933 - 850,000 fridges
1934 - Wright, Broadgate City
1936 - Two million fridges

1935

1936 - Charlie Chaplin, *Modern Times*
1936 - Wright, Johnson Wax
1937 - Wright, Falling Water
1938 - *Queen Elizabeth* (ship)
1940 - Rockefeller Centre
1941 - 3.5 million fridges

1945

11

12

Within the home, cooling has always been difficult. Ice could not be produced at home, and storage possibilities were limited. The development of electrical compressors allowed cooling for the storage of food, increasing capabilities in climate control. Electrical appliances were entering the home and would drastically change domestic life.

By the late 1920s, American companies were producing air conditioning units, originally invented by Carrier. In 1926, room air conditioning units were patented and utilised.

A New Agenda
The sunny side of heroic modernism

The feeling of this time is summed up in Sigfried Giedion's book *Befreites Wohnen*, which was published in 1929. It advocated 'light, air and opening' as new values of living. Architecturally, this idea found expression in large glass walls, terraces, and outdoor spaces. The stars of this new architectural style were Le Corbusier and Mies van der Rohe, shown walking through Weissenhof Siedlung in Stuttgart, Germany, in 1927.

The Bauhaus was not the only source of modernist thinking. The ideas and architecture were international, with practitioners coming from the Netherlands, Belgium, France, Britain, Denmark, Sweden, Italy, Austria, and Russia. Nevertheless, the Bauhaus was a powerhouse of extraordinary creativity. The institution and its building in Dessau, designed by its director, Walter Gropius, expressed the new agenda, a social vision of the future. They offered a new form of education which would sow the seeds for a new society. The Bauhaus brought together fine and applied artists to create a new breed of craftsmen.

1

2

3

4

The shock of the war and growing urban problems triggered one of the most radical and visionary periods in Europe this century. Walls dissolved into glass and light, and solar energy became a key element for health and education. With the new life-style, a new style was born for private, public, and industrial buildings.

New building types such as sanatoria were built throughout Europe. The modern movement wanted to create better and healthier buildings, letting in as much sunlight as possible to compensate for the lack of sunlight in the cities. The Colonia Elioterapica, designed by G.L. Banfi, L. Belgioso, E. Peressutti, and Ernesto Rogers, is a late example. Constructed in Lugano in 1938, it shows the direct link between the current architectural style and the philosophy of solar cures. This strong desire for sunlight, which is so integral to modernist architecture, was rooted in the cool, temperate climatic zone.

5

6

The sunbathing terrace of the sanatorium in Waiblingen, Germany, designed by Richard Döcker and constructed in 1926 (6), and the open-air school at Amsterdam (8) show similar design approaches. The Amsterdam school was designed by Johannes Duiker and constructed in 1930.

Duiker and Bernard Bijvoet's sanatorium built in 1927 in Hilversum was one of the first major projects expressing the ideas of the modern movement. Here, the main concern was to get as much daylight into the building as possible (7).

7

8

Le Corbusier's Pavilion de l'Esprit Nouveau was built for the Paris Exposition of 1925 (1). It was a prototype for the living and housing concept of Immeubles Villas, which dates from 1922 (3). The Immeubles Villas were designed to be stacked in blocks on six double floors with garden terraces. They were part of Le Corbusier's Ville Contemporaine, the contemporary city, which was a model for high-density living in an urban context. The Ville Contemporaine was designed to provide residents with a good quality of life. It was intended that housing blocks would offer hotel-style services to residents and would have their own outdoor recreational facilities.

1

2

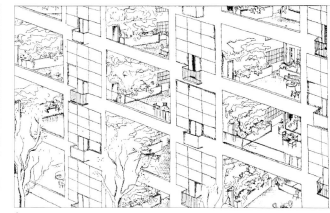

3

Frank Lloyd Wright's Falling Water placed bioclimatic design in the dramatic natural setting of Bear Run, Pennsylvania (4). The reinforced concrete house, constructed in 1937, brings its occupants close to nature, while there is ample shade from the huge cantilevered balconies. In the summer months, cooling air from the waterfall can be let into the building via the staircase. This extraordinary piece of architecture was designed specifically as a holiday residence and offers high comfort levels in the summer, but it is far less comfortable in winter. The luxury building cannot therefore be seen as an example for mass housing of the future.

4

Mies van der Rohe's German pavilion for the Barcelona Exhibition of 1929 can be seen as his vision of an ideal home. The simple building with its open plan has expanses of glass running from floor to ceiling and broad roof overhangs. It represented a new style of architecture for a new life. Note the overhang which shades the terrace and the glass wall.

5

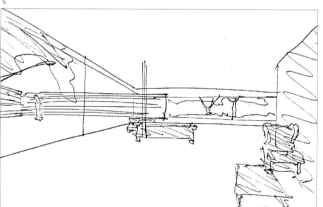

6

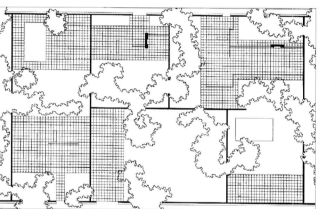

7

Mies Courtyard Houses
Three years later, Mies designed some courtyard houses. The architect's drawings relate to the traditional courtyard houses of China. Modern architects in Europe and America were looking to many sources for inspiration, and their awareness of solar design is evident from projects like this.

8

9

Richard Neutra believed there was a link between a building's design and the psychophysiological health of its users. One of Neutra's influences in this theory was Dr Philip Lovell, for whom he designed the Health House in Los Angeles. Constructed in 1927, this house was in fact a mixed-used development incorporating family accommodation and an open-air school. The steel frame was constructed in just over a week. In his book *Survival Through Design*, published in 1954, Neutra writes, 'It has become imperative that in designing our physical environment we should consciously raise the fundamental question of survival in the broadest sense of the term.'

Visions for Global Living
Buckminster Fuller's solar future

The 10-deck 4D apartment house of 1927 had pneumatic floor pads, vacuum-pane glass walls, and air conditioning that would filter out dust to save on housework. The 4D house was designed for mass production, and to keep costs down, utilities were factory installed in the tower's central mast. The house was also designed to be portable. Fuller intended that the block would be transported by zeppelin and simply dropped into position, like planting a tree. The name 4D came from the 'fourth dimension' in physics, the time-space dimension.

The tower was part of a greater vision for an Air Ocean World Town Plan, developed in 1927. The buildings were intended to house airline maintenance crews in the most hostile natural environments of the world, providing stepping stones for air travel. This project has proved inspirational to such architects as Sir Richard Rogers and Sir Norman Foster.

Streamlined shields were designed to reduce the air drag and hence the heat loss of the 4D house. By reducing air drag, the building's structure could be lighter in weight, an important factor for transportation. The effectiveness of the shield is shown in the diagrams. From the overhang deck of the 4D house, residents had a panoramic view of the landscape.

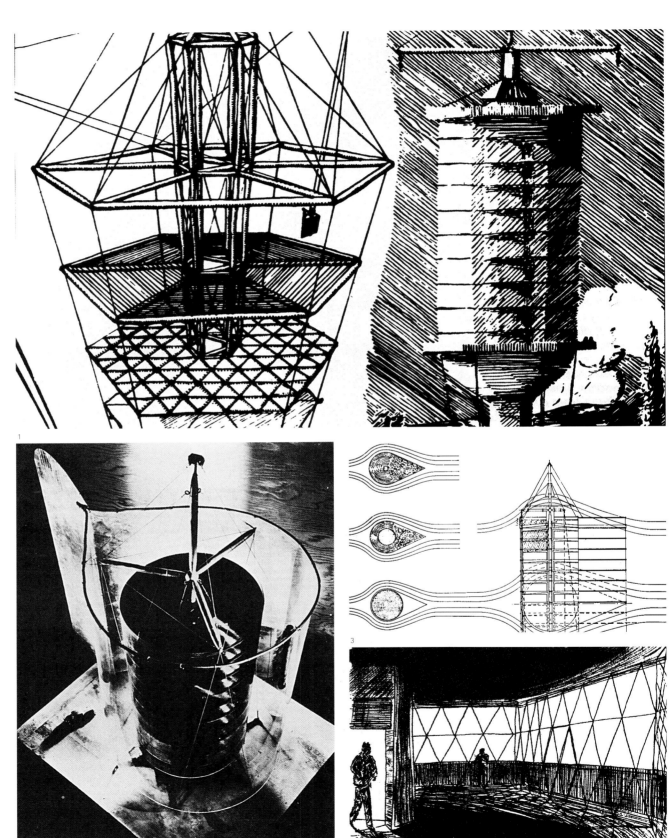

New concepts for living were expressed in the housing models of the visionary American designer Buckminster Fuller, which ranged from super-lightweight designs to aerodynamic forms improved for better insulation, wind resistance, and ventilation.

5

4D Dymaxion House
Fuller described his minimum 4D Dymaxion house of 1927 as combining an American skyscraper and an oriental pagoda. The house was hexagonal in plan and was suspended from a central mast that contained the building services. The masthead also contained lenses to take advantage of solar energy. It was anticipated that the temperature, humidity, and airflow inside the house would be kept at optimum levels so that occupants would not actually need to have blankets on their beds or wear clothes indoors. Inside, the house boasted such advanced features as a built-in pneumatic sofa, a suspended dining table, a dishwasher, and a clothes drier. Rooms were divided not by solid walls, but by partitions formed of prefabricated utility units — shelving and other useful facilities. The term *Dymaxion* was a fusion of the words *dynamism, maximum,* and *ions.*

The Dymaxion Dwelling Machine of 1944 had a rooftop ventilator that resembled a boat hull and rudder. The ventilator provided minimum drag and maximum exhaust efficiency.

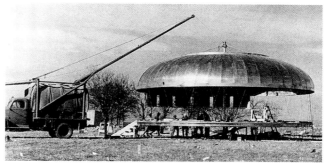

7

6

8

New technologies inspired architects, and concrete, steel, and glass became the predominant materials for construction. American high-rises excited architects around the world and set them a challenge. The glazed skyscraper with its unlimited light and view became a symbol of progress and of corporate success.

Mies van der Rohe's visionary design for a glass skyscraper in Berlin from 1922 is one of the clearest manifestations of the spirit of the age (1). It was a vision that clearly mirrored the idea of l'Esprit Nouveau and was years ahead of its time. Its successor, Lake Shore Drive, was not built until 1962. In his proposal for the Berlin project, Mies explained that the tower's curved plan was determined by three factors: 'Sufficient illumination of the interior, the massing of the building from the street, and lastly the play of reflections.'

Walter Gropius and Adolf Meyer produced the design for a competition for the Chicago Tribune building in 1922 (2). This design seems harsh in comparison to the light and airy designs of the time.

While architects were dreaming of visions of the future, the construction industry and its structural engineers developed spectacular factories with vast areas of glass, steel, and concrete. Albert Kahn's 1922 plant for the Ford Motor Company at Dearborn is still in good working condition (3).

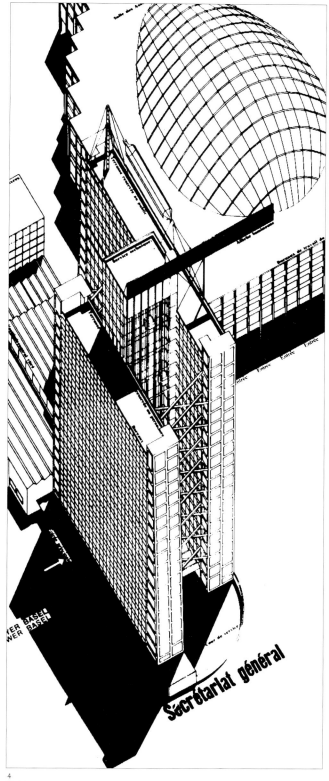

Hannes Meyer was a strong proponent of the solar orientation of buildings and a member of the ABC group, which was dedicated to designing socially relevant buildings according to certain scientific principles. Shown (4) is his 1927 competition entry with Hans Wittwer for the United Nations headquarters in Geneva. Meyer's principles are clear in his description of another project by the pair, the Petersschule project in Basel of 1926. Meyer said, 'The ideal would be to skylight all the rooms ... The school itself is raised as far as possible above ground to a level where there is sunlight and fresh air.'

Le Corbusier's Algier high-rise, designed in 1938, marked his first use of the brise-soleil (5, 6).

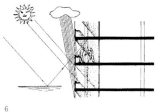

6

Brinkman and Van der Vlugt's Van Nelle packing plant in Rotterdam is clearly structured with a simple concrete skeleton. Built in 1927, the facade is independent of the structure and allows brilliant daylight into the building. The workers' canteen took pride of place. Located at the top of the building, it gave diners a panoramic view (7, 8).

7

8

Back to Nature
Different ideologies, similar concepts

Modernism was expressed in a contradictory, and increasingly reactionary, fashion in Germany under the Third Reich. Nazism rejected the bland universalisation of technology and the collapse of spatial distinctiveness and identity associated with modernity, emphasising instead the power of myth — connecting blood with soil, race and Fatherland, destiny and place — as the bases for social and political action. Through the aesthetisation of politics, city dwelling was characterised as a nomadic existence in which residents had lost any attachment to the soil and therefore to the Homeland. Disurbanisation and a rejection of modernism in architecture were pursued and a return to natural roots was favoured. A clear reflection of this was found in the shift from the cubic structures of the Bauhaus-influenced Weimar Republic to the pitched roofs that came to symbolise the Third Reich.

Ginzburg and Barshch's rather eccentric proposal for a 'Green City Competition' comprised housing units raised on stilts projecting like a spiral into the open countryside. Communal facilities were provided at 500-m intervals, and the continuous parkland and green space on either side offered sports fields, swimming-pools, and other healthy activities. These new arteries would act to decant population from the existing urban area (3).

Leonidov and Milyutin's proposals for the new city of Magnitogorsk reflect the dominance of linear city and green space principles in Russian planning during the early 1930s. Leonidov's plan emphasised social housing and transit links, with the city structured around a 32-km road joining the industrial plant to an agricultural commune in the interior. Milyutin's proposals advocated a linear city comprising six parallel strips (4, 5).

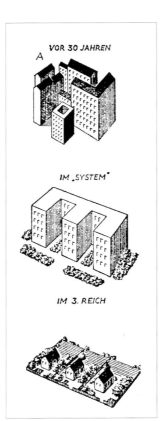

1

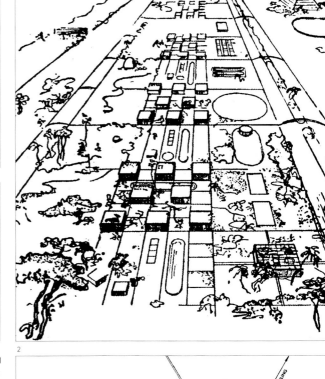

2

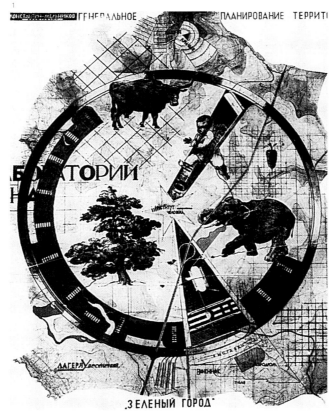

3

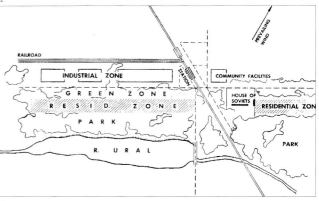

4

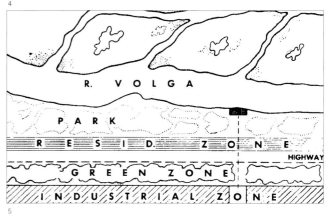

5

Parallel to the high-density and highly urban models put forward by figures such as Meyer and Le Corbusier during the 1920s and 1930s, an anti-urbanist tradition also received a wide following in a number of different contexts. As with support for high-density living, advocates of a return to nature cut across contrasting ideologies, from the Nazism of the Third Reich to the emerging suburbia of America.

6

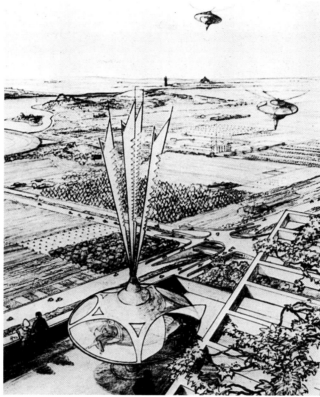

7

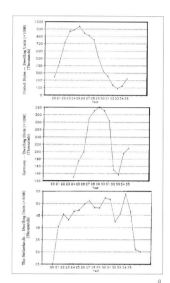

8

9

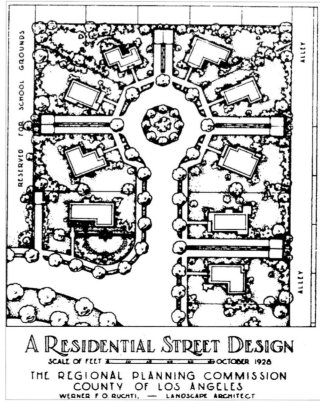

10

Housing Construction
The end of the 1920s and early 1930s represented a time of change in the urban landscape (8).

Frank Lloyd Wright's Broadacre City Project (1928–63) promoted a low-density future (sub)urban landscape. Wright proposed that each household unit would live on an acre of land and lead an independent, isolated life-style based upon individual freedom (7). A. Caldwell's proposals for the expansion of the city of Chicago (1942) illustrate the development of low-density residential networks surrounded by ample green space (6).

With the plan for Radburn, New Jersey (9), a number of innovative concepts were introduced into suburban design: pedestrian and vehicular traffic was segregated to promote greater safety; connected green spaces separated housing clusters; and the use of the cul-de-sac was much in evidence. This was promoted again in the residential street design for Los Angeles, California (10: as of 1930). Street designs developed out of the traditional gridiron framework and became increasingly curvilinear as housing communities grew less dependent upon public transport.

Solar Geometries for Healthy Living
High-density urban life

Simple diagrams by Ernst May illustrate the thinking in urban planning around the 1930s that led to the *Zeilenbau*, or slab building (1).

Ludwig Hilbersheimer was a promoter of high-density, high-rise slab housing. The plan illustrates how space efficient slab housing is in comparison to lower-density models and how much open space can be gained through building higher (2, 4, 5). At this time, urban planners only saw the extremes of low or high density; the advantages of the mixed-use compact city had not yet been discovered.

Walter Gropius took the principles of the *Zeilenbau*, the row houses developed in Germany to solve its housing shortage in the interwar years, and tried to optimise the relationships of spacing and height of the building blocks (6). *Zeilenbau* complexes were long, narrow apartment buildings with east–west orientation. Gropius' solar master plan for Dammerstock of 1929 is shown here (3). Unfortunately, the concept of the *Zeilenbau* soon showed its limitations.

6

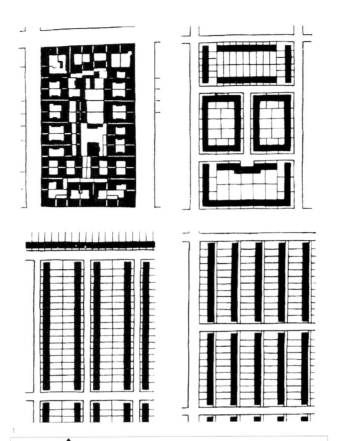

1

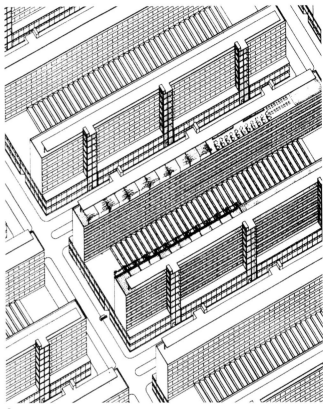

2

3

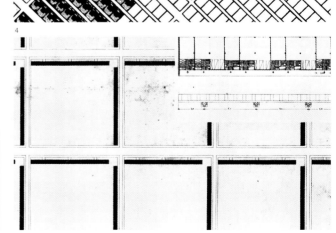

4

5

Architects around the world were engaged in the quest to find the right way of living in industrial society. Most were trying to find the optimum city and building form to allow maximum daylight, air, and space to each resident.

7

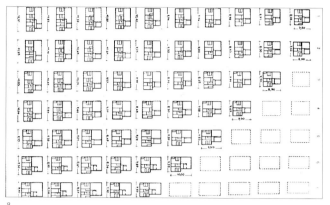

8

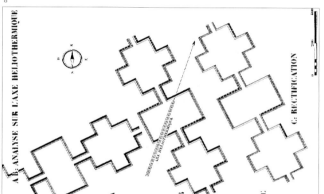

9

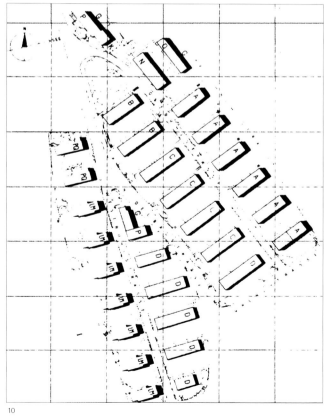

10

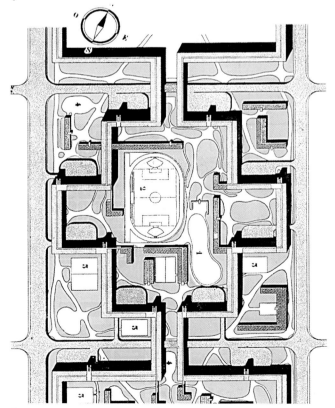

11

Alexander Klein was a true solar pioneer of the 1920s who tried to optimise land use, density, insulation, and ventilation in housing. This led to interesting urban geometries and building types (7, 8).

Le Corbusier developed his ideas for the Ville Radieuse, or Radiant City, from the principles of the heliothermic axis (9,11). CIAM's Athens Charter of 1933 set down a series of proposals for urban planning, including rigid functional zoning of the city separated by green spaces. The quantity and time of insulation each built surface in the town would receive and the solar optimisation were based on a density of a thousand people per hectare.

The Neubühl project, near Zurich, designed by seven young architects, was one of the more successful examples of solar housing (10). Constructed in 1932, it is located on a slope with buildings orientated to the south-east. Housing follows the topography and is grouped on a human scale.

World War Two
The war effort boosts mass production

World War Two changed the course of civilisation. Not only did it establish the US as the dominant world power; it also spurred advances in technology that had a major impact on every aspect of people's lives in peacetime.

Two areas of technological development had a particularly strong influence on postwar society: nuclear energy and the industrial environment as epitomised by the sealed, windowless, climate-controlled, black-box factory.

6

The US came into the war in 1941 at a time when its economy was still in depression and resources were far from plentiful. In order to quickly and efficiently produce the planes, weapons, and other paraphernalia of war, it applied its skills in production engineering to the industrialisation of war. Production rates for arms were increased dramatically. At the beginning of the war, the country was producing around 6,000 aircraft a year; by the end of the war, that figure had rocketed to more than 96,000. In 1941, four bomber assembly plants were constructed, and the total floor space of aircraft plants doubled between 1940 and 1941.

1

American Aircraft Production by Year	
Year	Number of Planes
1940	6 019
1941	19 433
1942	47 836
1943	85 898
1944	96 318
1945	47 714
1946	1 669
Total	304 887

7

2

3

4

5

The development of nuclear power during the war reinforced America's role as a world power. If the energy source that could effect total destruction could be harnessed for peacetime use, there should be no limit to the American Way of Life...

The American Age
Technology and building technology 1945–1970

The establishment of multi-national firms in almost all sectors of industry pointed the way to a new world order. Petrochemical companies controlled the most important energy source in this period: oil.

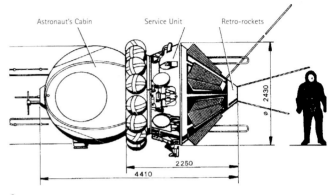

Astronaut's Cabin   Service Unit   Retro-rockets

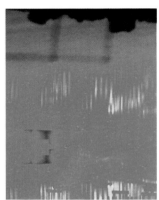

1945

1946 - MIT Solar Houses
1946 - Oil drilling in Arab countries
1947 - Case Study Houses, US
1947 - Neutra, Desert House
1949 - Rudolph, Florida House
1949 - Craig Elwood
1951 - Mies, Lake Shore Drive

1951

1952 - Jet airliner
1952 - United Nations Headquarters, N.Y.
1953 - Transistor radios
1955 - American freeway programme
1956 - Le Corbusier, Villa Shodan
1957 - Sputnik

19

Technological development following World War Two allowed the populations of industrialised countries to enjoy a boom in tools and appliances for the home. The downside of these new 'gadgets' was that most of them required electricity to operate, thus causing energy consumption to escalate.

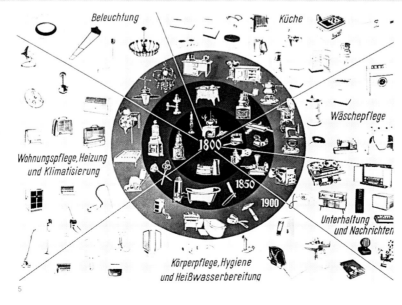

Beleuchtung   Küche

Wohnungspflege, Heizung und Klimatisierung

Wäschepflege

Unterhaltung und Nachrichten

Körperpflege, Hygiene und Heißwasserbereitung

Technological advances made during World War Two were developed further in peacetime. It became clear that human beings could exist in the most hostile environment of all — outer space.

7

8

The spaceship Vostock I was the first to make a journey around the world in outer space. The Russian cosmonaut Yuri Gagarin orbited Earth on 12 April 1961.

Friendship 7 was the first American spaceship to orbit Earth, on 20 February 1962.

First Man on the Moon
In 1969, the first man walked on the moon's surface. The spacesuit is a custom-made life-support system. The long johns worn underneath were equipped with ribbed panels to facilitate the circulation of air. A well-dressed space explorer would wear a rubber aluminised suit, a fibreglass helmet with acrylic visor, and a life-support system in a rucksack.

57

1958 - Le Corbusier, Chandigarh
1960 - First satellite in space
1961 - Gagarin is first man in space
1961 - Atelier 5 and Archigram
1964 - Capsule Homes and Megastructures
1965 - First floppy disc

1965

1967 - Buckminster Fuller, Montreal
1968 - Ron Herron, Walking City
1969 - Jumbo jet
1969 - Concorde
1969 - Man on moon
1969 - Hancock Tower, Chicago
1970 - Osaka Expo

1970

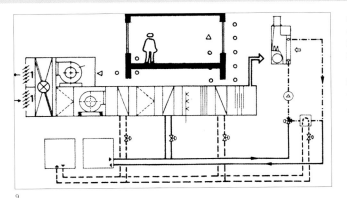

9

Air Conditioning Boom
After World War Two, air conditioning was extended into almost all building types. Because it was costly to install systems of ducts and fans exclusively for cooling, warm-air heating methods were customarily used in buildings that were to be air conditioned.

New Cities in the Making
The American sprawl

Throughout the 20th century, no technological partnership has been as significant as that of oil and the car in reshaping urban landscapes. Mussolini's autostrada and Hitler's autobahns provided models that were replicated throughout the industrialised world. High-speed roads unhindered by urban congestion provided new freedom to an increasingly automobile-dependent public. Spatial expansion through sub-urbanisation marked the widespread implementation of concepts after relatively little activity during the Depression years. Clearly World War Two was the catalyst fuelling suburban growth in a number of ways.

The end of the war symbolised a fresh start. The promise of good homes in healthy environments provided a vehicle for suburban expansion. Posters such as *It's a promise!* symbolised these new hopes for the future. The single, pitched-roof house and the large display of new domestic goods to mechanise the new property are typical. The new environments of suburbia reflected visions of a new society, centred on the Middle American home.

Wartime production of military hardware necessitated the expansion of the country's industrial base and a redirection into other forms of manufacturing. A variety of strategies were employed to redirect capacity into stimulating consumption — for example, the acceleration of the suburbanisation process. New investment itself acted to stimulate fresh areas of demand for the products of industrial capital: urban sprawl made a car essential. Technological innovation and expertise gained in the war were also applied in developing new products for the mechanised home.

1

2

3

4

5

The middle-class dream ot the small house in the country sounded a death knell for traditional cities thoughout the world and led to the development of urban sprawl with all its side-effects.

6

7

8

9

Industrial expansion during the war had also led to extreme housing demand in parts of the country and the construction of new company towns, such as Vanport in Washington State. New methods of design, production, and construction utilised in these developments proved important for subsequent suburban development.

The downsides of uncontrolled sprawl and supra-metropolitan systems were recognised during the 1960s, and despite the implications of rising pollution and energy crisis scares, this trend continues. Ownership of a detached structure surrounded by a piece of private greenery with easy access to work and facilities remains a common aspiration, and in the search for ideal community living, the quarter-acre suburban plot provides a certain benchmark. As a consequence, it is difficult to live with fewer than two cars per family, since few trips can be made within walking distance. Furthermore, the levels of density resulting from development requiring such space standards effectively rule out public transport, making it both uneconomic and difficult to provide a local service to all residents, given the curvilinear and variegated nature of suburban street design. The car has come to dictate, rather than act as a facilitator of, our towns and cities. This dependency is reflected not only in residential patterns, but equally through the suburban and exurban relocation of other sites of production and consumption. Multinational headquarters have followed, typically into landscaped parkland locations. Shopping malls have competed with city centre activities. Indeed, it is within so-called 'edge' or 'sprawl' cities emerging on the periphery of large metropolitan areas that the most rapid growth in commercial floorspace has taken place in recent years.

The Jewels of a New Life-Style
Elegance in industrialised building technologies

The Charles and Ray Eames House in California was constructed four years after the end of World War Two and was one of the first products of the Case Study House programme (1, 3). One aim of the programme was to find new housing models that used the construction materials available in this time of postwar shortage. The house can be seen as a prototype for mass-produced prefabricated houses.

Pierre König Case Study Houses
Another designer of Case Study Houses was Pierre König. Case Study House No. 22 (2) dates from 1959. The houses blur the distinction between inside and outside to give open living environments and magnificent views. The Case Study programme was initiated by John Entenza, editor and publisher of the magazine *Arts and Architecture*. In 1945, he commissioned eight architectural practices to design experimental homes that would offer good living environments and use the limited construction materials available. The steel-framed house was pioneered in this programme.

Marcel Breuer House
This era of construction is firmly associated with steel, glass, and concrete, but Marcel Breuer chose wood for his house at New Canaan, Connecticut, constructed in 1947 (4, 6). The modernist Breuer incorporated shade in his design from quite early in his career.

The Farnsworth House by
Mies van der Rohe, near Fox River, Illinois, was designed in 1950 and is an excellent example of the transparent homes being built at that time for the wealthy few (5).

1

2

3

4

5

6

The dramatic improvement in industrial productivity achieved during the war and the scarcity of materials in postwar America resulted in some of the most elegant and balanced solar buildings, with new approaches to the articulation of inside/outside space.

7

8

9

10

11

12

The Hiss Residence in Lido Shores illustrates Paul Rudolph's skills in designing shade and cross-ventilation for the humid climate of Florida. The house was constructed in 1954 and offers the ultimate in inside/outside space (7, 12).

The Healy House in Siesta Key, Florida, by Rudolph and Twit-chell is an excellent example of bioclimatic architecture. Constructed in 1949, the house takes advantage of the breeze from the south-west. Walls are made from wood slats and glass to give variable levels of shade (8, 9).

Rudolph's Wacker Guest House in Sanibel Island, Florida, has a multipurpose, dynamic wall with wood flaps that can be lowered to provide shade. The house was constructed in 1952 (10, 11).

The 'Brise-Soleil'
Shade and the glass box

The 1936 design for the Salvation Army in Paris must have been a turning point in Le Corbusier's thinking. The initial design (1, 2) shows a fully sealed glass wall, which created unbearable internal comfort conditions — overwhelming in summer and too cold in winter. Even though Le Corbusier had intended mechanical ventilation, this was never installed. The cladding had to be removed and rebuilt with brise-soleils.

The mur neutralisé was a concept Le Corbusier had tried to develop with the French glass-maker Saint-Gobain. The two drawings show the test chamber with two panes of glass that form a cavity (3). This cavity is ventilated mechanically. The ultimate dynamic wall (4) could be used as cupboard, desk, ventilation, lighting — a true mixture of furniture and building component.

The Unité building in Marseille was revolutionary and took the use of brise-soleils to a new level (6). They were ideally suited for south-facing walls and less successful for east- or west-facing facades, where they blocked the winter sun and let afternoon summer sun in.

The Villa Shodhan in Ahmadabad, India, designed by Le Corbusier in 1951, shows elegant simplicity in plan. Interior and exterior spaces are handled with striking plasticity. The brise-soleils and roof gardens form wonderful compositions of shade and comfort (5).

1

2

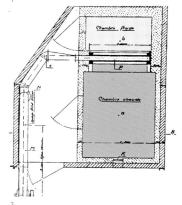
3

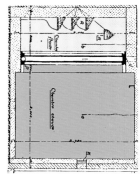

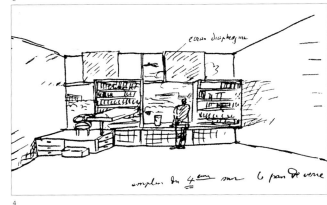
4

5

6

Realising the insufficiency of the simple glass wall, Le Corbusier developed a wide range of solutions to incorporate shade into designs for the glass box — brise-soleils. Climatically responsive, interactive architecture adopted the brise-soleil as an integral part of the building. This was Le Corbusier's *mur ambivalent.*

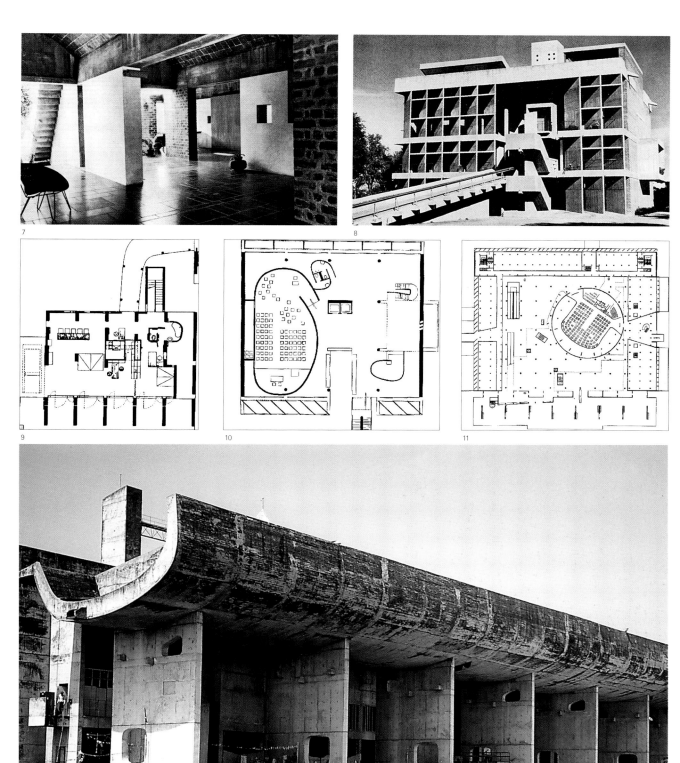

7

8

9

10

11

12

Le Corbusier's Chandigarh Legislative Assembly, constructed from 1956 to 1970, became the testing ground for many of the architect's ideas on how to design for the combination of extreme summer heat and cool winters. Huge brise-soleils dominate the parliament building (11, 12). The device for creating shade had come of age. Chandigarh was the administrative capital of the Punjab, and the complex comprised a series of buildings: the Secretariat, the Assembly, the Governor's Palace, and the High Court. In developing his design for the complex, Le Corbusier drew on the skill of traditional Mogul building, notably Fatehpur Sikri.

The Villa Sarabhai in Ahmadabad is situated according to the prevailing winds for cross-ventilation (7, 9). Its facades are furnished with brise-soleils. It was designed by Le Corbusier in 1955. Villa Sarabhai and the Villa Shodhan both illustrate how shade can be integral to a building. There is complete harmony of building and natural environmental performance.

Le Corbusier's 1954 building for the Mill Owners Association in Ahmadabad has walls of brise-soleils on the east and west facades; the facades' function is to shade the building occupants (8, 10). The hall is indirectly lit by reflections from the curved ceiling, which is kept cool by two gardens and a water reservoir on the roof.

The Johnson Wax Research
Tower in Racine, Wisconsin was
added by Frank Lloyd Wright to
the Johnson Wax Building in
1950. Wright himself called the
tower a 'heliolap' and a 'sun
worshipper.' He experimented
with glass tubes to create a
translucent skin by stacking
them on top of each other,
using this technique in the
tower and the roof lights of the
main office space. The experiment was not entirely successful, and most of the glass tubes
had to be replaced because of
water leakage.

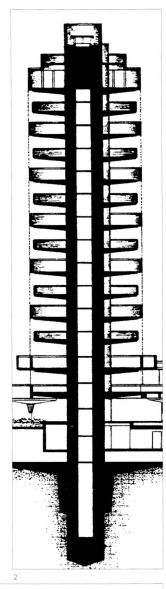

One of the great American
architects of this century dealt
very consciously with the bioclimatic factor in his work. The
Solar House, designed by
Wright for the Jacobs family
in Madison, Wisconsin (3-5),
mirrored a plan of the solar
hemicycle. The module of the
house was a six-degree sector
of a circle, measured from a
post in the centre of the
grounds. The house formed a
virtual half-circle. With big
windows at the front, the low-
lying winter sun's rays would
penetrate into the house and
provide warmth on cold days.
The high summer sun would be
kept out by the deep roof overhang. This design clearly maximises heat gain in a cold continental climate.

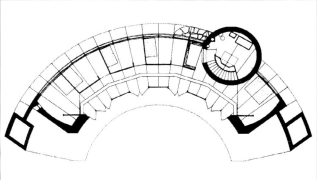

6

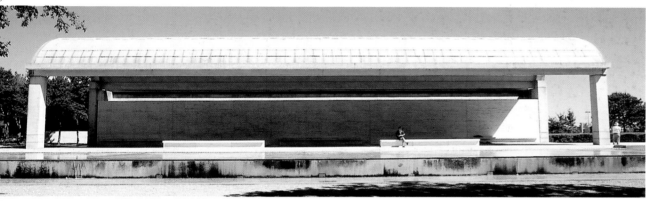

7

The Kimbell Art Museum in Texas, built in 1966 by Louis Kahn, is a masterpiece in its use of natural daylight. The reflectors below the slit in the vaults were of great importance. Kahn said about his design, 'I am designing an Art Museum in Texas, where the light in the rooms ... will have the luminosity of silver ... The scheme of enclosure of the museum is a succession of cycloid vaults ... each forming the rooms with a narrow slit to the sky... this will give the comforting feeling of knowing the time of the day' (6, 7).

8

9

Kahn displayed his mastery of bioclimatic design in the parliament building for Dacca, constructed in 1962. Cool, dramatic spaces were created by turning the whole focus of the building inwards (8, 9).

In South America, architecture was combined with ingenious means of solar control. A. E. Reidy and O. Niemeyer developed one of the first modern brise-soleil facades for the Ministry of Education and Health building in Rio de Janeiro, Brazil, in 1937.

Reidy's design for an insurance building in Rio de Janeiro in 1957 took the concept further. The west facade is strongly exposed to the sun and is equipped with a special sun-screen system, a fixed reinforced concrete lattice with broad and narrow openings, allowing the air to circulate directly in front of the window areas (2-4).

Bioclimatic design principles were applied by Reidy in the Pavilion on the Lagoon Rodrogo de Freitas in Rio de Janeiro. Cross-ventilation of the pavilion is elegantly achieved by the raised roof design. The roof structure is separated from the rooms below, so the heat from the sun generated from the roof cannot be transmitted there. The air circulating under the roof and under the raised floor ensures pleasant climatic conditions. The sides of the pavilion receiving most sunlight are protected by adjustable venetian blinds on the outside (5).

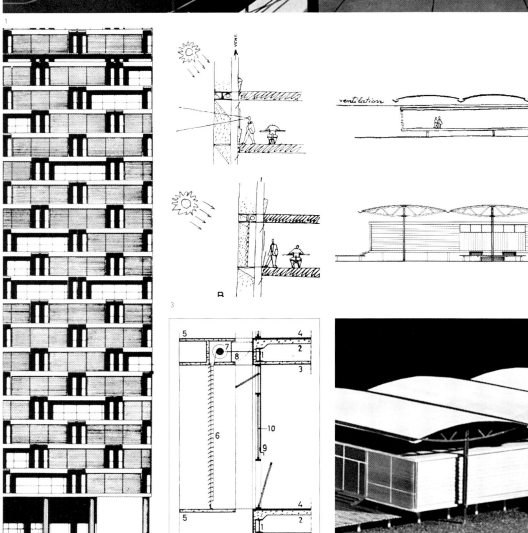

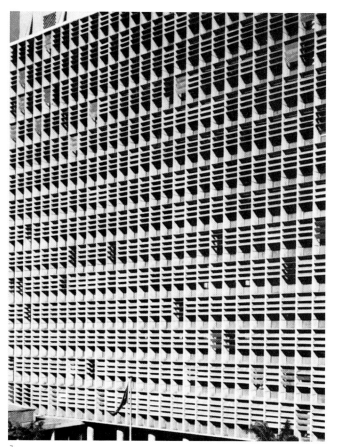

6

7

Oscar Niemeyer's design for Un Emprezas Graficas in Brazil is characterized by the use of shading devices on the outside. The eastern facade has a fixed honeycomb shade boxes for protective screening. The north facade has adjustable horizontal louvers.

The Ministry of Education in Rio de Janeiro designed by Niemeyer and Reidy has shades on the north facade which consists of fixed vertical concrete fins with three movable horizontal panels. The entire system is very close to the form of Persian blinds.

The Mexican architect Luis Barragan has mastered the skill of modelling daylight, as can be seen in the swimming pool of the Casa Gilardi, Tacubaya, Mexico, dating from 1970. This project illustrates how solar power can be used to create drama and pleasure in very small spaces. Barragan has always had a close link with the natural world, formed in the pueblo where he spent his childhood, and he has lamented modern people's remoteness from nature: 'Before the machine age, even in the middle of cities, nature was everybody's trusted companion — nowadays the situation is reversed.'

8

In Europe, **Brutalism** showed a more gentle, human, and solar aspect in Atelier 5's Siedlung Halen housing complex near Bern, Switzerland, constructed in 1961. The compact design, the orientation of the buildings, the careful balance of private and public space, and its energy performance have made this estate a role model for postwar housing. Shown is an overall view of the estate, the south-facing elevation with brise-soleils, and the roof terraces and sun space (1-3).

1

2

3

Alvar Aalto was well known for his use of daylight modelling. Working in the testing environmental conditions of Finland, he had to concentrate on maximising winter daylight in buildings without overheating spaces in summer. The Paedagogical University in Jyvaskyla, constructed in 1953, has large windows, but plentiful shade (4). Aalto's facade for the Villa Mairea illustrates the use of various types of wood for shading (5).

4

5

6

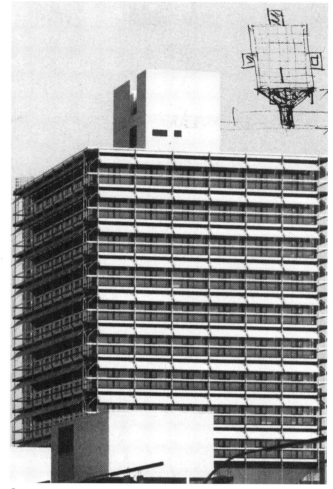

7

Egon Eiermann developed multi-layered, elegant, and lightweight brise-soleil facades that were very different from the heavy concrete shade creating devices adopted by Le Corbusier. Eiermann's approach can be seen in his Olivetti building in Frankfurt, Germany, which was constructed in 1968 (6, 7). Almost all of Eiermann's designs were later equipped with this extra layer of shades.

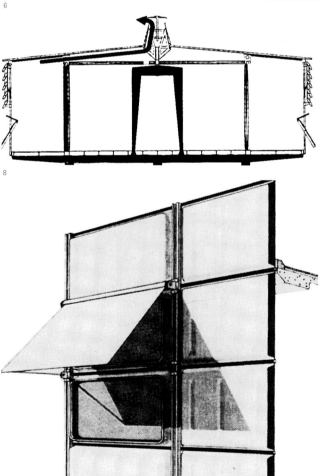

8

9

Jean Prouvé's 1949 designs for a prefabricated, demountable tropical house that could be air-freighted around the world is based on a similar concept to Buckminster Fuller's Dymaxion House, especially in its ventilation and shades. The many constraints on the design did not result in a bland structure. On the contrary, it is interesting to see how refreshing designs can be when they are constrained by material efficiency and climatic performance (8, 9).

Engineer Prouvé was an expert in metal construction, particularly cladding. He was a leading proponent of prefabrication and the use of dynamic metal and glass facades. The facade of the CCC building in Paris has integrated movable solar shades (10).

10

11

Solar Building for the Poor
Hassan Fathy's Egyptian vernacular

The evolution of the typical **Arab house** began with the Arab tent, which then was combined with a big enclosing wall and later became a court-yard house, as is shown in this sequence of drawings by Hassan Fathy (1).

1

Measurements of Temperature Fluctuations
Comparison of indoor and outdoor air temperature fluctuations within a 24-hour period for a mud brick vault (3, 4) and a prefabricated concrete test model shows superiority of adobe construction.

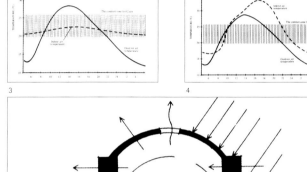

3   4

Heat gain and loss are illustrated in the schematic diagram (5).

2

5

The optimal orientation of a row of houses in regard to sun and wind and the plan for two row-houses showing the *malgaf*, or wind-catcher, of each arranged to bring breezes into the dwelling are illustrated by two other diagrams (7, 8).

The principles of solar urban design in a hot and arid country can be analysed in Fathy's design for Gourma Village (9).

6

7   8

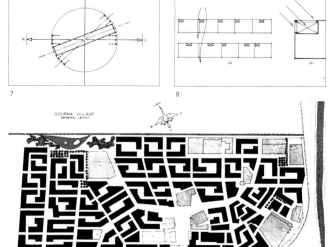

GOURNA VILLAGE
GENERAL LAYOUT

88 Master plan 1948

9

Hassan Fathy has taken the traditions of Arab architecture and applied them to housing for the poor. The result has been high levels of comfort and spatial quality.

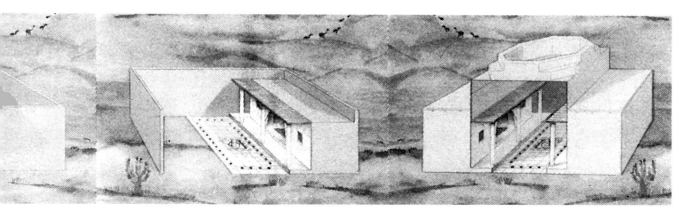

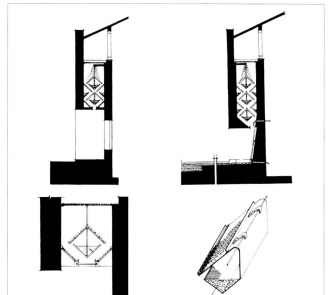

10

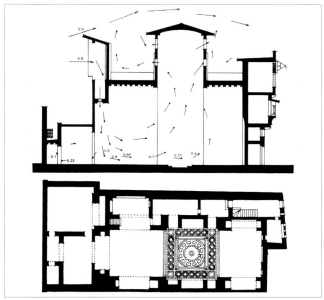

11

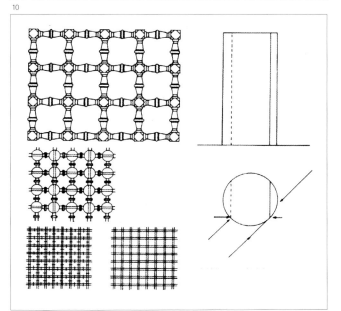

12

13

The **Villa Al–Kufa** in Iraq has *malgafs* and wind escapes. A *malgaf* is a shaft rising high above the building with an opening facing the prevailing winds. It traps wind from high above the building, where it is cooler and stronger, and channels that current down into the building. This technique has long been employed in vernacular buildings of the steppe.

The cooling of air can be improved by using water-filled clay vases, which create evaporative cooling on their surfaces as the water diffuses through the clay. Fathy has developed special techniques based on the same principle, using charcoal-filled containers and water (10).

Screens designed by Fathy in Cairo (12, 13) and his detailed analysis are illustrated at the bottom. Light falling on the screens has an effect on the cylinder, whose graduated light and shade subdue the dazzling effect of dark-light contrast which occurs when looking from the inside towards the light outside..

Pioneers of Efficiency
Form generation through new structures

Engineering has been the major force behind the design of new forms generated by structural efficiency and logic. Buckminster Fuller's dome for the Montreal Expo in 1967 has dynamic shading devices that can be unrolled in each triangle (1). The parachutes on the dome have no function, but show the similarity of structural forms. The integrity of form of Fuller's geodesic dome is evident when the structure is viewed from a distance (2).

Solar Cloud
Fuller worked out that a 30-m 'tensegrity' sphere weighing 1.5 tons would enclose 3.5 tons of air. Doubling the diameter of this cloud would raise the weight of the structure to 3 tons and the weight of the enclosed air to 28 tons. By enlarging the sphere to almost one km, Fuller believed that the ratio of structural weight to enclosed air volume would become negligible, and the warming effect of the sun upon the enclosed air would allow the sphere to rise like a cloud (3).

The structural principle of 'tensegrity' was exploited by Fuller in various experiments. He claimed that he could enclose large areas of Manhattan in order to create better living conditions and reduce heat loss (4, 5).

Experiments in architecture, building technology, and materials brought visionary designers to the verge of a new solar architecture. Innovations in engineering produced light-weight structures built from new materials. Here, form follows function.

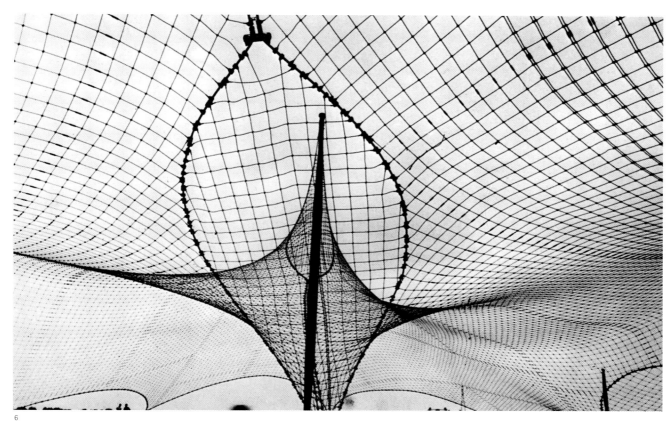

6

The German exhibition pavilion for the Montreal Expo was designed by engineer Frei Otto. Stretched high above the seating is a light-weight, tensile roof that makes highly efficient use of materials. The roof's form follows the constraint of structural efficiency (6, 7).

7

8

Frei Otto's design for the Indian exhibition for the Expo in Osaka was a further development in light-weight structures (8).

9

The tent structure for the German landscape exhibition held in Cologne in 1957 by Frei Otto was a spectacular example for its time.

Sealed Glass Boxes and Indoor Cities
A multinational corporate building style

Modernism found its purest expression in the world of commerce, where the new breed of multinational conglomerates was hungry for buildings that reflected their status. A steel frame clad in glass represented the modern business environment perfectly; this was the corporate mind freed from the traditions and trappings of the past, freed from sentiment, and focusing on the future. The concept of the stalked floor plate could be utilised in the same manner as in wartime factories.

The UN Building in New York It is important to remember that the development of curtain-wall buildings was the subject of great debate. For example, during the design of the United Nations building by Wallis K. Harrison, Le Corbusier, who had learned his lessons with his Salvation Army Cité de Refuge in Paris and who now believed in the *mur neutralisant*, wrote to the American Senator Warren Austin: 'My strong belief, Mr. Senator, is that it is senseless to build in New York, where the climate is terrible in summer, large glass areas which are not equipped with a brise-soleil. I say this is dangerous, very seriously dangerous.'

1

2

3

4

America produced an international architectural style for the business community. Businesses turned their backs on nature, and buildings became completely dependent on a huge energy supply.

4

In American cities, the glass tower came to represent both corporate and individual prestige. Purity of form took precedence over human comfort and pleasure. Even for low-rise buildings, the sealed steel and glass box was the only design option. In the city, of course, there was some justification for sealing a building to shield occupants from urban noise and pollution. On the inside, the modern office was a deep-plan space, artificially lit and ventilated all day.

The glass box ruled. Its hard-headed perfection and precision became the modern metaphor for power. In buildings, almost any environment could be produced within a sealed space, but they depended on machinery to achieve it, and the machines ran on energy. It is not surprising that these were the highest energy-consuming buildings ever created, and this fact was integral to their, and their occupants', status. People no longer interacted with the built environment to find an acceptable level of comfort; the building took care of everything. No one opened a window; there was air conditioning. Central heating compensated for the heat loss from glass facades in winter, while in summer chillers worked overtime refrigerating the air to cool the interior, which collected solar heat as efficiently as Paxton's palmhouses. Technical dexterity in manipulating and controlling the environment was demonstrated daily.

Mies van der Rohe's collage, *Loop near North Side* presents his image of high-rise living, with the view outside as the real focus of the home. His Seagram Building in New York, with interiors by Philip Johnson, typifies the thinking of the time. The building was constructed in 1958.

Energy End Uses Ranked by Energy Consumption and Expenditures, 1989	a. Energy Consumption		b. Energy Expenditures
	19	District Heat Cooking	0.08
	26	Fuel Oil Water Heating	0.13
	31	Fuel Oil Other Uses	0.16
Primary Energy (11.7 Quadrillion Btu)	73	Electric Water Heating	0.49
	136	District Heat Other Uses	0.59
	169	Electric Cooking	1.13
	197	District Heat Water Heating	0.85
■ Site Energy (5.8 Quadrillion Bt	198	Natural Gas Cooking	0.88
□ Energy Losses (5.9 Quadrillion Btu)	290	Electric Space Heating	1.93
	290	Natural Gas Other Uses	1.29
	301	Fuel Oil Space Heating	1.53
	320	Natural Gas Water Heating	1.42
	543	District Heat Space Heating	2.34
	566	Electric Refrigeration	3.77
	841	Electric Ventilation	5.61
	852	Electric Cooling	5.68
	1147	Electric Office Equipment	7.65
	1265	Natural Gas Space Heating	5.62
	1356	Other Electric Uses	9.05
	3093	Electric Lighting	20.63

3000   2000   1000   0
Trillion Btu

0   5   10   15   20
Billion Dollars

5

6

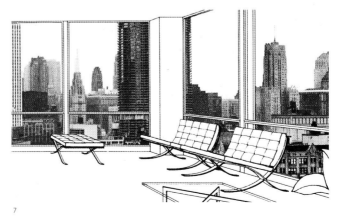

7

Changing Architecture for a Sustainable World

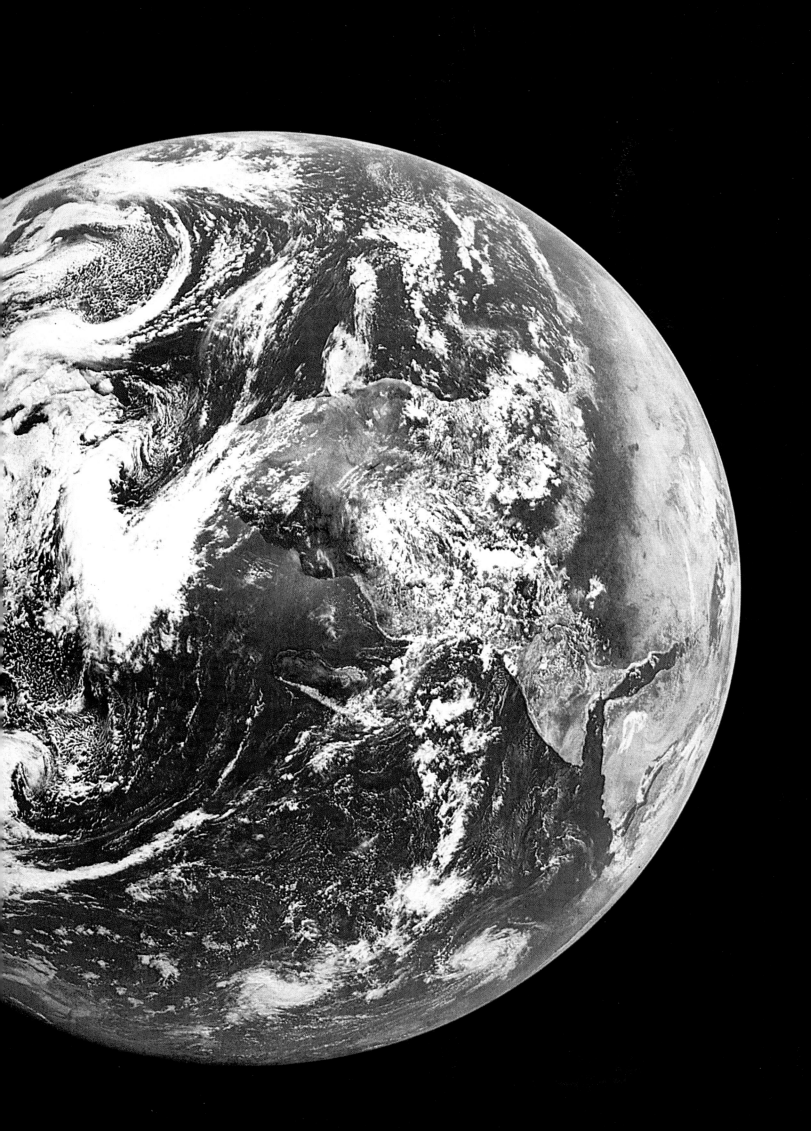

A New Agenda
The overview effect

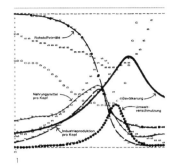

The **Club of Rome** and the results of their research led to a major change in thinking in the early 1970s regarding the limits on natural resources and the impact of their use on the environment.

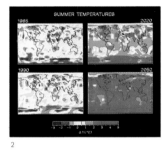

Global warming and the resulting changes in the atmosphere were recognised early in the 1970s, illustrating the irreversible impact of human consumption patterns on the atmosphere and therefore on our living environment.

The project of modernity, grounded in Enlightenment reasoning and driven by technological and industrial progress, began to show signs of faltering towards the end of the 1960s. A series of events took place at this time that challenged the long-held trust in innovation and scientific development to overcome all difficulties in the human pursuit of ever-increasing standards of life. The period of postwar optimism became eclipsed by a growing feeling of uncertainty and pessimism.

The strong and consistent economic growth experienced, in the wealthier nations at least, since the late 1940s was beginning to slow down. The security this growing prosperity had created, and the life-styles it had fostered, showed signs of strain. Many industrialised countries faced social unrest as traditional norms were rejected and Government policies came increasingly to be questioned. The US experienced civil disorder on a large scale as the poverty and disadvantage of many inner-city areas became clearly visible as the cities burned. Important political figureheads were lost through the assassinations of John Kennedy and Martin Luther King. The response to the war in Viet Nam reflected a nation at growing unease with itself: mass demonstrations against involvement were staged, and the actual outcome of the conflict represented a failure by the most advanced technocrats to account for and overcome their opponents. Riots and civil disturbance spread throughout the industrialised world during 1968–69, and the rise of new political organisations, focusing on issues such as women' rights, racial equality, and the environment, became increasingly prominent.

The collapse of traditionally held notions increasingly pervaded all aspects of life. As the modern movement came under attack, the values and modes of organisation associated with modernity became strained. Work practices and labour organisations started to undergo dramatic shifts (a process that continues today) as the forces of globalisation and new technologies challenged the need for labour-intensive activities in the industrialised world where labour costs are high. Fordist methods of production began to be replaced by more flexible forms, and industrial centres began to shift to reflect the global nature of the market, in terms both of production and of consumption. Our global interdependence was further highlighted by the energy crisis in 1973: the life-styles that had been enabled by an unhindered rise in energy consumption in advanced economies were directly challenged.

The widespread implementation of modernist principles in both architecture and urban planning following World War Two also came under strong critique as a number of problems became apparent. Although the dramatic skyscrapers of downtown districts had come to represent symbols of corporate wealth, many of the modernist high-density housing projects found world-wide, particularly in European cities, soon deteriorated to such an extent that they were uninhabitable. To a large extent, these estates suffered due to their loss of human scale, the lack of clearly defined public and private space, and the use of poor-quality construction techniques. Although it is necessary to guard against any form of environmental determinism, one may observe that these modernist projects failed to deliver the New Jerusalem they promised: instead of representing new homes to build a new society, social poverty has continued and in fact has become increasingly ghettoised through redevelopment of this kind. The sprawling suburban environments dictated by rigid functional zoning practices, which came to typify postwar American cities, have also been criticised, both in terms of their energy inefficiency (since such form necessitates almost universal car ownership) and also as a result of their homogeneity and lack of cultural vibrancy. Once again, faith in progress and technology to act as the guiding mechanism in improving our quality of life was directly questioned: the universalising, rationalising, and standardising instincts of modernism could not provide solutions for human living.

The pictures of the Earth transmitted back from US space missions provided a profound symbol of the planet as an interconnected, dynamic system, yet at the same time illustrated its fragility. Buckminster Fuller's notion of Spaceship Earth reflected calls for a more comprehensive understanding of our environment and its complexity. The recognition that the environment was a key component affecting our quality of life, and that it was something that should be protected and valued in its own right, translated into a variety of institutional measures. For example, through the 1972 Stockholm Conference and the establishment of the United Nations Environment Programme (UNEP), the foundations were laid for a plethora of international environmental accords which have since been established. Additionally, this period marked a growth in public awareness and the formation of environmental pressure groups such as Greenpeace and Friends of the Earth.

Scientific reasoning holds a spurious position in contemporary environmental debates. On the one hand, the questioning of the rational and objective bases of knowledge has undermined notions of truth and reason; on the other, improved techniques of scientific investigation and analysis have enabled a greater understanding of how the environment works. Therefore whilst technological advances have provided better models and means of explanation regarding the detrimental effects human activity is having on the environment, it is recognised that forms of technological domination traditionally employed to overcome

In the 1970s, the overview effect fundamentally changed our view of the world as an interconnected integral system.

these detrimental effects are no longer valid. Until recently, our relationship with nature was based upon the uncertainties of trial and error, but was always underscored by the belief that human superiority and separation from nature would enable us to control the physical environment to our advantage. Mounting evidence of environmental destruction on a global scale – for example, climate change resulting from the accumulation of carbon dioxide and other greenhouse gases, acid rain deposition, and the depletion of the stratospheric ozone layer – has illustrated the complexities and interconnected nature of the global environmental system. Models like Lovelock's Gaia thesis have helped to promote greater understanding in this regard and have focused public and political attention upon recognising the need to work with, rather than against, nature.

It is increasingly acknowledged that technology can no longer provide wholly satisfactory solutions to the detrimental environmental consequences of human activity. Within such a framework, the continued resistance towards 'hard technologies' such as nuclear energy, with its undetermined long-term consequences, can be understood. The two sides of technology – the light and the dark – have always paralleled one another closely, although the 'dark' effects have typically been subsumed in the pursuit of continued and ever-increasing technological progress. While technology has enabled higher standards of living and saved more lives this century than at any other time in history, technology's dark side has also led to mass killing and devastation on a scale not previously experienced. A growing mistrust of governments, and major companies' assurances of 'acting in the public good' has fuelled greater participation in pressure groups and green party politics.

The questioning of our relation to nature reflects the need for new values and approaches to the environment: notions of stewardship, trusteeship, and sustainability need to replace the accepted doctrine of human superiority. As such, the natural environment should be respected in itself, and not simply as a means of satisfying our needs. Presently, we are drawing upon the ecological capital of future generations knowing that we are unable to repay it: this relates not only to the extraction of fossil fuels but also to the loss of biodiversity. The Commission for the European Communities (CEC) suggest that a new direction based upon a code of environmental ethics to guide our behaviour in activities that may have an environmental impact is increasingly appropriate. This will necessitate a redefinition of our responsibilities not only to the natural environment but also to future generations. An ethical approach recognises that technology can no longer be assumed to provide solutions; rather, the key lies in re-evaluating our own ways of life, our production and con-

sumption practices. Such decisions will require life-style changes and will necessitate new forms of organisation in our present economic structures. Despite this, the role of technology remains paramount: indeed, it may be argued that the increasingly dialectical relationship between our understanding of the environment and technology will be a defining factor of the new solar age. While technological advances enable a more accurate understanding of the complexities that condition global environmental systems, continued research into the actual structures and organisation of natural phenomena, which has so far helped us to better understand notions of chaos and the occurrence of fractal geometries, will provide the greatest challenge driving future innovation. For example, the structure of cells, skins, and shells, or the ability of DNA to store vast quantities of data, will shape future directions in efficient technological design.

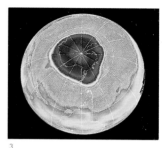

3

Air Pollution in Cities and the Depletion of the Ozone Layer
The irreversible depletion of the ozone layer and its causes in human behaviour in terms of consumption and material use were discovered in 1983.

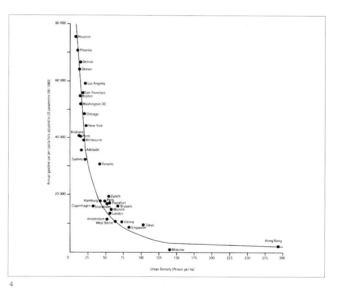

4

5

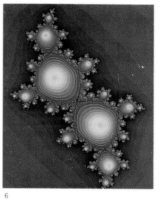

6

New Sciences
Chaos theory and the theory of complexity have brought the matter of unpredictability to many people's attention. The predictability of science has been thoroughly questioned, and this has led to a more holistic approach to thinking about the world and about relationships and systems within it.

A rise in the use of the car
rather than public transport in the booming areas of the world has contributed to our environmental problems, especially in the area of carbon-dioxide emissions.

Harvesting Wind Energy
Wind farms, turbines, and towers

Wind power is gaining in popularity, and that is not surprising. It is the most cost-effective way of producing energy from renewable sources. Every year, enough wind turbines are installed worldwide to generate 4750 MW of electricity. The wind power pioneers carried out much of their research in the ideal testing ground of the Mojave Desert in California. These windmills near the Edwards Air Force Base were built as part of an experiment in the 1970s in which different wind-turbine styles from around the world were tested (1).

Modern turbines are formidable machines — the rotor blades of the turbines at the E45 wind park, near Emden in Germany, are up to 40 m in diameter (2).

The epoxy resin rotor blades resemble the wings of a glider and have to be designed with care. There are more than 50 turbine manufacturers worldwide. These turbines were manufactured by a German company, Enercon.

There have been some revolutionary developments in wind-turbine technology in recent years. For example, designers have eliminated the gearbox and developed new directly driven generators that run efficiently on a wider range of wind speeds (4).

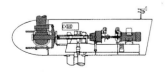

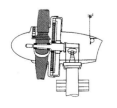

The first agricultural revolution changed the face of the Earth by deforesting vast areas of land to harvest solar energy through natural collectors. A new perspective for farmers, landscape designers, architects, and engineers might be to ensure that new technologies like windmills are well designed and integrated into our environment.

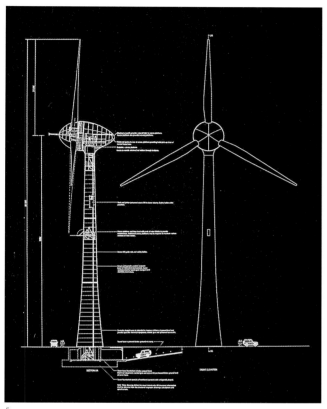

5

6

Turbines are growing in height. The one shown here is 80 m high. As wind turbines have increased in size, the public has become more and more aware of their presence. The impact of windmills on the landscape has to be carefully considered, and there is scope for architects to work alongside engineers in doing this. Sir Norman Foster & Partners were involved in the design of this new wind turbine.

7

9

The thermal power plant in Spain, designed by the German engineer Jörg Schlaich, works on the principle of thermodynamics (7-9). Heat behaves in a predictable way — it rises. This installation basically uses artificially created thermal energy to drive a turbine. A large area is covered by a transparent roofing material and traps heat like a greenhouse. The only way the hot air can escape is by rising through the lightweight turbine tower/chimney.

8

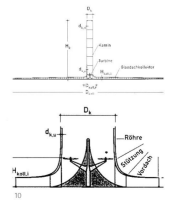

10

Buildings Using Wind
Aerodynamics as a form-generating factor

In a visionary scheme by Richard Rogers (1), the wind-mills have become part of the buildings. Although problems of noise and vibration from the turbines would have to be overcome in realising such a project, the design shows an imaginative approach to using wind power.

The design by one of the leading Malaysian practices, T.R. Hameah + Yeang in Kuala Lumpur, features the use of natural ventilation, sky gardens, and a geometry generated from the local environment (2).

Richard Rogers 'Turbine Tower' in Tokyo is designed to be capable of generating enough energy to power itself. Wind-tunnel tests have been carried out to analyse wind conditions on the urban site. These show how flexible the building is for the varying wind conditions of Tokyo (3-5).

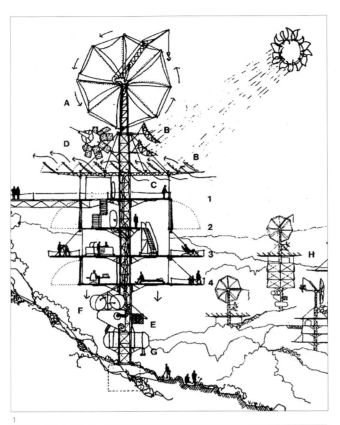

1

2

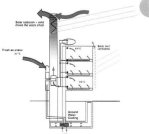

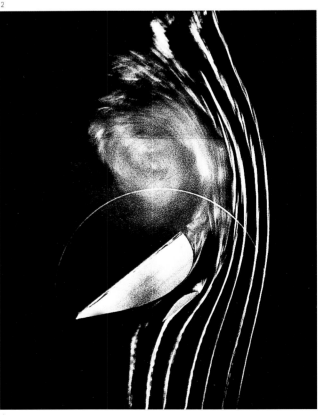

5   3

4

Building forms should relate to local climatological conditions. Wind is crucial for natural ventilation and fresh air supply, but it also causes drafts and adds additional wind loads to structures. Wind can be harnessed by a building itself, through integrated turbines or other wind-catching devices.

6

The Duisburg Microelectronic Centre tries to optimise the flow of natural ventilation and smoke extraction through the two atria. The performance of the concepts was tested in a wind tunnel.

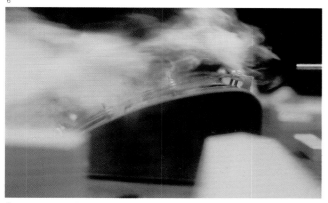

7

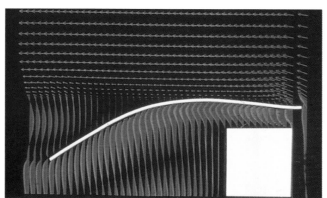

8

The behaviour of wind and the aerodynamic performance of buildings are explored through wind-tunnel testing and computer simulation using fluid dynamics.

9

10

New Caledonia Cultural Centre
The distinctive shape of Renzo Piano's Cultural Centre for Noumea was generated by the need to maximise ventilation in a humid climate (9).

Richard Rogers' design for the competition for the Inland Revenue headquarters, UK, has an aerodynamic feel. The built form has been used to accelerate the south-westerly winds to assist in the natural cooling of the building (10, 11).

11

Learning from the Masters of Wind
Coherent design for solar energy

The design of sailboats and the optimisation of their performance has evolved over approximately five thousand years. Very rarely does boat design look 'designed' or 'fashionable'. The forms are a direct product of their function. Even though buildings are immobile, architects can learn from the design processes employed in other industries such as boatbuilding.

The windsurfer, the paraglider, and the hang-glider are brilliant examples of the synergy of humans and materials and also of the use of solar energy for recreation. Such equipment is constantly being improved to achieve higher performance levels using little energy.

Form generation, not design, is the name of the game. Computer programs have been developed to simulate the stress of the wind on every cm^2 of a sail. In order to create optimum efficiency, sails are fabricated with their 'shape' built in. Scientists and engineers are constantly experimenting with new materials, construction methods, and shapes. The race to build the highest-performance boat and sails is as hard as the actual regatta itself.

1

2

5   3

4

The technological development of moving vehicles has always been ahead of that of structures. In the design process, forms are found and developed as a direct product of their expected performance, taking ergonomic criteria and environmental forces into account.

6

The design process in other industries is aimed at functionality and efficiency, particularly for those who deal with such natural energies as wind and water. The beauty of these structures is apparent to everyone, but they are also functional. Here, humans learn to fly with an ingeniously tailored piece of high-tech fabric, using thermals like birds.

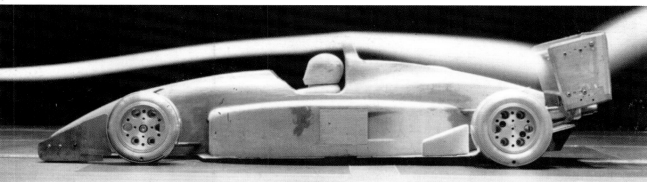

7

Even though this car does not use solar energy, it is still an example of highly sophisticated form generation, combining beauty and the lowest drag factor to achieve high efficiency.

8

Designing the Airbus depended on simulation of the forces of solar energy. This aeroplane model in a wind tunnel clearly illustrates the importance of integrating the effects of natural power into the design process. The little fins on this plane's wings were designed to optimise fuel consumption, resulting in savings of up to 10%.

The Ventilated Cavity
New concepts in cladding design

The Hooker buildings in Buffalo, New York, (1, 3, 4) was one of the first buildings in the world to apply a double-skin technology. Built in 1981, it has since proven very effective in reducing energy consumption. The structure is air conditioned nonetheless.

The Business Promotion Centre in Duisburg, by Sir Norman Foster & Partners (2, 5, 6#) is a stepping stone for high-performance cladding systems using the principle of double skins and a ventilated cavity. The external planar facade protects very finely computer-controlled perforated aluminium blinds, that still allow views out in when closed. Behind them is a highly insulated double-glazed argon-filled facade for thermal comfort. The building's design concept was to try to create the best level of comfort under artificial conditions. Each room has individual controls in addition to computer-controlled light and temperature sensors.

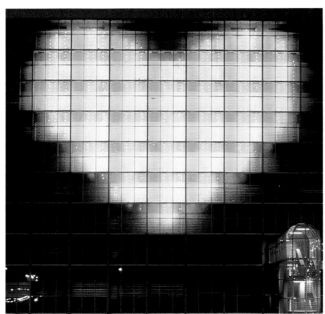

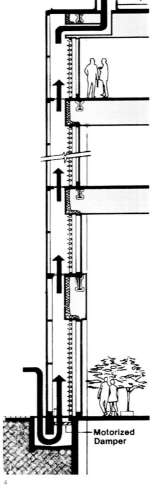

Motorized Damper

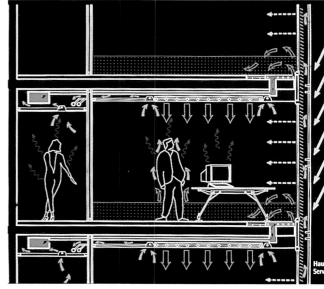

Wind shields and double-skin facades not only protect a building from heat loss but also protect external shades from damage. The thermodynamics of the cavity can be used to cool the building and shades, whilst heat can be recovered.

7

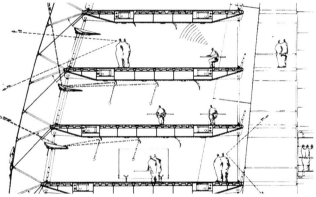
8

9

Future Systems' design for a Green Building in 1990 also plays with the idea of the second skin. In this case, it is used mostly as an exhaust air system, utilising the stack effect to suck air out of the perimeter offices. Fresh air supply reaches the occupants through an atrium in the middle of the building. The project is the result of a close collaboration with the engineers Guy Battle and Chris McCarthy (7, 8).

The roof of an atrium designed by Nikken Sekkei in Japan is a curved double facade with integrated shading systems (9). The glass roof permits the careful use of daylight, and the built-in ventilation system cools the building as needed.

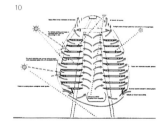
10

S.I.T.E.'s design for a Supermarket illustrates the vision of a natural green wall. In a buffer between two glass walls, the architects created a linear greenhouse, partly filled with plants and earth material. This design illustrates how magnificent the use of the cavity of double-glazed facades might be in the future. The external use of water running down the facade has an additional cooling effect (11, 12).

11

12

Natural Ventilation for Extremes
The wall becomes a membrane

Ventilating Skins

It has long been the dream of architects and engineers that buildings walls should act as natural skins. This is still far from being realised, but recent developments in the field of multilayered facades are an important step forward towards a fully responsive semi-permeable building skin.

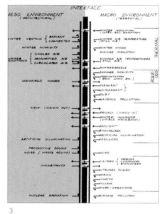

3

The new headquarters for the **Commerzbank Frankfurt** by Sir Norman Foster & Partners is the first of a new generation of high-rise buildings. These buildings do not depend on full artificial climatisation to provide the highest possible comfort, but explore ways of using natural energies and particularly high-performance skins to satisfy the requirements of their occupants. With this aim in mind, extensive simulations have been carried out to study the environmental behaviour of wind and light to ensure that the building maximises the time that natural ventilation and lighting can be used. The Commerzbank has openable windows, sky gardens, and natural ventilation throughout (1, 3, 5). The design of the wall is the result of a close collaboration with the cladding manufacturer Gartner.

The **ARAG Headquarters in Düsseldorf**, designed by Sir Norman Foster & Partners, in collaboration with RKW (Rode, Kellermann, Wawrofski) makes use of the same principle (2, 5, 7).

1

2

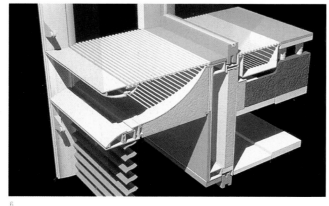

4

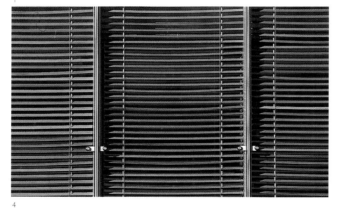

5

6

7

Although high-rises are problematic in some ways, many advances have been made. High-performance cladding systems provide more comfort than ever before by allowing carefully controlled natural ventilation, dynamic shade variation, and glare control, and integrated individual control systems for the user — drastically reducing energy demands of future buildings.

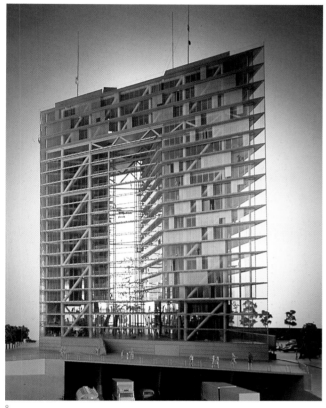

The climate facade for the RWE Headquarters in Essen, Germany, has been developed by the architects Ingenhoven Overdiek & Partner. The detail shows the air in- and outlet at every slab level and the 50-cm cavity (9, 11, 12).

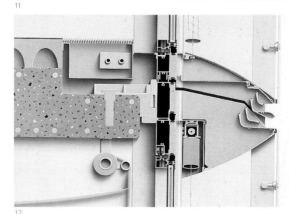

The City Gate in Düsseldorf by Petzinka Pink & Partner follows a similar concept. The cavity between the inside and the outside wall is approximately 1.5 m deep (8, 10).

Much of today's outdoor equipment is made using breathable materials. Mountaineers wear a system of layered clothing, the outer layer of which keeps water out while allowing water vapour from the body to escape. Modern materials use body heat to drive moisture vapour out through the fabric. This is a high-tech solution that relies on a natural energy source, the heat of the human body (13).Fabrics and Materials such as Gortex or Trevira (following page) perform in ways building walls still have to achieve.

Collecting Solar Heat
The beauty of true solar geometries

The beauty of thermal collectors can be experienced at Kraemer Junction in California's Mojave Desert (1-5). Here, five solar electric generating systems constructed between 1984 and 1990, produce 90% of the world's commercially available solar thermal electric power serving approximately 50,000 American households. Each plant has a solar field made up of rows of parabolic trough solar collectors, which have mirrors and track the sun. Sunlight reflected off the mirrors is focused onto steel tubes containing a heat-transfer fluid. This fluid travels through heat exchangers to produce steam, powering a turbine generator, which then creates electricity. The roofs of factories could be covered with similar systems. Shown here (5) is the precise fabrication of the curved glass reflector at the plant.

1

2

3

4

5

It is possible to harvest solar heat with collectors and generators. We should not let the heat that we already have escape. New forms of thermal insulation and the efficient and more creative use of heat are major goals for building design in the future.

6

These collectors are the result of a design collaboration between one of Germany's leading engineers, J. Schlaich, and cladding manufacturer Fischer. The concave dishes (6) are made of sheet aluminium, which is formed by a vacuum created behind them to a geometry that can focus rays onto one spot in order to power a motor.

Solar One, also in the Mojave Desert, is a field of computer-controlled mirrors (7, 8). These mirrors direct light onto a single point on a central plane, which produces heat and drives turbines. The image of pure solar power is shown at the far right, as the mirrors are focused on two points away from the actual generator. Virtual stars are created.

7

8

9

10

Hot water collectors for domestic use have been in existence for more than a century (9). In warmer countries like Israel or Greece, they are a major source of energy. Nevertheless, architects seem to ignore them. There are hardly any examples of well-integrated collectors. Meanwhile, heating is still one of the major energy demands in residential buildings all over the world. Well-designed hot water collectors and their integration into architecture should be of major interest to architects and designers. An example of poor integration can be seen in Santorini, where useful collectors destroy the beautiful architecture of houses.

Sophia University in Tokyo has been using solar collectors to generate its own heat for some time. The roof installation has proved to be a viable source for energy over the years (10).

Insulation and Conservation
New technologies for highest thermal performance

There are a multitude of good insulation materials available, ranging from polystyrene foam to mineral woods and natural materials like wood, cork, and straw. Even stone in a certain thickness is a good insulator. But none of these materials lets light through.

Glass in layers and in combination with other materials has experienced a dramatic increase in performance in the last 20 years. Simple float glass has an insulation value of 5.8; simple double glazing 3.0; good double glazing 1.1; double glazing with low-e coatings and gas 0.7; and triple glazing with low-e coatings and gas 0.4. This is more than 14 times better than before.

Transparent Insulation
Materials now available include TWD honeycomb structures, capillary structures, Basogel granular aerogel, and glass tubes (5).

Extruded Honeycomb
Transparent insulation materials are placed between two sheets of glass. This combination has high values, but still allows diffuse daylight into space. It can even be used as a light-guiding system projecting light deep into space (1, 2, 4, 7).

Aerogel products like Basogel are small beads of insulation material, up to six mm in diameter (6). They are placed between two sheets of glass. Glass tubes can be placed between glass panes to trap heat and allow light to penetrate (5).

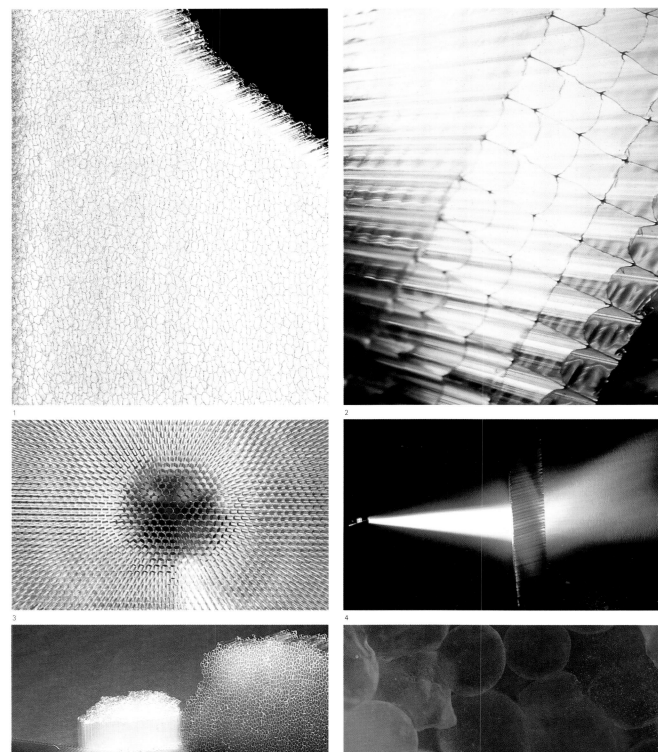

1

2

3

4

7   5

6

The careful use of our resources is a prime goal, conservation and storage of energy, a must, — in this context insulation is crucial.

8

9

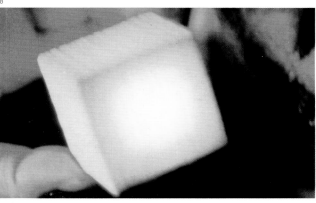

10

11

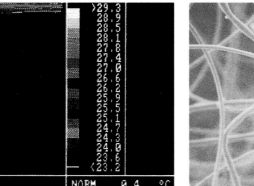

12

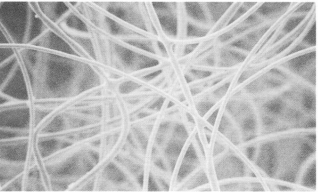

13

The insulation of a spacesuit maintains all life-supporting features for our bodies in outer space. The range of performance is extremely high — from 230 degrees on the sunny side to about -230 degrees on the shaded side. These requirements are so high that no single material would be able to meet them. Therefore multilayered active systems like a water circulating system incorporated into the underwear are necessary.

The insulation of an aircraft is an excellent example of high performance in the field of mobile design. It permits people to lean back in a comfortable armchair, sip champagne, and adjust a fresh air nozzle while the aircraft flies through temperatures of -40 degrees Celsius, leaving New York in a snowstorm only to arrive in the heat of the desert.

The nose and underside of the space shuttle have to be covered with a special highly refined silica to insulate the astronauts from a few thousand degrees of heat as they dive back through the Earth's atmosphere. This material has such low thermal conductivity that a person can hold a small cube of it even though the inside is still red-hot.

Sleeping bags are sophisticated pieces of equipment, but their prime insulator is the simple natural resource, air. They envelop the body in a layer of air, which is kept still to combat convection. Research and development in materials and their performance in other industries could be used by architects and designers. Manufacturers carry out extensive testing on their products to check on aspects, such as insulation levels, so that the body's essential organs are kept at the required temperature of 37 degrees Celsius.

Guiding Daylight
Efficient use of natural energies

The idea of optimising the relationship of shade and daylight guidance leads to new forms. The big prefabricated concrete baffles that Renzo Piano developed for the Menil Collection in Houston, Texas, show the beauty of the shapes that can evolve (1, 2). It is interesting that a miniature version, which was developed independently by the German designer Köster in collaboration with Okalux arrived at similar forms as they tried to balance shade and daylight control (5, 6).

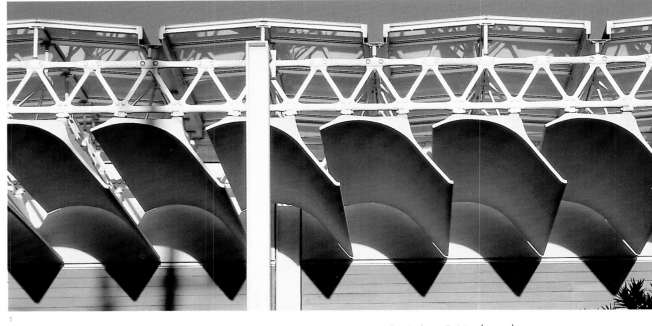

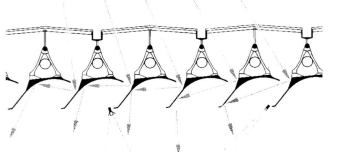

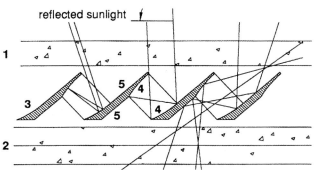

reflected sunlight

Thomas Herzog's Design Centre in Linz, Austria, is an example of the use of reflecting and neutralising light diffusion systems. Developed in collaboration with Christian Bartenbach, it has epitomised the microgeometry of each baffle (3, 4).

The single most efficient use of solar energy is the use of daylight for lighting. The best light bulb needs far more watts per m² and produces far more heat than the sun does for the same amount of light. Therefore, the incorporation of daylight in every building must be balanced against unwanted heatgain.

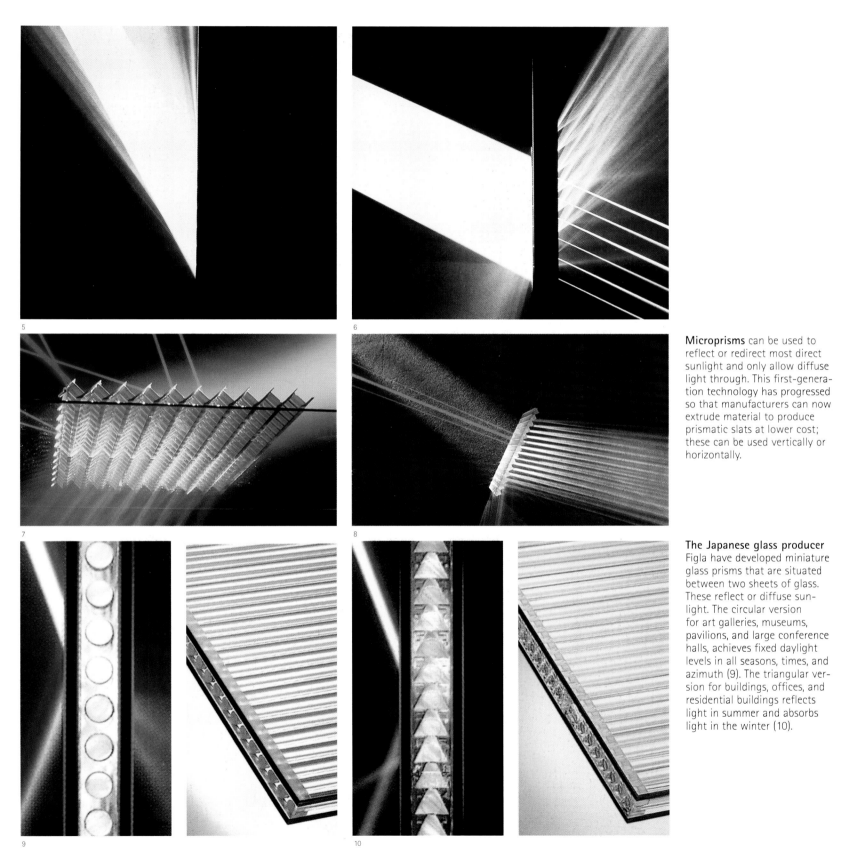

Microprisms can be used to reflect or redirect most direct sunlight and only allow diffuse light through. This first-generation technology has progressed so that manufacturers can now extrude material to produce prismatic slats at lower cost; these can be used vertically or horizontally.

The Japanese glass producer Figla have developed miniature glass prisms that are situated between two sheets of glass. These reflect or diffuse sunlight. The circular version for art galleries, museums, pavilions, and large conference halls, achieves fixed daylight levels in all seasons, times, and azimuth (9). The triangular version for buildings, offices, and residential buildings reflects light in summer and absorbs light in the winter (10).

Transparent Daylight Control
Sculpting light with glass

James Carpenter, architect and light and glass designer from New York, uses diachromic glass for light-guiding effects. In his working model for a Methodist church, one can see that the envisaged light pattern is a design goal from the very beginning. While this design does not necessarily optimise kW consumption, it clearly explores new ways of utilising glass as a building material (1, 2).

The use of holographic coatings on glass to redirect sunlight has been explored in this project for the garden exhibition in Stuttgart by two professors from Cologne (3, 4).

Electrochromic glass is the amazing result of adding dynamic properties to a stable material. Electrochromic glass can turn opaque within a few seconds when electrical current is applied (5).

The concept of the multi-layered, fully dynamic wall, that can respond to the environment like a chameleon has been investigated by Mike Davies from Richard Rogers Partnership (6).

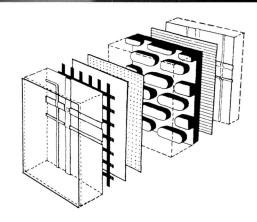

The development of glass has influenced architecture of this century more than that of any other material. Even though it might have caused problems in the 1950s and 1960s, glass is still one of the most promising high-performance materials in solar architecture.

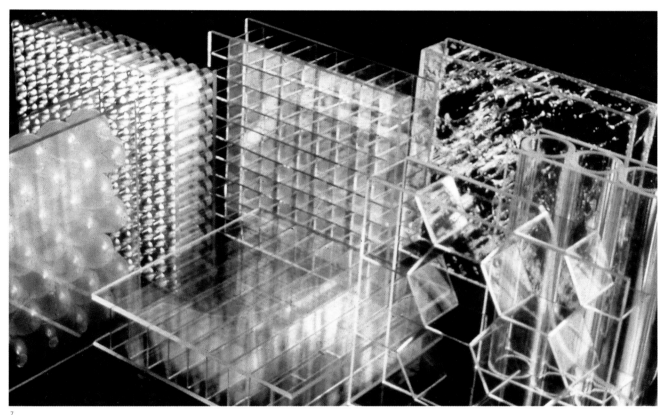

7

Mike Davies at Richard Rogers Partnership has been a leading figure in the exploration of new glass technologies. Various studies for multi-skin glazing prototypes for the Pilkington Bros. research project218 have been carried out.

8

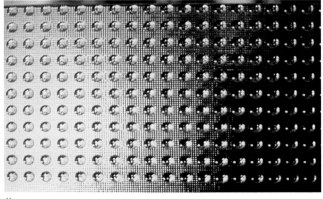

9

The ventilated cavity wall of the Lloyds building in London not only achieves a high thermal performance but also creates optimum diffuse daylight conditions inside (8, 9).

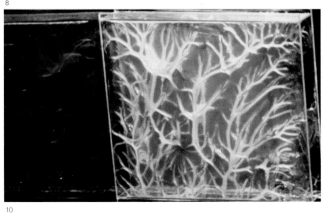

10

11

An open field for research includes the potential of gases and liquids or even organic substances to be integrated between glass panels or of glass to be sculpted, as in this pane for the Lloyds building in London.

Dramatic Daylight
Contemporary spectacular structures

The **Reichstag in Berlin** will house the new German parliament. Sir Norman Foster & Partners are designing the conversion of the existing building. The development of an innovative energy concept culminated in an exuberant daylight-guiding structure at the top of the building. This modern interpretation of a dome will not only include a visitors' platform but also will reflect light into the parliament chamber by means of a central cone with hundreds of mirrors. Extensive tests have been carried out using computer simulation as well as a 1:20 model of the entire dome and chamber in real conditions. Shown here is the model view looking up into the 'daylight chandelier' (1). The computer simulation (2) shows the view down from the visitors' ramp. Other views show the model (3), a cross-section (4), a photomontage (5), and the initial sketch (6).

1

2

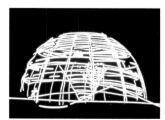

4

6   3

5

The art of using daylight to create theatrical effects is still alive. New technologies have opened up new possibilities.

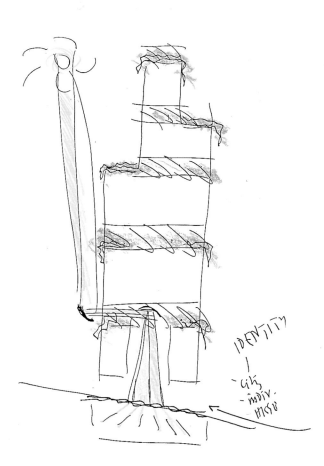

9

One of the features of the Hong Kong Bank, designed by Foster Associates, is the daylit atrium in the middle of the building. This was achieved by redirecting sunlight with two giant mirrored surfaces. The external sun scoop is covered by hundreds of small mirrors which follow the path of the sun, reflecting the daylight towards another concave reflector zone at the top of the atrium which guides the light into the space and, even further, through the glass floor. The initial sketch by Norman Foster still shows the idea of guiding the daylight all the way down into the basement.

7

8

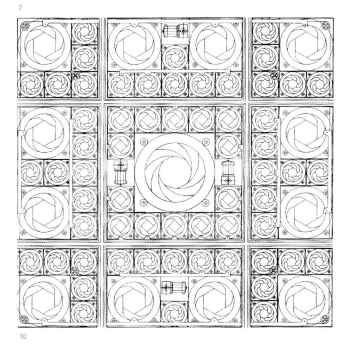

The extraordinary daylight control for the Institute du Monde Arab by Jean Nouvel consist of thousands of dynamic sensory shutters that are computer controlled.

10

11

Converting Daylight into Electricity
The evolution of photovoltaic integration

Free Electricity from the Sun
The physicist Henri Becquerel discovered that when light hits a combination of materials including silicon, electric volt age is produced. This was a revolutionary discovery, be cause it triggered the idea that one could produce energy from light by an artificial process similar to photosynthesis.

There are several types of photovoltaics. There are single crystalline cells that look almost homogeneously grey/black; there are poly-crystalline cells that look like enlarged bits of granite; and there is also the possibility of applying very thin layers of silicon onto a carrier such as glass or metal.

The production of photovoltaic cells begins with silicon crop, which is a byproduct of the computer industry. This silicon is melted and formed into ingots, which are then trimmed into blocks and sliced into thin wafers (3).

Crystalline photovoltaics come in thin wafers and are mostly used under plastic or glass covers for protection, thus permitting external use. Each panel of cells can vary in size and output according to customer needs.

Amorphous silicon has the advantage that it is easier to produce in large quantities/ areas. It is currently less efficient but considerably cheaper than poly-crystalline cells. Amorphous silicon also makes it possible to create a film, which can be applied in a pattern in order to create translucency.

1

2

3

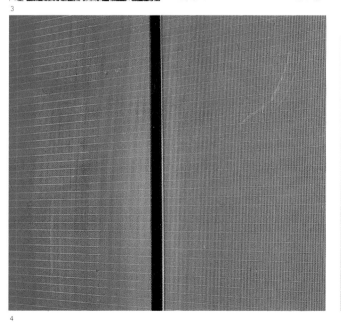

4

5

Light is probably the most obvious of renewable energies. New transformation processes – i.e., photovoltaics – are now capable of converting this energy into electric current.

6

7

All man-made objects in space are powered by solar energy through photovoltaic (PV) cells. On the Hubble telescope, non-crystalline PV cells are used, the highest-efficiency cells to date. If it had not been for a few scientists at NASA who were looking for a sustainable power supply for satellites and manned containers in space, the PV movement would have collapsed. Through the Apollo programme, PV technology experienced an amazing boost. The cells' performance since then has quadrupled.

8

9

The photovoltaic industry profits from technological developments in other fields. The development of silicon coated drums for colour photocopiers is now applied to the production of continuous metal strips covered with amorphous silicon (8, 9).

PV panels ideally want to be focused on the sun as long as it shines. As the sun's position changes, this can be difficult. Panels can be tilted according to the altitude and then pointed in the most advantageous direction. It is obviously also possible to place PV panels flat or vertically on roofs and facades, but this will always reduce the efficiency and output of the cells slightly.

The use of PV panels is determined by the set-up in panels made up of various cells. These cells can be joined together in almost any configuration and size. It is possible to use a tiny PV cell to power an electric calculator or to connect thousands of big panels to create a PV farm.

This big photovoltaic installation is part of the HYSOLAR Institute in Stuttgart Germany.

10

The introduction of PV in buildings has fascinated architects around the world. The most successful projects have managed to make the PV panels an integrated part of the cladding or roofing system. The design challenge lies in the use of a completely new material, which also has requirements of its own, particularly in regard to orientation.

Nick Grimshaw's pavilion for the EXPO in Seville in 1992 explores the use of PV cells on beautifully shaped roof collectors to act as shade, but also to power water pumps that cool the facade (1).

The costs of PV cells have been so high, as they are mostly produced in small numbers. If demand were increased, the price could be brought down dramatically. Various governments have now produced PV subsidy programmes in order to raise production levels. In Germany, a thousand-roof programme was launched in 1990, and Japan followed suit in 1995 with a seventy-thousand-roof programme.

Two of the latest Japanese developments are amorphous photovoltaic roof panels by Canon and PV rooftiles by Sanyo (3, 4).

This fully integrated PV facade for the Aachen power utilities in Germany, in collaboration with Flagsol, was the first of its kind in the world (5). The Flachglas AG Headquarters in Gelsenkirchen show a further Development in PV cladding (6).

1

2

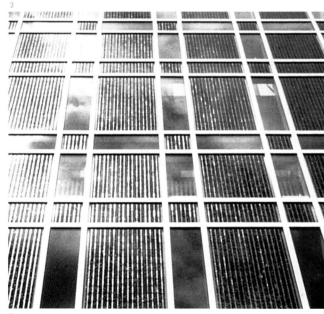

3

4

5

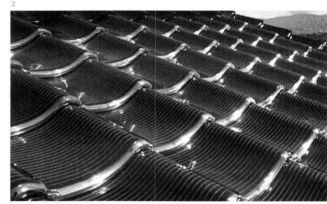

6

7

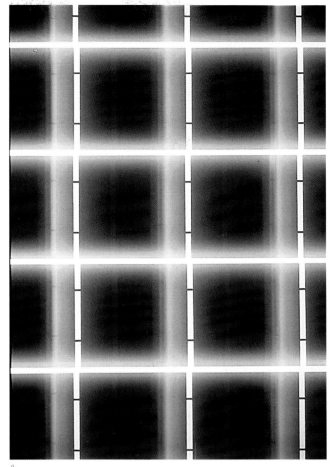

8

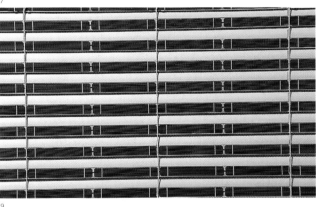

9

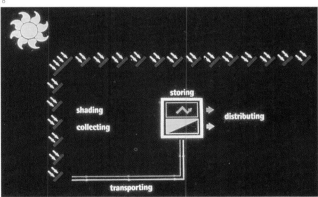

10

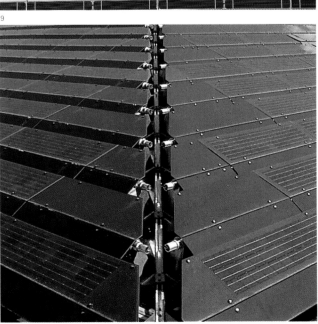

11

12

The possibility of laminating PV cells between two pieces of glass permite another fascinating application, in which the panel can act as a shading device and only let light through the gaps between the cells. The library illustrated at the top of this page shows how this technology can be integrated into architecture.

Sir Norman Foster & Partners in collaboration with Norbert Kaiser have developed prototypes for PV-covered blinds that could be used for old buildings as modifications to shutters or as venetian blinds of any kind. Shading devices are ideal carriers for cells as they face the sun or even follow its path according to daylight conditions. For this, sophisticated computer controls should be able to prioritise the use of daylight, the necessary shading, and the potential for energy harvesting through the blinds (9, 10).

The DEC Digital Equipment Corporation in Geneva illustrates an attractive PV application (11, 12). The 15-kW shadow voltaic power generator can produce up to 16,000 kWh per year. This application was developed in collaboration with the companies Solution and Colt.

Learning from Solar Cars and Planes
Designing with new parameters creates new forms

The Spirit of Biel won the solar race, which runs 3,013 km across Australia, in 1993. It crossed the continent in hours, with an average speed of 72 km/hr. For the entire race, the car required approximately the same amount of energy as five l of petrol would produce.

1

The Solar Racer, designed by the American engineer Paul MacCready, won the same solar car race in 1987. The project was realised with the cooperation of General Motors. The optimisation of shape and performance was intensively tested in wind-channel and other simulation programmes.

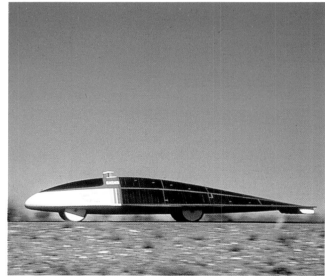

2

3

The latest winner of the solar car race was Honda, in 1993. It follows the aerodynamic principles set out by Paul MacCready and General Motors in 1987.

4

5

The best examples of the integration of photovoltaic cells, aero-dynamic forms, and super-lightweight structures can be found in the world's leading solar cars and planes. New shapes of logic and beauty are developed without being 'designed.'

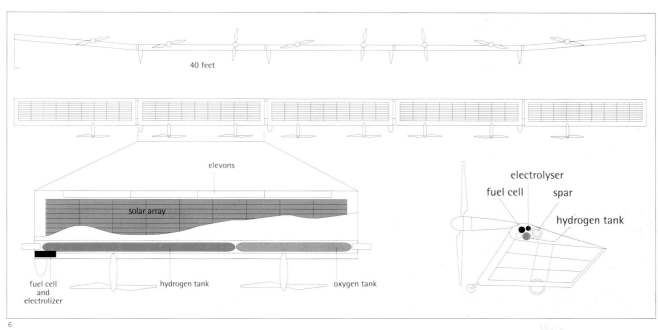

40 feet

elevons

solar array

fuel cell and electrolizer

hydrogen tank

oxygen tank

electrolyser

fuel cell

spar

hydrogen tank

6

7

8

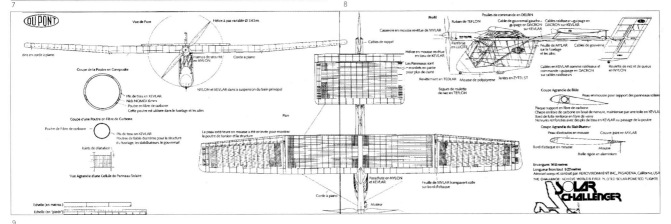

9

The Pathfinder is one of the latest achievements in solar high-performance design (6, 8). The goal was to create an aero-plane that could be remote-controlled and that could stay in the air for months testing high-altitude air pollution for NASA. The tests undertaken so far did prove a plane's ability to fly driven by PV cells only. In September 1995, the aeroplane reached the record-breaking altitude of 50,000 ft.

The Solar Challenger was the first manned plane that was fuelled by direct solar energy (7, 9). Designed by Paul MacCready in collaboration with Dupont, it managed to fly from Dover to Paris in 1981. The PV cells were integrated on the top of the wings and a spe-cial rear wing in order to gene-rate the electricity to power a propeller. Sir Norman Foster noted about this plane: 'I think it was relevant that Paul MacCready achieved the first solar powered flight, because, unlike everybody else, he did not try to copy what everybody else thought such a craft should look like. He went back to basics. As Lilientahl did in 1880, he used new material — carbon fibre and honeycomb. Paul MacCready spoke to an audience of architects and designers in Aspen in 1980. We all thought that his design pro-cess was highly creative, but Paul MacCready did not agree. He felt that Mr. Kraemer, who set the goal and price for the first solar-powered flight, was evoking the truly creative act. I think that says a lot about architecture today. Where is the patronage, where is the equivalent today of Kraemer setting goals, quality standards, inspirations, and challenges to the spirit?'

Efficient Structures and Materials
Reducing embodied energy

Stansted, London's third international airport not only is an example of a highly efficient structure but also — by concentrating all services at ground level, has a very lightweight roof. The roofline acts as an enormous daylight-guiding system. This permits the airport to be daylit for most of its operating time and results in a huge energy saving.

This light-weight dome was constructed by Mero for the German pavilion of the 1970 EXPO in Osaka (2). The new connection methods developed by Mero allowed complex space frames and geometries to be constructed with a minimal, versatile kit of multifaceted connecting bails and sticks, allowing a reduction of material consumption.

The concert hall in Mannheim designed by Frei Otto explores the potential of wood, and the complex geometries of bubbles to create a new type of shell construction (3).

The Pavilion of IBM designed by Renzo Piano combines materials like wood and metal in an extraordinary manner in oder to achieve light weight as well as demountability (4, 5). This minimal use of materials had mainly been employed in sailboat construction prior to the construction of Piano's building.

Efficient structures and materials are crucial if we want to reduce the overall energy consumption of buildings. Energies embodied in materials and in the construction process, as well as the materials' longevity and performance, all contribute to total life-cycle cost.

6

The **Olympic Stadium** in Munich, by Günther Behnisch and Frei Otto, built in 1972, is a light-weight tensile structure on large scale. A concept that provides for more with less (6).

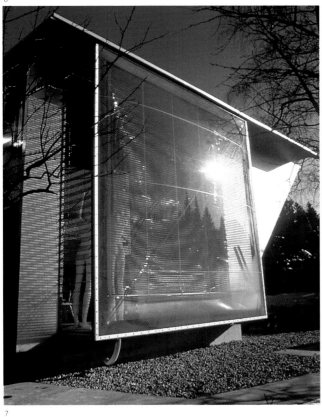

7

8

Koch Hightex have been developing cushion constructions out of hostaflow for years. The vela glass shown here (7) illustrates a unique example of a cushion with integrated shade for an artist's studion in Munich.

Paul MacCready's development of the human-powered aeroplane, the Gossamer Albatross, was made possible through the innovative use of new materials (8). These combined mylar skins with carbon-fibre structures and honeycomb material.

Suppliers of equipment for such outdoor activities as mountaineering, skiing, etc. have been quick to explore the potential of new materials and structures. The new generation of tents can be seen as great examples for super-light-weight structures.

Environmentally Responsive Structures
Doing more with less

The Autonomous House designed for Buckminster Fuller and his wife by Foster Associates in 1982 was a lightweight, high-performance structure. The inner and outer domes floated on a low-friction, sealed hydraulic race. The external skin was to be a fly-eye dome capable of rotating independently around a similar inner dome, which could support the space-deck living floors. Each dome was to be half glazed and half clad in aluminium panels, so that the house could be completely closed at night and track the path of the sun during the day, similar to eyeball and lid. The cavity would have been used to circulate air.

1

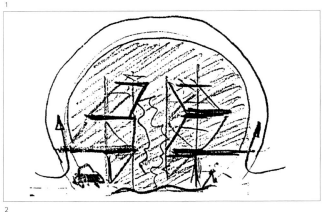

2

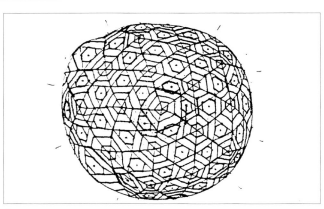

3

Among the various applications of sculptor and engineer Charles Hoberman's research is the Iris Dome Retractable Roof.

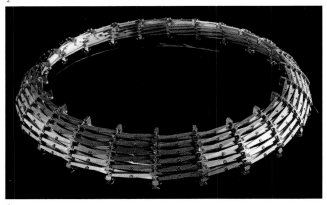

4

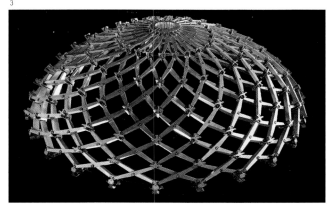

5

Umbrellas creating shade
were designed by Bodo Rasch,
Germany, as a prototype for a
mosque in Mecca. The mosque
was supposed to have an
adaptable roof-shade that
could not rest on an existing
structure and therefore had to
be an independent part of the
complex. Rasch did one design
integrating solar cells into his
shade umbrellas so the mechanism of opening and closing
could be performed without
electricity.

6

7

8

9

10

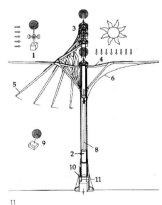

11

227

New Tools for Environmental Design
Visualising the invisible flows of energy

New Planning Tools
This approach requires a clear understanding of how different buildings perform under various circumstances, be they externally or internally generated. A better understanding of both people and building behaviour and the application of sophisticated computer modelling techniques are the key to a successful low-energy ecological design. Typical computer modelling tools available to today's engineers and architects include dynamic thermal modelling, computational fluid dynamics and daylighting/artificial lighting modelling.

The building context must be studied to maximise the benefits of natural resources and provide a clear understanding of the comfort expectations of the occupants, their social lifestyle and living patterns.

For the Commerzbank Headquarter in Frankfurt, various tests have been carried out in order to assess the building's performance. Fluid dynamic simulations carried out by the engineers J. Roger Preston & Partners not only illustrate the tower in its urban context (as a photomontage could) but also show the patterns and intensities of wind energy around the building at different levels. Through the 'virtual reality' of computer simulation it is possible to zoom in and out from the global movements of energy down to the individual distribution of, for example, ventilation and daylight. These are unique possibilities that were never available before.

1

2

3

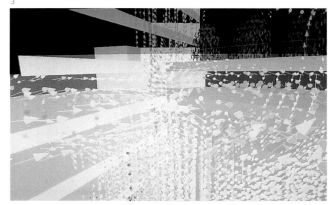

4

5

Recent developments in the fields of computer-aided design, virtual reality, fluid dynamics, and light modelling allow the visualisation of invisible performance. This helps to achieve higher quality, efficiency, and design in buildings.

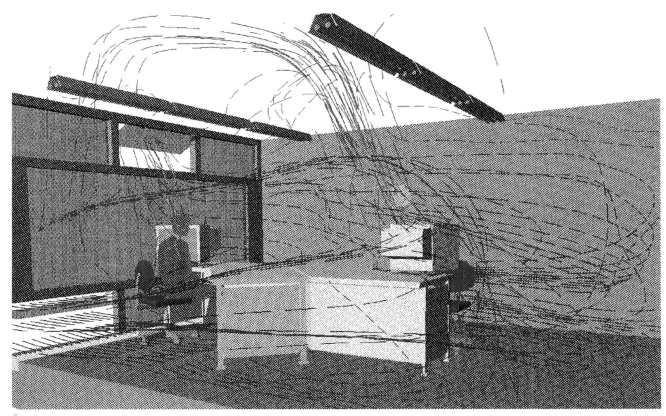

6

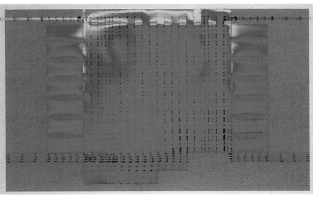

7

8

9

10

The Potsdamer Platz in Berlin is one of the biggest high-quality speculative office developments in Europe. It uses natural ventilation and maximises daylight. Computer simulations are used to optimise natural airflow through varying window positions.

Fluid dynamic computer simulations are used to optimise natural airflow through varying window positions (8, 9).

11

Computer software can simulate the distribution of daylight in spaces and therefore allows the designer to optimise his design (10, 11).

What Can We Expect from Buildings?
High performance and efficiency

Our goal for buildings must be to create good environments for individuals as well as for large groups in a sustainable way. To achieve this, we must define our internal individual performance expectations and external environmental energy performance.

Architecture is voodoo. The architects don't initiate anything; they just go to work when the client says so. They know how to draw, but they don't know how to design an airplane. They don't go to Douglas and say tell me what you've found out today about the tensile strength of that new steel aluminium. They have approximately nothing to do with evolution. I think the younger architects may be changing. I think they understand what I am saying.
(Richard Buckminster Fuller, New York Times 23.4.1967).

Aeroplanes fly, cars drive, boats float. What do we expect from buildings? The high performance and efficiency to maintain comfort and ethics inside and outside.

Even though buildings are immobile, we can learn from the way planes, cars, and boats are designed in order to achieve a certain level of performance. Often their shapes are generated with an eye to optimising their ability to deal with natural elements and energies.

This approach requires a clear understanding of how different buildings perform under various circumstances. A better understanding of both people and building behaviour and the application of sophisticated computer-modelling techniques are key to a successful low energy/ecological design. Typical computer-modelling tools available to today's engineer/architect include dynamic thermal modelling, computational fluid dynamics, and daylighting/artificial lighting modelling.

This interactive design process, coupled with the search for and application of new man-made smart materials, such as carbon fibre technology/lightweight structures, phase-change materials, and thermal storage, is what we need to come to terms with when taking energy conservation that one step further.

Buildings need the least amount of energy for their own 'survival'; almost all energy *consumed* is used by the occupier, in order to satisfy his or her expectations. Therefore energy consumption itself depends on the building technology that was applied to create specific structural conditions. Buildings are built for people in order to maintain comfort and the well-being of their occupants and users. The ability of the occupant to control (i.e. influence, change, and adapt the environmental parameters affecting comfort) has the most crucial influence on occupant satisfaction. Control is more important than actual comfort conditions.

The need to minimize the energy consumption of buildings has often led to solutions potentially in conflict with the providing of individual control. For example, a building designed for both natural ventilation and air conditioning

by providing personalized controls to the occupants can result in part of a building operating in air-conditioned mode when it doesn't need to.

The first questions have to be:
What do we expect from a building?
What are the internal conditions that should be created?
What are the activities envisaged and the comfort desired?
Later, the question of *how* one can or should achieve these objectives is to be considered.

2

The challenge for the future will be to create the best possible environments inside and outside — comfortable and healthy, using highly efficient technologies that create affordable structures for a sustainable life-style. This can be achieved by drawing upon what we know of both vernacular and spectacular building successes and by exploring new materials, technologies, and tools.

Several reasons exemplify why such a change is long overdue:
1. 30-40% of energy is consumed in buildings. Solar energy in architecture and urban planning can create the biggest and therefore the most important contribution to an environmentally sound energy system.
2. Because architecture always symbolises and represents the mind set of a culture and its dominant ideas, we have to recognise that the main political and sociological aim of our time is democratisation. Democracy requires communication, and there can be no communication without transparency. Solar architecture leads to more transparency and enhances communication. In other words, solar architecture corresponds with the predominant ideas of our time.
3. We are living in a world experiencing increasing tension between individualism and society. The general, and perhaps the most serious, question is how to create individualism which does not conflict with common responsibility. Solar architecture offers an opportunity to overcome this contradiction by creating more individuality — but always in harmony with the social needs of the present and future society.
(Herrmann Scheer, German parlamentarian and president of Euro Solar, European Conference on Solar Energy in Architecture and Urban Planning, Florence 1993).

3

The Quality of Space
Establishing internal performance specifications

In most cultures, paradise represents the ultimate in human comfort and quality of space. Harmony with nature and the "ideal" stimulation of all senses render shelter and the need for any compensation in building form unnecessary.

Even though no clear or uniform definition of paradise is possible, most individuals probably have some sort of picture in their minds.

Comparing the quality of such an ideal environment with the environment we live in today raises many questions.

Spaces created by human beings should provide the highest levels of practicality, satisfaction, and appropriate stimulation. Not the compromise on quality, but the challenge of more comfort with less energy, is the goal for future solar architecture

Quality has always been the goal of good architects and builders, but it is difficult to define. Nevertheless, millions of kilowatt hours and pounds are spent to achieve it. It seems necessary to attempt an evaluation of the criteria applied to buildings and their performance.

Human physiology enables us to judge the quality of our internal/external environment in a direct, interactive manner, whether consciously or unconsciously. The main tools for this are our senses, whose joint action allows human perception. Our senses react to external stimulation in a complex way. If all or one are over-stimulated, our brain is warned until the senses deteriorate. If they are under-stimulated or even suffer under sensual deprivation, our brain starts to hallucinate until the senses are damaged. Ideally, we remain balanced between too little and too much stimulation. The term *comfort* has been commonly used to relate to 'thermal comfort' and not 'human comfort' in the true sense of the word. True comfort is more psychological than physiological. Owing to the uniqueness of personal perception there exists no singular benchmark figure defining comfort.

The difficult aspect of designing quality space is that people do have different expectationns. Individual variations can sometimes be greater than the variation within a group of people. To satisfy these expectations is a problem for designers, because even an ideal design cannot please one persn, let alone a group of people. The solution seams to be to create adaptable spaces that can take into account changes in the environment. Internal climate control was first developed after the Second World War, ideally providing unprecedented comfort for a large number of people. It would be difficult and possibly wrong to expect people give up this luxury. Our goal must be to achieve this ideal comfort for the largest number of people, but based on our new understnading of the environment.

The pioneering role of the Danish Professor P.O. Fangers in attempting to define optimum comfort scientifically resulted in the internationally recognised ISO Standard 7730 of 1984 for moderate thermal environments. This standard has the advantage of being deterministic, quantifiable, and measurable. However, its very objectivity is its greatest shortcoming.

Psychological parameters are far more complex to assess. They are time-dependent and closely linked to individual background. They are also linked to locale. What is defined as comfort for moderate temperature climates is not identical with that in arctic or tropical climates. The importance in addressing and satisfying all the five senses when designing a space was discussed already in the 18th century. The term *aesthetics* relating to all sensual knowledge was defined by A.G. Baumgarten in his work *Aesthetica*

(1750/58). If comfort can be defined as an individual''s perception of the aesthetics of space, then we must revert to Baumgartens definition in which all senses are to be addressed. The complex anture of personal behaviour leaves no option but to recognise the impact physiology has on every one of us in our perception of space and, subsequently, comfort.

2

Modern and contemporary commercial buildings, in particular, with their homogenous conditions, are problematic for the human senses. Research undertaken by the Martin Centre of Architectural and Urban Studies, University of Cambridge, has shown that the existence of adaptive opportunity reduces stress and hence leads to an increase in comfort. This suggests that the ability of the occupant to control (i.e., influence, change, and adapt the environmental parameters affecting comfort) has the most crucial influence on his or her satisfaction. The act of control appears to be more important than the actual comfort condition itself.

Exerting an influence on the overall individual perception of space is only possible by giving people the freedom of choice and mechanisms of individual control. This idea has major implications for the architectural design process, space organisation, and building systems. Ultimately, it allows the occupier of a building to interact with that building and with the environment. The stimulation and satisfaction such an interaction can give is closer to sailing, surfing, or hang-gliding than flying on a jumbo jet or being in a submarine.

The noises of a stream or the wind in a tree, the light filtering through a tree top are complex sources for human stimulation, oscillating in the most pleasant ways. Our senses were developed for outdoor life, the set-up of our senses has not changed. There is no better light than daylight, no better air than fresh air. We should use these external qualities as much as we possibly can in order to gain comfort.

Natural stimulation and comfort conditions are not only better for our health and well-being; they are also energy-conserving, as we do not have to produce them artificially. For the artificial creation of natural comfort conditions, energy is needed. Each cubic metre of energy that comes through an openable window does not have to be pumped through the building; each kilowatt hour of light that reaches a desk does not have to be generated through electricity. To maintain a balance between the maximum use of naturally available comfort conditions in a building and the artificial generation of additional comfort through machines can help to keep the energy consumption of a building low and efficient.

Environmental Ethics
High-performance structures for sustainability

Built structures must have a reciprocal relationship with their environments and the rest of the world. The environmental imperatives of today are the challenge for the building industry, high performance is the goal. This requires a close collaboration of coherent teams and an integrated design method.

Two aspects of technology, the light and dark sides, have come to appear in even sharper contrast in the 20th century. We may safely say that in this century more human lives have either been saved or destroyed by the instrumentality of science and technology than in the whole of the rest of human history. How are we to deal with this dilemma? This is the historic task of all of us living in this century and about to enter a new century.
(Prime Minister Nakasone, Conference on Life, Science, and Man, 1984).

As sustainability is our goal, the criteria for the external energy performance of a building are ultimately based upon a responsibility to society and the environment.

The freedom of the individual and the performance of the building he or she lives in ends when the effects of the individual or the building impinge on other people's freedom or endanger their bases of life. This is also true of cities.

Ideally, this means that buildings should not use more energy to satisfy their occupants' expectations than they can harvest from renewable energies surrounding them. Ultimately, buildings and cities should have a positive total-life-cycle energy balance. This would include the embodied energy in materials (from cradle to grave) as well as refurbishment and recycling or reusability, and, obviously, the energy requirements for the building's actual operation. This will only be possible if resources and all renewable energy available are used, stored, and managed to their full potential.

This might be a mere vision at the moment, but it is certain that the building industry will go through an unprecedented efficiency revolution, and that the performance of buildings and all their systems and components will be evaluated.

The first and fundamental step is not to block positive renewable outside energies if they are available and useful.

Designers of the future will need to learn from natural structures that deal with environmental energies and study how form truly follows function. Other rich areas of inspiration are those structures that have evolved over thousands of years, whether agricultural, stabiles, or mobiles. For example, sailboats represent a sophisticated design solution to a complex problem. How can one use the varying strengths and directions of wind to move a boat and reduce its loads as fast and as much as possible? The hull and the steering, the mast, the sail and the rigging, all have to perform in the most efficient way. They are designed to fulfil a task, and their form and shape are

generated by practicality and natural challanges. One should study the design process and evolution of shapes in relation to technological change.

Today, the world of sports equipment provides astonishing examples of high performance. Comparing a sports shoe of today with one of 50 years ago illustrates that we are living in a time when high efficiency and performance are recognised disciplines. We must apply this knowledge to our building design practice.

All those involved in the building industry will have to face the challenge of high-performance buildings in a responsible way. What is needed is the commitment to an integrated, shared effort.

Future design challenges, encompassing an ever-increasing number of inter-related components, will necessitate new forms of organisation to facilitate the successful orchestration of the many different actors involved in any one project. This trend reflects the fact that the architect no longer works in isolation, but is dependent upon a plethora of other expert groups as well as the lay public.

With ever-increasing complexities involved in building design and construction, the role of specialist groups outside the architectural practice will grow both in size and in importance. Each person or sub-group will have specific responsibilities within the overall task; however, it is in the interaction of the team as a whole, with different actors from a variety of fields, that the challenge lies.

However, if architects do recognise the importance of designing structures that meet the objectives previously discussed, then a greater level of teamwork involving a host of specialist groups is imperative. Architects will need to interact with structural engineers, M&E consultants, lighting and energy consultants, health and safety experts, and the growing field of experts involved in assessing the living and working qualities of buildings. Promoting development based upon environmental ethics will necessitate architects working closely with urban planning agencies, climatologists, and environmental groups, sociologists, and geographers. In addition to their expert knowledge, such groups also provide an important relation with local lay public opinion, which must have some form of input into the design process.

2

3

European Charter for Solar Energy

Preamble

Roughly half of the energy consumed in Europe is used to run buildings. A further 25% is accounted for by traffic. Large quantities of non-renewable fossil fuel are used to generate this energy, fuel that will not be available to future generations. The processes involved in the conversion of fuel into energy also have a lasting negative effect on the environment through the emissions they cause. In addition to this, unscrupulous, intensive cultivation, a destructive exploitation of raw materials, and a worldwide reduction in the areas of land devoted to agriculture are leading to a progressive diminution of natural habitats.

This situation calls for a rapid and fundamental reorientation in our thinking, particularly on the part of planners and institutions involved in the process of construction. The form of our future built environment must be based on a responsible approach to nature and the use of the inexhaustible energy potential of the sun.

The role of architecture as a responsible profession is of far-reaching significance in this respect. In future, architects must exert a far more decisive influence on the conception and layout of urban structures and buildings on the use of materials and construction components, and thus on the use of energy, than they have in the past.

The aim of our work in the future must, therefore, be to design buildings and urban spaces in such a way that natural resources will be conserved and renewable forms of energy – especially solar energy – will be used as extensively as possible, thus avoiding many of these undesirable developments.

In order to attain these goals, it will be necessary to modify existing courses of instruction and training, as well as energy supply systems, funding and distribution models, standards, statutory regulations and laws in accordance with the new objectives.

Planners

Architects and engineers must design their projects with a knowledge of local conditions, existing resources, and the main criteria governing the use of renewable forms of energy and materials. In view of the responsibility they are thus required to assume, their role in society must be strengthened in relation to that of non-independent planning companies and commercial undertakings. New design concepts must be developed that will increase awareness of the sun as a source of light and heat; for an acceptance of solar technology in construction by the general public can only be achieved by means of convincing visual ideas and examples.

This means:
– cities, buildings and their various elements must be interpreted as a complex system of material and energy flows;
– the use of environmentally friendly forms of energy must be planned from a holistic point of view. A professional knowledge of all functional, technical and design relationships, conditions and possibilities is a precondition for the creation of modern architecture;
– the extensive and constantly expanding body of knowledge about the conditions governing the internal climate of buildings, the development of solar technology, and the scope for simulation, calculation and measurement must be systematically represented and made available in a clear, comprehensible and extendible form;
– the training and further education of architects and engineers must be related to future needs and should take place within mutually related systems on various levels, using the facilities afforded by the new media. Schools, universities, and professional associations are called upon to develop relevant options.

Building sites

The specific local situation, the existing vegetation and building fabric, climatic and topographical factors, and the range and availability of ecologically sustainable forms of energy seen in relation to the duration and intensity of their use, as well as local constraints, all have to be analysed and evaluated as the basis for each individual planning project.

The natural resources available in a given location, especially sun, wind and geothermal heat, should be harnessed for the climatic conditioning of buildings and should be reflected in the design of their layout and form.
Depending on the geographical situation, the physical form, the material composition and the use to which a structure is put, the various existing or emerging patterns of building development will enter into a reciprocal relationship with the following local factors:

– climatic data (elevation of the sun, seasonal and regional range of sunlight, air temperatures, wind force and direction, periods when winds occur, quantities of precipitation, etc.);
– the degree of exposure and aspect of open spaces and the surface of the ground (angle of slope, form, contour, proportion, scale, etc.);
– the location, geometry, dimensions and volume of surrounding buildings, topographical formations, areas of water and vegetation (changing patterns of shade, reflection, volume, emissions, etc.);
– the suitability of existing earth masses as thermal storage bodies;
– human and mechanical patterns of movement;
– existing building conventions and the architectural heritage.

Materials and forms of construction

Buildings and urban open spaces should be designed in such a way that a minimum of energy is needed to light and service them in terms of harnessing heat for hot water, heating, cooling, ventilation and the generation of electricity from light. To cover all remaining needs, solutions should be chosen that meet the criteria of an overall energy balance and that comply with the latest technical knowledge on the use of environmentally compatible forms of energy.

The use of materials, forms of construction, production technology, transport, assembly and dismantling of building components must, therefore, take account of the energy content and the life cycle of materials.
– Regenerable raw materials that are available in adequate quantities and forms of construction that have a minimal primary energy/"grey" energy content should be given preference.
– The recycling of materials should be guaranteed, with scope for eventual reuse or for ecologically sustainable disposal.
– Load-bearing structures and the skins of buildings must be of great durability so as to ensure an efficient use of materials, labour and energy, and to minimize the cost of disposal. An optimal relationship between production or embedded energy, (also known as enbodied energy), and longevity should be achieved.
– Building elements that serve the passive or active harnessing of solar energy and that can be easily accommodated to constructional, design, modular and dimensional requirements

in Architecture and Urban Planning

should be subject to further development and given priority in use.
– New systems and products in the field of energy and construction technology should be capable of simple integration into a building and should be easy to replace or renew.

Buildings in use

In terms of their energy balance, buildings should be regarded as self-contained systems with an optimal exploitation of environmentally sustainable forms of energy to meet various needs. They should be developed as permanent systems that will be capable of accommodating different uses over a long period.

– Functions should be laid out in plan and section in such a way that account is taken of changes of temperature and thermal zones.
– The planning and execution of buildings and the choice of materials should be based on a flexible concept, so that later changes of use can be accommodated with a minimum expenditure of materials and energy.
– The permeability of the skin of a building towards light, heat and air, and its transparency must be controllable and capable of modification, so that it can react to changing local climatic conditions (solar screening, protection against glare, light deflection, shading, temporary thermal protection, adjustable natural ventilation).
– It should be possible to meet comfort requirements largely through the design of the building by incorporating passive measures with a direct effect. The remaining energy needs in terms of heating, cooling, electricity, ventilation and lighting should be met by active systems powered by ecologically sustainable forms of energy.
The technical and energy resources used in a building should be appropriate to its function. Graphs showing the requirements for different user categories should be reconsidered and, where appropriate, modified. Buildings with special uses, such as museums, libraries, hospitals, etc., should be considered separately, since specific climatic constraints exist for these types.

The city

Renewable forms of energy present an opportunity to make life in cities more attractive. In the realms of energy supply and transport infrastructures, the use of these kinds of energy should be maximized through the actual form of the building. The existing building fabric should be used as far as is practical and possible. The combustion of fossil fuels must be drastically reduced.
The relationship between cities and nature should be developed to achieve a symbiosis between the two. Alterations and other measures carried out in public spaces or existing buildings, or caused by new construction, must take account of the historical and cultural identity of the location and the geographic and climatic conditions of the landscape.

The city must be comprehended in its entirety as a self-contained long-living organism. It must be possible to control the constant changes in its use and appearance, as well as in technology, in order to ensure a minimum of disturbance and a maximum conservation of resources.
Cities are resources in built form and have a high primary energy content. To achieve a closer integration with the overall balance of nature, their various neighbourhoods, buildings and open spaces, their infrastructures, and their functional, transport and communication systems must be subject to a constant process of modification and reconstruction that follows natural cycles of renewal.
The form of the urban and landscape structures that man creates must be governed by the following environmental and bioclimatic factors:
– orientation of streets and building structures to the sun;
– temperature control and use of daylight in the public realm;
– topography (land form, overall exposure, general situation);
– direction and intensity of wind (alignment of streets, sheltered public spaces, systematic ventilation, cold-air corridors);
– vegetation and distribution of planted areas (oxygen supply, dust consolidation, temperature balance, shading, windbreaks);
– hydro-geology (relationship to water and waterway systems).

Urban functions such as habitation, production, services, cultural and leisure activities should be

co-ordinated with each other where this is functionally possible and socially compatible. In this way the volume of vehicular traffic can be reduced. Production and service facilities can complement each other and be used more intensively and efficiently.
Pedestrians, and vehicles that are not propelled by the combustion of fossil fuels must be given privileged treatment in urban areas. Public transport should enjoy special support. Parking needs should be reduced and the consumption of petrol and other fuel minimized.
An economic use of land, achieved through a reasonable density in new planning schemes coupled with a programme of infill developments, can help to cut expenditure for infrastructure and transport and reduce the exploitation of further areas of land. Measures to restore an ecological balance should also be implemented.
In the public spaces of towns and cities, steps should be taken to improve the urban climate, temperature control, wind protection and the specific heating or cooling of these spaces.

Berlin 3/1996

Signatories:
Alberto Campo Baeza, Madrid E · Victor López Cotelo, Madrid E · Ralph Erskine, Stockholm S · Nikos Fintikakis, Athens GR · Sir Norman Foster, London GB · Nicholas Grimshaw, London GB · Herman Hertzberger, Amsterdam NL · Thomas Herzog, Munich D · Knud Holscher, Copenhagen DK · Sir Michael Hopkins, London GB · Françoise Jourda, Lyon F · Uwe Kiessler, Munich D · Henning Larsen, Copenhagen DK · Bengt Lundsten, Helsinki FI · David Mackay, Barcelona E · Angelo Mangiarotti, Milan I · Manfredi Nicoletti, Rome I · Frei Otto, Leonberg D · Juhani Pallasmaa, Helsinki FI · Gustav Peichl, Vienna A · Renzo Piano, Genoa I · José M. de Prada Poole, Madrid E · Sir Richard Rogers, London GB · Francesca Sartogo, Rome I · Hermann Schröder, Munich D · Roland Schweitzer, Paris F · Peter C. von Seidlein, Stuttgart D · Thomas Sieverts, Berlin D · Otto Steidle, Munich D · Alexandros N. Tombazis, Athens GR

This document was drawn up by Thomas Herzog in 1994–95 in the context of READ project supported by the European Commission DG XII. The contents were discussed and the wording agreed with leading European architects.
READ = **R**enewable **E**nergies in **A**rchitecture and **D**esign

Selected Bibliography

The Need for Change
Chermayeff, Serge, and Christopher Alexander, *Community and Privacy. Towards a New Architecture of Humanism*, New York 1963
Commission of the European Communities. Environmental Ethics, Brussels 1990
Energy. Facing up to the Problem, Getting down to Solutions, Special Report. National Geographic, February 1981
Fuller, Buckminster R., *Critical Path*, New York 1981
Fuller, Buckminster R., and Robert Marks, *The Dymaxion World of Buckminster Fuller*, London 1973
Gore, Al, *Earth in the Balance. Forging a New Common Purpose*, London 1992
Harrison, Paul, *The Third Revolution – Population, Environment and a Sustainable World*, London 1993
Lovelock, James, *The Ages of GAIA. A Biography of Our Living Earth*, Oxford 1988
Meadows, Daniel et al., *Die Grenzen des Wachstums*, Bericht des Club of Rome zur Lage der Menschheit, Stuttgart n.d.
Patterson, Walter, *The Energy Alternative. Changing the Way the World Works*, London 1990
Rosenkranz, Gerd, *Spezial. Energie*, Reinbeck 1995
Scheer, Herrman, *Sonnenstrategie – Politik ohne Alternative*, Zurich 1993
Schlaich, Werner and Sybille, *Erneuerbare Energien Nutzen – Bevölkerungsexplosion und globale Umweltzerstörung. Läßt sich der Energiebedarf wesentlich durch erneuerbare Energien stillen?* Düsseldorf 1991
Spurgon, Richard, and Mike Flood, *Energy and Power. A Practical Introduction with Projects and Activities*, London 1990
Vester, Frederic, *Unsere Welt. Ein vernetztes System*, Munich 1983
Weizsäcker, Ernst Urich von, *Erdpolitik*, Darmstadt 1994
Winter, Karl-Jochen, *Die Energie der Zukunft heißt Sonnenenergie*, Munich 1993

Learning from Natural Systems
Bender, Michel, *Miracle of Life. Discover Patterns of Behaviour in the Living World*, London 1992
Bionik. Patente der Natur, ed. by WWF and Pro Futura, Munich 1991
Calder, Nigel, *Spaceship Earth*, London 1991
Friedmann, H., *Die Sonne, Spektrum der Wissenschaft*, Heidelberg 1987
Galston, J.W., *Life Process of Plants*, Scientific American Magazine, New York 1994
Hancocks, David, *Masterbuilders of the Animal World*, London 1973
Harlow, William M., *Art Forms from Plantlife*, New York 1976
Klima, die Kraft mit der wir leben, ed. by WWF and Pro Futura, Munich 1994
Living Races of Mankind, 2 vols, London n.d.
Stevens, Payson R., and Kevin W. Kelly, *Embracing the Earth*, London 1992
Weisheit der Wildnis, ed. by WWF and Pro Futura, Munich 1993

Responsive Solar Buildings
Bier, Michael, *Asien: Straße, Haus*, Stuttgart 1990
Blaser, Werner, *Elementare Bauformen*, Düsseldorf 1982
–, and Chang Chao-Kang, *China – Tao in Architecture*, Basel/Boston 1987
Bourgeois, Jean-Louis, and Carolee Pelos, *Spectacular Vernacular. The Adobe Tradition*, New York 1993
Davoli, Pietromaria, *Architettura senza impianti*, Florence 1993
Denyer, Susan, *African Traditional Architecture. An Historical and Geographical Perspective*, New York 1978
Fathy, Hassan, *Natural Energy and Vernacular Architecture. Principles and Examples with Reference to Hot Arid Climates*, Chicago 1986
Goldfinger, Myron, *Villages in the Sun. Mediterranean Community Architecture*, New York 1993
Guidoni, Enrico, *Architettura Primitiva*, Milan/Stuttgart 1979
Izard, Jean-Louis, *L'Architecture d'Été. Construire pour le comfort d'été*, Paris 1993
Knevitt, Charles, *Shelter*, London 1994
Matus, Vladimir, *Design for Northern Climates. Cold Climate Planning and Environmental Design*, New York 1988

Muthesius, Stefan, and Hans Koester, *Das englische Reihenhaus. Die Entwicklung einer modernen Wohnform*, Königstein, Taunus 1990
Olgyay, Victor, *Design with Climate. Bioclimatic Approach to Architectural Regionalism*, New York 1963
Oliver, Paul, *Dwellings*, London 1987
Perry, C., Gore, A., and L. Fleming, *Old English Villages*, London 1986
Rudowsky, Bernhard, *Architecture without Architects. A Short Introduction to Non-Pedigreed Architecture*, London/ New York 1964
Rudowsky, Bernhard, *The Prodigious Builder*, Eugene, Or. 1977
Slesin, Suzanne et al., *Caribbean Style*, London 1985
Trebersburg, M., *Neues Bauen mit der Sonne*, Berlin 1994
Warren, John, and Ihsan Fethi, *Traditional Houses in Baghdad*, Horsham, England 1982
Wright, David, *Sonne. Architektur. Natur. Anleitung zum energiebewußten Bauen*, Karlsruhe 1984

The First Solar Structures
Gerster, Georg, *Grand Design*, London 1976
Rivals, *Claude, Le Moulin à vent et le meunier*, Ivry 1976

Solar Cities
Benevolo, Leonardo, *Storia della città*, Rome/Bari 1982
Cruickshank, D., and N. Burton, *Life in the Gregorian City*, London 1989
Knoll, Michael, and Rolf Kreibich, *Solar City. Sonnenenergie für die lebenswerte Stadt*, Basel 1992
Singh, Madanjeet, *The Sun and Myth in Art*, London 1993
Weltgeschichte der Architektur, 17 vols., Stuttgart 1985-88

Architecture for the Agricultural Age
Architecture in India, exh. cat. Association Française d'Action Artistique, Paris 1986
Butti, Ken, and John Perlin, *A Golden Threat*, London 1981
Dal Maso, Leonardo B., *Das Rom der Cäsaren*, Florence 1974
De Luca, Leonardo, and Cettina Gallo, *Bioclimatic Architecture*, Rome 1992
Jellicoe, Geoffrey and Susan, *The Landscape of Man*, London 1987
Kimpel, Dieter, Suckale, Robert and Albert Hirmer, *Die gotische Architektur in Frankreich 1130-1270*, Munich 1985
Klassische Chinesische Architektur, ed. by Chinesische Architekturakademie, Stuttgart 1990
Norberg-Schulz, Christian, *Vom Sinn des Bauens. Die Architektur des Abendlandes von der Antike bis zur Gegenwart*, Stuttgart 1979
Pevsner, Nikolaus, *A History of Building Types*, London 1976
Sauermost, Heinz Jürgen, and Christian von der Mülbe, *Istanbuler Moscheen*, Munich 1981

Architecture for an Industrial Age
Ackermann, Karl, *Industriebau*, exh. cat. University of Stuttgart, Institut für Entwerfen und Konstruieren, Stuttgart 1984
Albrecht, Donald, *World War II and the American Dream*, Cambridge, Massachusetts 1995
Banham, Rayner, *The Architecture of the Well-Tempered Environment*, London 1969
–, *Brutalismus in der Architektur*, Stuttgart 1966
–, *Design by Choice*, London 1981
Beaver, Patrick, *The Crystal Palace*, London 1970
Blaser, Werner, *Architecture and Nature*, Basel/Boston 1984
Chan-Magomedow, Selim O., *Pioniere der sowjetischen Architektur*, Dresden 1983
Danz, Ernst, *Sonnenschutz. Sun Protection*, Stuttgart 1967
Elliott, Cecil D., *Technics and Architecture*, Cambridge, Massachusetts 1992
Fathy, Hassan, *Architecture for the Poor*, Chicago 1973
Hitchcock, Henry, R., and Phillip Johnson, *Functional Architecture. The International Style 1925-40*, New York n.d.
Geist, Johann Friedrich, *Passagen. Ein Bautyp des 19. Jahrhunderts*, Munich 1979
Giedion, Sigfried, *Die Herrschaft der Mechanisierung. Ein Beitrag zur anonymen Geschichte*, Hamburg 1994
Hellmann, Ulrich, *Künstliche Kälte – Die Geschichte der Kühlung im Haushalt*, Gießen 1990
Herzog, Thomas, *Pneumatic Structures. A Handbook for the Architect and Engineer*, London 1977
Hilpert Thilo, *Le Corbusier. Charta von Athen*. Texte und Dokumente, Wiesbaden 1984
Huber Dorothee (ed.), *Sigfried Giedion – Befreites Wohnen*,

Frankfurt a.M. 1985
Hütsch, Volker, *Der Münchner Glaspalast 1854-1931. Geschichte und Bedeutung*, Munich 1980
Jacobs, Herbert, *Building with Frank Lloyd Wright. An Illustrated Memoir*, San Francisco 1978
Jencks, Charles, *Current Architecture*, London 1982
Klotz, Heinrich, *Vision der Moderne*, Munich 1986
Koppelkamm, Stefan, *Glasshouses and Wintergardens of the 19th Century*, London 1982
Le Corbusier, *The Radiant City*, London 1964
Lissitzky-Küppers, Sophie, *El Lissitzky*, Dresden 1978
McCoy, Esther, *Case Study Houses 1945-1962*, Los Angeles 1977
Miljutin, Nikolaj A., *Sozgorod. Die Planung einer neuen Stadt*, Basel/Berlin/Boston 1992
Obra Construida Luis Barragan Morfin 1902-1988, exh. cat., Dirección General de Arquitectura y Vivienda, Seville 1991
Olgyay, Aladar and Victor, *Solar Control and Shading Devices*, Princeton 1957
Öttermann, Stephan, *Das Panorama*, Frankfurt a.M. 1980
Pawley, Martin, *Buckminster Fuller*, London 1990
Portoghesi, Paolo, *Bernardo Vittone*, Rome 1966
–, *Guarino Guarini 1624-1683*, Milan 1956
Rowe, Peter G., *Making a Middle Landscape*, Cambridge, Massachusetts 1991
–, *Modernity and Housing*, Cambridge, Massachusetts 1992
Simmons, Jack, *A Visual History of Modern Britain. Transport*, London 1962
Smithson, Alison and Peter, *Die heroische Periode der Modernen Architektur*, London 1991
Steele, James, *Hassan Fathy Monographs*, New York 1988
Stierlin, Henri (ed.), *Architektur der Welt*, 16 vols., Lausanne/Cologne n.d.
–, *Architektur des Islam*, Zurich 1979
Troitzsch, Ulrich, and Wolfhard Weber, *Die Technik von den Anfängen bis zur Gegenwart*, Stuttgart 1987
Winkler, Klaus Jürgen, *Der Architekt Hannes Meyer. Anschauung und Werk*, Berlin 1989
Woods, Marey, and Arete Warren, *Glass Houses*, London 1988
Ungers, Liselotte, *Die Suche nach einer neuen Wohnform*, Stuttgart 1983

Changing Architecture for a Sustainable World
Allen, John, *BIOSPHERE 2, The Human Experiment*, London 1991
Andritzky, Michael, and Beate Hentschel et al., *Wieviel Wärme braucht der Mensch? Die Geburt der Kultur aus dem Feuer und das Energieproblem heute*, exh. cat., Stuttgart 1995
Barker, T.C., Pilkington. *An Age of Glass. The Illustrated History*, London 1994
Flagge, Ingeborg, *Annual of Light and Architecture* (Jahrbuch für Licht und Architektur), Berlin 1992
Friedrichs, Kai, and Fritz Haller, *Zweites Symposium Intelligent Building*, Karlsruhe 1991
Fuller, R. Buckminster, *Operating Manual for Spaceship Earth*, Arkansas 1963
Gnan, Karl Heinz, *Glas in der passiven Solar Architektur*, Wiesbaden/Berlin 1986
Goulding, J.R., Lewis, J.O., and Theo Steemers, *Energy Conscious Design. A Primer for Architects*, Brussels 1992
Howard, Rob, and Eric Winterkorn, *Building Environmental and Energy Design Survey*, Watford 1993
Humm, Othmar, and Peter Toggweiler, *Photovoltaics and Architecture. Photovoltaik und Architektur*, Basel/Boston/Berlin 1993
Imamura, M.S., Helm, P., and W. Palz, *Photovoltaics System Technology*, Brussels 1992
Kodama, Yuichiro, Cook, Jeffrey, and Simon Yannas, *Passive and Low Energy Architecture*, Process Architecture, no.88, Tokyo 1991
Lam, William, *Sunlight as Formgiver for Architecture*, Atlanta 1986
Lewis, Owen, *Energy in Architecture. The European Solar Passive Handbook*, Brussels 1986
Natterer, Julius et al., *Gebäudehüllen aus Glas und Holz, Maßnahmen zur energiebewußten Erweiterung von Wohnhäusern*, Cologne 1984
Plummer, Henri, *Poetics of Light*, Tokyo 1987
Røstvik, Harald, *The Sunshine Revolution*, Stavanger 1992
Sala, Marco, and Lucia Ceccherini Nelli, *Technologie Solari*, Florence 1993
Solar Architecture in Europe. Design, Performance and Evaluation, Brussels 1991
Tuckey, Bill, *Sunracer*, with photographs by Ray Berghouse

We wish to express our gratitude to numerous museums, libraries, photographic agencies, individuals, and other organisations named or quoted in the book, for having provided excellent ideas and illustrations for *Sol Power*, and for extending the courtesy of either waiving entirely or substantially reducing charges. Due credits are appropriately indicated. All other photographs are taken from the authors' archives. However, should any acknowledgement inadvertently have been overlooked or mentioned incorrectly, the error will be rectified in subsequent editions..

Alvar Aalto, vol.1 1922-1962, (Les Éditions d'Architecture Artemis) Zurich 1963: p.182/4-5
Gerald M. Ackermann, *Les Orientalistes de l'Ecole Britannique*, vol. 9, (ACR Édition Internationale) Paris 1989: p.113/8
K. Ackermann, *Industriebau*, exh. cat. University of Stuttgart, Institut für Entwerfen und Konstruieren, (DVA) Stuttgart 1984: p.135/6-7, p.135/9
Aerovironment, Palo Alto, California: 222/2-5, p.223/2, p.225/8
Donald Albrecht, *World War II and the American Dream*, (MIT Press) Cambridge, Massachusetts 1995: p.161/5, p.172/1, p.172/3, p.172/5
Architekt. Urbanist, Lehrer. Hannes Meyer 1889-1954, exh. cat. Bauhaus Archiv, Berlin 1989: p.163/4
Art through the Ages, (Harcourt Brace) Fort Worth 1987: p.100/4
Angewandte Solarenergie — ASE GmbH, Putzbrunn: p.218/2, p.218/5
Reyner Banham, *The Architecture of the Well-Tempered Environment*, (Architectural Press) London 1969: p.136/7, p.145/15, p.176/1-2
—, *Brutalismus in der Architektur*, (Karl Krämer) Stuttgart 1966: p.182/1-3
Obra Construida de Luis Barragan Morfin 1902-1988, Dirección General de Arquitectura y Vivienda, Consejeria de Obras Públicas y Transportes, Seville 1991: p.181/7
Bartenbach Lichtlabor, Aldrans, Innsbruck: p.213/7-8
Bautek Fluggeräte GmbH, Kenn: p.201/6
Bavaria Bildagentur: p.2, p.5, p.27/7, p.29/9, p.30/1, p.33/6, p.33/8, p.34/1, p.34/5, p.36/2, p.36/4, p.39/6, p.70, p.211/8
Patrick Beaver, *The Crystal Palace*, (Hugh Evelyn) London 1970: p.140/3-4
Mitchell Beazley (ed.), *The World Atlas of Architecture*, (Portland/Reed) London 1988: p.94/1, p.95/12. p.96/1, p.100/2, p.101/10
Behnisch & Partner, Stuttgart: p.225/6
Leonardo Benevolo, *Storia della Città*, (Editori Laterza) Rome/Bari 1982: p.39/4, p.82/1-2, p.83/4-5, p.84/3, p.114/1, p.124/1, p.124/3, p.150/3
—, *I confini del passagio umano*, (Laterza) Rome 1994: p.81/9, p.84/3
Ingenieurschule Biel, HTL Bern: p.222/1
Michael Bier: p.59/8
Werner Blaser: p.50/1, p.51/4, p.53/6, p.54/3
Werner Blaser, *Elementare Bauformen*, (Beton) Düsseldorf 1982: p.54/2
—, *Mies van der Rohe — less is more*, (Waser) Zurich 1986: p.159/5-7, p.189/7, p.109/9
—, *Architecture and Nature*, (Birkhäuser) Basel 1984: p.165/7
W. Boesiger, O. Stonorov (ed.), *Le Corbusier. Œuvre Complète*, vol.1. 1919-1929, Les Éditions d'Architecture, (Artemis) Zurich 1991: p.154/5, p.158/1-3
W. Boesiger (ed.), *Le Corbusier. Œuvre Complète*, vol.4. 1938-1946, Les Éditions d'Architecture, (Artemis) Zurich 1991: p.163/5-6
—, H. Girsberger (ed.), *Le Corbusier 1919-1964*, Les Éditions d'Architecture, (Artemis) Zurich 1991: p.176/6
Auguste Boppe, *Les Orientalistes. Les Peintres du Bosphore au XVIIIe Siècle*, vol.8, (ACR Édition Internationale) Paris 1989: p.113/3
Jean Louis Bourgeois, Carollee Pelos, *Spectacular Vernacular, The Adobe Tradition*, (Aperture) New York 1989: p.63/4
Bruno Bushart, Bernhard Rupprecht (ed.), *Cosmas Damian Asam. Leben und Werk*, (Prestel) Munich 1986: p.122/1-3
M. Bussagli, *Weltgeschichte der Architektur. Indien, Indonesien, Indochina*, (Electa/DVA) Milan/Stuttgart 1985: p.82/3
Ken Butti, John Perlin, *Golden Threat*, (Marion Boyars) London 1980: p.144/3-6, p.145/11
Cannon Architecture, Engineering, Planning, Design, Grand Island, NY: p.202/1, p.202/3-4
Canon, Solar Cell Business Centre, Tokyo: p.219/8-9, p.220/3
Selim O. Chan-Magomedow, *Pioniere der sowjetischen*

Architektur, (Verlag der Kunst) Dresden 1983: p.164/3-4
James Carpenter Design Ass. Inc., New York: p.214/1-2
Cities of Childhood. Italian Colobie of the 1930's, (Architectural Association) London 1988: p.157/5
Classical Chinese Architecture, ed. by Chinese Academy of Architecture, (Joint Publishing) Hong Kong 1986: p.106/1-2, p.106/5-6, p.108/1-3
Flavio Conti, *Weltwunder der Baukunst. Stille der Klöster und Glanz der Paläste*, (Bertelsmann) Augsburg 1987: p.125/5
Le Corbusier, *The Radiant City*, (Faber & Faber) London 1967: p.167/10-11
D. Cruickshank, N. Burton. *Life in the Gregorian City*, (Penguin) London 1989: p.55/5
Daimler-Benz Aerospace Airbus GmbH: p.201/8, p.211/8
Francesco Dal Co, *Kevin Roche*, (Electa) Milan 1985: p.173/6
Leonardo Dal Maso, *Das Rom der Caesaren*, (Bonechi Edizioni "Il Turismo") Florence 1974: p.97/9, p.97/12
Richard Davies: p.226/1
Hans D. Dossenbach: p.35/9
Du Pont/Aerovironment, Monrovia, CA: p.223/6-9
Götz Eckhardt, Roland Handrick, *Sans Soucci*. Die Schlösser und Gärten,(Henschel) Berlin 1990: p.125/6-8
Cecil D. Elliott, *Technics and Architecture*, (MIT Press) Cambridge, Massachusetts 1992: p.137/9, p.137/12, p.155/12
Enercon GmbH, Aurich: p.196/2-4, p.197/6
Fanatic Sports: p.200/2, p.200/5, p.231/3
Hassan Fathy, *Architecture for the Poor*, (University of Chicago Press) Chicago 1973: p.184/4
—, *Natural Energy and Vernacular Architecture*, (University of Chicago Press) Chicago 1986: p.185/10
C. Falkenhorst, *Luftfahrten*, *Klassiker der Technik*, (VDI) Düsseldorf 1987: p.130/5, p.144/7
Andreas Feininger, *Industrial America 1940-1960*, (Dover) Mineola, New York 1981: p.170/3
—, *Nature in Miniature*, (Thames & Hudson) London 1989: p.32/2, p.72/1
FIGLA Ltd., Tokyo: p.213/9-10
Fischer von Erlach — Entwurf einer historischen Architektur, (Harenberg) Dortmund 1978: p.81/7
FlagSol — Flachglas Solartechnik, Gelsenkirchen: p.208/5, p.220/6
Agentur Focus: p.13/2, p.17/5, p.27/8, p.30/5, p.169/7, p.194/2, p.195/3
Foster and Partners, London: p.197/5, p.199/6-8, p.202/2, p.202/5-6, p.204/1-3, p.204/5-7, p.216/1-6, p.217/7-9, p.221/9-10, p.224/1, p.226/2-3
Foster and Partners, London/Rode, Kellermann und Wawrofski, Düsseldorf: p.204/4, p.204/6
Foster and Partners, London/J. Roger Preston and Partners, Maidenhead, Berkshire: p.228/1-5
Charles Fowkes, *The Illustrated Kama Sutra*, (Reed) London 1987: p.116/5, p.233/2
Frauenhofer Gesellschaft, Institut für solare Energietechnik, Freiburg: p.210/5-6
© 1960 Allegra Fuller Snyder. Courtesy, Buckminster Fuller Institute, Santa Barbara: p.17/3, p.160/1-4, p.161/6, p.161/8, p.186/4-5.
© 1990 Allegra Fuller Snyder. Courtesy, Buckminster Fuller Institute, Santa Barbara: p.161/7, p.186/2-3
For more information about the work of Buckminster Fuller contact: The Buckminster Fuller Institute, 2040 Alame
Future Systems, London: p.203/7-8, p.203/10
Grimshaw & Partners, London: p.220/1
J.W. Galston, *Life Process of Plants*, Scientific American Magazine, New York 1994: p.31/7
Johann Friedrich Geist, *Passagen. Ein Bautyp des 19. Jahrhunderts*, (Prestel) Munich 1979: p.146/2
Johann Friedrich Geist, Klaus Kürvers, *Das Berliner Mietshaus 1862-1945*, (Prestel) Munich 1984: p.150/1
Georg Gerster, *Grand Design*, (Weidenfeld & Nicolson) London 1976: p.73/5-6, p.173/7, p.173/9
Sigfried Giedion: *Die Herrschaft der Mechanisierung. Ein Beitrag zur anonymen Geschichte*. Edited and with an essay by Henning Ritter. With an epilog of Stanislaus von Moos, (Europäische Verlagsanstalt, Europäische Bibliothek vol.8) Hamburg 1994: p.137/14, p.145/14, p.156/1
Rainer Graefe: p.95/9
—, *Vela erunt. Die Zeltdächer der römischen Theater und ähnlicher Anlagen*, 2 vols, Mainz 1979: p.97/6, p.97/11
Bruce Graham of SOM, Monographie, (Electa) Milan 1989: p.172/4, p.189/6
Will Grohmann, *Was Hände bauten*, (Éditions du Pont Royal/Scherz) Zurich 1962: p.144/9-10, p.154/1-2, p.154/6
Große Architekten. Menschen, die Baugeschichte machten,

Photo Credits

(Gruner + Jahr) Hamburg 1990: p.183/6-7
Max Gschwend, *Bauernhäuser der Schweiz*, (Schweizer Baudokumentation) Blauen 1988: p.50/2-3, p.51/6
Enrico Guidoni, *Architettura Primitiva*, (Electa) Milan 1979: p.49/9, p.52/1, p.53/4, p.60/2, p.62/1-2, p.63/3, p.67/7
Bildagentur Anne Hamann: p.13/1
David Hancocks, *Masterbuilders of the Animal World*, (Hugh Evelyn) London 1973: p.35/7
William M. Harlow, *Art Forms from Plant Life*, (Dover) New York 1976: p.30/4
Stefan Hartmaier: p.38/2
Duncan Haws, *Schiffe und Meer*, (Orbis) Munich 1992 (Original: Nordbok, Gothenburg, Sweden 1975): p.144/8
Bildagentur Hecht & Zimmermann: p.200/1 (Photo: Guy Gurney), p.234 (Photo: Guy Gurney)
Herzog + Partner, Munich: p.212/3, p.212/4
Thomas Herzog (ed.), *Solar Energy in Architecture and Urban Planning*, (Prestel) Munich 1996: p.195/4 (Norbert Kaiser)
Thilo Hilpert (ed.), *Le Corbusier Charta von Athen*. Texte und Dokumente, (Friedrich Vieweg & Sohn) Munich 1984: p.167/9, p.167/10-11
Hirmer Fotoarchiv, Munich: p.103/4, p.104, p.105
Henry R. Hitchcock, Philip Johnson, *Functional Architecture. The International Style 1925-1940*, (W.W. Norton) New York n.d.: p.156/8, p.157/6-7, p.163/7, p.163/8
John D. Hoag, *Weltgeschichte der Architektur. Islam*, (Electa/DVA) Milan 1978/Stuttgart 1986: p.100/5, p.101/7-8
Charles Hobermann: p.226/4-5
Hoechst AG, Frankfurt: p.206-207
W. Hoepfner, Ernst L. Schwandner, *Haus und Stadt im klassischen Griechenland*, (Deutscher Kunstverlag) Munich 1994: p.86/1-5, p.87/6-9
Brian Holme, *Princely Feasts and Festivals*, (Thames & Hudson) London 1988: p.124/4
Dorothee Huber (ed.), *Sigfried Giedion. Befreites Wohnen*, (Syndikat) Frankfurt a.M. 1985: p.154/3, p.166/6
Hans Ibelings, *Niederländische Architektur des 20. Jahrhunderts*, (Prestel) Munich 1995: p.157/7
The Image Bank: p.235/2 (Photo: Gianni Cigolini), p.235/3 (Photo: Alan Becker)
Ingenhoven, Overdiek & Partner, Düsseldorf: p.205/9, p.205/11-12 (Photos: Holger Knauf)
Integrated Environemental Solutions Ltd., Glasgow: p.229/9-10
Herbert Jacobs, *Building with Frank Lloyd Wright*, (Chronicle) San Francisco 1978: p.178/3, p.178/5
100 Jahre Architektur in Chicago, exh. cat. Neue Sammlung München, Staatliche Museen für angewandte Kunst 1973: p.148/1
Susan and Geoffrey Jellicoe, *The Landscape of Man*, (Thames & Hudson) 1987: p.124/2
Albert Kahn/Ford Foundation: p.148/3-4
Kahn in the Realm of Architecture, (Rizzoli) New York 1991: p.179/9-10
Kaiser Consult, Düsseldorf: p.210/2, p.210/4
Gottfried Knapp (ed.), *Engel*, (Prestel) Munich 1995: p.122/4
Charles Knevitt, *Shelter*, (Polymath) Streatly-on-Thames 1994: p.47/7
Koch HighTex, Rimsting/Chiemsee: p.225/7
Wilfried Koch: p.95/11
Georg Kohlmaier, Barna von Sartory, *Das Glashaus*, (Prestel) Munich 1981: p.138/2-3, p.139/6, p.140/1-2, p.141/5-6
Stefan Koppelkamm, *Glasshouses and Wintergardens of the 19th Century*, (Granada Technical Books) London 1982: p.139/8, p.141/7
Ulrich Krings, *Bahnhofsarchitektur. Deutsche Großstadtbahnhöfe des Historismus 1866-1906*, (Prestel) Munich 1985: p.141/8
Vittorio Magnago Lampugnani (ed.), *The Architecture of the Window*, (YKK Architectural Products) Tokyo 1995: p.156/3-4
Alfred Limbrunner: p.34/3
Living Races of Mankind, 2 vols., (Hutchinson) London n.d.: p.39/5, p.46/5, p.48/2, p.48/5, p.58/6
Paul Logsdon: p.85/4
3M, Thinsulate Liteloft: p.211/13
Esther McCoy, *Case Study Houses 1945-1962*, (Hennesy & Ingalis) Los Angeles 1977: p.174/5
Kenneth Macksey, *Technology in War*, (Guild Publishing) London 1986: p.152/3, p.152/5-6, p.168/2
Cyril Mango, *Weltgeschichte der Architektur. Byzanz*,

(Electa/DVA) Milan 1978/Stuttgart 1986: p.98/1
Bernard Marais, *Les Grands Magasins des origines à 1939*, (Picard) Paris 1979: p.147/6-7
Mauritius Bildagentur: p.189/4
Daniel Meadows et al., *Die Grenzen des Wachstums*, Bericht des Club of Rome zur Lage der Menschheit, Stuttgart n.d.: p.194/1
MERO-Raumstruktur, Würzburg: p.224/2
Claude Mignot, *Architektur des 19. Jahrhunderts*, (Office du Livre) Fribourg 1983: p.132/5, p.139/4, p.141/9
Nikolaj A. Miljutin, *Sozgorod: die Planung einer neuen Stadt*, (Birkhäuser) Basel/Berlin/Boston 1992: p.164/5-6
George Mitchell, *Architecture of the Islamic World*, (Thames & Hudson) London 1978: p.115/10
Mario Morini, *Atlante di Storia dell'Urbanistica*, (Hoepli) Milan 1963: p.95/6-7, p.95/10
Wolf Christian von der Mülbe: p.92/2, p.112/1
Peter Murray, *Weltgeschichte der Architektur. Renaissance*, (Electa/DVA) Milan 1978/Stuttgart 1989: p.120/4
Museum of the City of New York, „Court at Baxter Street", The Jacob A. Riis Collection, # 107/108: p.150/2
NASA p.24, p.26/1, p.26/3, p.28/1, p.28/3, p.29/5, p.73/7-8, p.171/7-8, p.192-193, p.211/10-11, p.219/6-7
NGM Energy 1981/02 14-5: p.19/1
Christian Norberg-Schulz, *Vom Sinn des Bauens. Die Architektur des Abendlandes von der Antike bis zur Gegenwart*, (Electa/Klett-Cotta) Milan/Stuttgart 1979: p.151/9
Jean Nouvelle, Emmanuel Cattani et Associes, Paris: p.217/10-11
Stephan Oettermann, *Das Panorama*, (Syndikat) Frankfurt a.M. 1980: p.130/6, p.131/10, p.133/7-9
Okalux Kapillarglas GmbH, Marktheidenfeld-Altfeld: p.210/1, p.213/5 (Photo: Lukas Roth), p.213/6 (Photo: Lukas Roth)
Victor and Aladar Olgyay, *Solar Control and Shading Devices*, (Princeton University Press) Princeton 1957: p.175/7-8, p.175/10-11, p.181/6-7, p.188/2
Paul Oliver, *Dwellings*, (University of Texas Press) London 1987: p.46/2, p.49/6, p.49/8, p.60/1, p.67/5
Frei Otto, Leonberg: p.224/3
C. Perry, A. Gore, and L. Flemming, *Old English Villages*, (Weidenfeld & Nicolson) London 1986: p.54/1
Nikolaus Pevsner, *A History of Building Types*, (Thames & Hudson) London 1976: p.132/1-4, p.134/1-2, p.134/5
Petzinka, Pink und Partner, Düsseldorf: p.205/8 (Photo: Tomas Riehle), p.205/10
Renzo Piano, Genova: p.199/9, p.212/2, p.224/4-5
Pilkington Glass Ltd., St. Helens, England: p.170/4, p.214/5
P.M. Magazin, Perspektive Energie, 29. Oktober 1986: p.209/8
Richard Pommer et al., *In the Shadow of Mies. Ludwig Hilbersheimer. Architect, Educator, and Urban Planner*, (The Art Institute Chicago) Chicago 1988: p.166/2
Paolo Portoghesi, *Bernardo Vittone*, (Edizioni del Elefante) Rome 1966: p.123/6
Paolo Portoghesi, *Guarino Guarini 1624–1683*, (Electa) Milan 1956: p.123/7
Anthony Preston, *Aircraft Carriers*, (Hamlyn) London 1979: p.168/2
J. Roger Preston & Partners, Maidenhead, Berkshire/Richard Rogers, London: p.229/6-8
Jean Prouvé Architecture/Industrie, (Klient, Entreprise idée produit) Paris n.d.: p.183/6, p.183/8, p.183/9-11
Rasch, SL Sonderkonstruktionen und Leichtbau GmbH, Leinfelden-Oberaichen: p.227/6-11
Alfonso Eduardo Reidy. Bauten und Projekte, (Hatje) Stuttgart 1969: p.180/1-5
Paolo Riani, Paul Goldberger, and John Portman, *John Portman*, (L'Arcaedizioni) Milan 1990: p.189/7
R.M. Richards, I. Seralgdin, and D. Rastdorfer, *Hassan Fathy*, (Concept Media) Singapore 1985: p.184/2
Claude Rivals, *Le Moulin à vent et le meunier*, (Edition Serg) Ivry 1976: p.74/1
Richard Rogers and Partners, London: p.198/1, p.198/3-5, p.199/10-11, p.214/6, p.215/7-11
Norbert Rosing: p.34/2
Peter G. Rowe, *Making a Middle Landscape*, (MIT Press) Cambridge, Massachusetts 1991: p.170/6, p.172/2, p.173/8
–, *Modernity and Housing*, (MIT Press) Cambrigde, Massachusetts 1993: p.165/11
Royal Geographic Society, London: p.100/3
Bernard Rudowsky, *Architecture without Architects*, (Academy Editions) London 1964: p.63/5, p.64/1
Bernard Rudowsky, *The Prodigious Builder*, (Harvest House) Eugene, Oregon 1977: p.46/1, p.48/1

Salewa, Munich: p.211/12
Sanyo Electric Co. Ltd., Osaka: p.220/4
Schott-Rohrglas GmbH, Bayreuth: p.210/3
Der Schrei nach dem Turmhaus, exh. cat. Bauhaus Archiv, Berlin 1989: p.148/2
Julius Shulman, Los Angeles: p.174/2
Nikken Sekei, Tokyo: p.203/9
Klaus Jürgen Sembach, *Into the Thirties. Style and Design 1927–1934*, (Thames & Hudson) London 1986: p.231/2
Schlaich, Bergermann und Partner, Stuttgart: p.197/7-10, p.209/6
Dennis Sharp, *A Visual History of 20th Century Architecture*, (New York Graphic Society/Bulfinch) Greenwich, Connecticut/Boston 1972: p.149/6, p.156/2, p.162/2-3, p.174/1, p.174/3, p.174/5-6, p.175/9
Jack Simmons, *A Visual History of Modern Britain. Transport*, (Longacre) London 1962: p.136/1, p.136/3-4, p.137/10-11, p.144/1, p.145/13
Madanjeet Singh, *The Sun and Myth in Art*, (Thames & Hudson) London 1993: p.80/3, p.80/6, p.84/1
SITE – James Wine, New York: p.203/11-12
Susan Slesin, et al., *Caribbean Style*. Copyright © 1985 by Susan Slesin, Stafford Cliff, Jack Berthelot, Martine Gaume, Daniel Rozensztroch and Gilles de Chabaneix. Reprinted by permission of Clarkson N. Potter Inc., a division of Crown Publishers Inc., London: p.61/5-7
Solarex, Frederick, MY: p.218/3, p.220/2
Solution AG für Solartechnik, CH - Härkingen: p.220/5, p.221/11-12
Peter Stache, *Raumfahrer von A-Z*, (Militärverlag der DDR) Berlin 1988: p.170/2
James Steele, *Hassan Fathy Monographs*, (Academy Editions) London 1988: p.184-85/1
Henri Stierlin (ed.), *Architektur der Welt. China*, (Compagnie du Livre d'Art, S.A., Éditions Office du Livre) Lausanne n.d.: p.72/3-4, p.108/4
–, *Architektur der Welt. Japan*, (Compagnie du Livre d'Art, S.A., Éditions Office du Livre) Lausanne n.d.: p.107/10, p.107/12, p.109/6-7
–, *Architektur der Welt. Ägypten*, (Compagnie du Livre d'Art, S.A., Éditions Office du Livre) Lausanne n.d.: p.80/1, p.80/4
–, Ulya Vogt-Göknil (ed.), *Architektur der Welt. Osmanische Türkei*, (Compagnie du Livre d'Art, S.A., Éditions Office du Livre) Lausanne n.d.: p.113/5-7
Henri Stierlin (ed.), *Architektur der Welt. Islamisches Indien*, (Compagnie du Livre d'Art, S.A., Éditions Office du Livre) Lausanne n.d.: p.116/2, p.117/6-7
–, *Architektur des Islam*, (Atlantis) Zürich 1971: p.100/1, p.114/2, p.114/4
–, *Architektur der Welt. Angkor Watt* (Taschen) Cologne n.d.: p.75/6-7
Joshua Stoff, *Picture History of World War II*, (Dover) Mineola, New York 1993: p.168/1
Manfredo Tafuri, Francesco Dal Co, *Weltgeschichte der Architektur. Klassische Moderne*, (Electa/DVA) Milan 1978/Stuttgart 1988: p.149/8, p.151/6-8, p.151/10, p.167/7-8
Ulrich Troitzsch, Wolfhard Weber, *Die Technik von den Anfängen bis zur Gegenwart*, (Westermann) Stuttgart/Braunschweig 1987: p.129, p.130/1-4, p.131/7-9, p.135/8, p.136/5-6, p.137/8, p.137/10, p.144/2, p.145/12, p.152/1-2, p.152/4, p.155/7-11, p.168/4-5, p.170/1, p.170/5
Liselotte Ungers, *Die Suche nach einer neuen Wohnform*, (DVA) Stuttgart 1983: p.164/1-2, p.165/10, p.166/1, p.166/3
U.S. Office of History/Army Corp. of Engineers, Washington D.C.: p.168/6
Vienna Racing GmbH, Oberstenfeld: p.201/7
Der vorbildliche Architekt. Mies van der Rohes Architektur-unterricht 1930-1958 am Bauhaus und in Chicago, exh. cat. Bauhaus Archiv, Museum für Gestaltung, Berlin1986: p.166/4-5
John B. Ward-Perkins, *Weltgeschichte der Architektur. Rom*, (Electa/DVA) Milan 1978/Stuttgart 1986: p.95/9
John Warren, Ihsan Fethi, *Traditional Houses in Baghdad*, (Coach) Horsham, England 1982: p.65/5
Stuart Cary Welch, *Persische Buchmalerei*, (Prestel) Munich 1976: p.115/6-7
Karin Wilhelm, *Portrait Frei Otto*, Architekten heute, vol.2, (Quadriga Verlag J. Severin) Weinheim 1985: p.187/6-9
Marey Woods, Arete Warren, *Glass Houses*, (Aurum Press) London 1988: p.138/1, p.139/7
Ken Yeang, Kuala Lumpur: p.198/2
John Zukowsky (ed.), *Chicago-Architektur 1872–1922*, (Prestel) Munich 1987: p.147/8